CALLED TO WATCH FOR CHRIST'S RETURN

Martyn McGeown

REFORMED
FREE PUBLISHING
ASSOCIATION
Jenison, Michigan

Scriptures cited are taken from the King James (Authorized) Version

Reformed Free Publishing Association
1894 Georgetown Center Drive
Jenison, Michigan 49428
rfpa.org
mail@rfpa.org
616-457-5970

Cover design by Erika Kiel
Interior design and typesetting by Katherine Lloyd, The DESK

ISBN 978-1-944555-14-6
Ebook 978-1-944555-15-3
LCCN 2016957809

I dedicate this book with much love to my family: my parents, Ernie and Sally; my siblings, Jason and Shelley; my brother-in-law, Michael; and my nieces, Anna, Lily, and Hope

Contents

Preface

This book began as a series of sermons that I preached in Limerick, Ireland, between August 2011 and January 2012, to the saints of the Limerick Reformed Fellowship.

I divide the material into two parts. The first, an explanation of Matthew 24:1–31, deals with the signs of Christ's coming. The disciples asked for signs, and Christ gave signs to them and to us. The second, an explanation of Matthew 24:32–25:46, applies what Christ has taught in the first part of the Olivet Discourse. Christ never teaches us about the signs of his coming merely to satisfy our idle curiosity. The truth is practical, for it concerns our hope. Therefore, I have entitled the second part, "Watching for Christ's Return." If we know about the signs but do not live watchfully, we will be like the fools described in the parables toward the end of the discourse.

Let us watch and pray, therefore, and wait for that great day with a most ardent desire!

THE APPROACH
TO THE
OLIVET DISCOURSE

Matthew 24–25 is called the Olivet Discourse, because Christ spoke these words from the Mount of Olives. The discourse is one of Christ's longest recorded speeches in the four gospels, and it is his most detailed treatment of eschatology, or the subject of the last things. In this important speech, Jesus proclaims his second coming, an event with which history will come to a dramatic and sudden close. Some commentators have called the discourse a "mini apocalypse," because it is parallel to the book of Revelation, given to John by the exalted Lord Jesus Christ on the island of Patmos.

Like every major eschatological passage—especially the book of Revelation and the important passages in Paul's Thessalonian correspondence—the Olivet Discourse is the subject of theological contention and debate. To understand what Christ is teaching here, we need to know the context. Without a careful examination of the context, we will become mired in useless questions, and we will miss the vital instruction and warning, which Christ gives his disciples and us about the signs of his coming.

There are three different approaches to the Olivet Discourse that reflect three different millennial schools of eschatology. If one has a certain conviction about eschatology, Christ's words will be interpreted to fit that position. Sometimes Christ's words will be forced into an eschatological and millennial mold that Christ never intended. The three schools of thought concerning Revelation and the Olivet Discourse are premillennial dispensationalism, postmillennialism, and Reformed amillennialism (the position that I will advocate in this book).

The millennium as such does not concern us here, because the term *millennium* only appears in Revelation 20 and is utterly absent from the Olivet Discourse itself. Nevertheless, millennialism will make a difference in one's interpretation of the discourse.

Pivotal to the discourse is the year AD 70. That was the year the city of Jerusalem and, more importantly, Jerusalem's temple were destroyed by the Romans. That date was a turning point in Jewish history, after which the Jewish nation for all intents and purposes ceased to exist. The unbelieving Jews were scattered, enslaved, and slaughtered in huge numbers. It cannot be denied that such a tragedy for the nation of Israel is part of the discourse, as well as part of the teaching of John the Baptist and the Lord Jesus Christ. For example, John the Baptist warned unbelieving Israel, "The axe is laid unto the root of the trees: therefore every tree which bringeth not forth good fruit is hewn down, and cast into the fire" (Matt. 3:10). The nation of Israel was hewn down with the Roman ax in AD 70. God, as John the Baptist warned, "is able of these stones to raise up children unto Abraham" (v. 9).

Moreover, Jesus both cursed the barren fig tree, which represented fruitless Israel (Matt. 21:19), and warned that fruitless nation, "The kingdom of God shall be taken from you, and given to a nation bringing forth the fruits thereof" (v. 43). Jesus even said about AD 70, "Verily I say unto you, This generation shall not pass, till all these things be fulfilled" (Matt. 24:34).

To deny that AD 70, with its dreadful fall and destruction of Jerusalem, was part of Christ's focus would be to deny the obvious. For one thing, that is exactly what the disciples asked. When Jesus warned, "There shall not be left here one stone upon another, that shall not be thrown down," a clear reference to AD 70, the disciples anxiously asked, "Tell us, when shall these things be?" (Matt. 24:2–3).

However, the question that divides the premillennial dispensationalists, the postmillennialists, and the (Reformed) amillennialists, and especially the question that divides the postmillennialists from the (Reformed) amillennialists, is this: Does AD 70 *exhaust* the fulfillment of the Olivet Discourse? Is the discourse a prophecy about *only* the events of AD 70, or is there more here?

The Postmillennial and Premillennial Dispensational Interpretations

Postmillennialism argues that the discourse, at least up to Matthew 24:35, is exclusively about AD 70. Some postmillennialists argue that the whole discourse, including the description of the final judgment in Matthew 25, treats exclusively the events of AD 70. This view is called *preterism*, a word derived from the Latin for "past." A preterist view of Christ's words sees them exhaustively fulfilled in the past. The reason postmillennialists find such a preterist view attractive, and even necessary for their whole eschatological system, is that the discourse contains prophecies that do not fit a "positive" view of the future.

David Chilton is emphatic: "*Everything* Jesus spoke of in this passage, at least up to verse 34, *took place before the generation then living passed away.*" 'Wait a minute,' you say. 'Everything? The witnessing to all nations, the Tribulation, the coming of Christ on the clouds, the stars falling...*everything*?'" Yes.[1]

Postmillennialism teaches that before Christ returns the church will enjoy a long period of unprecedented peace, prosperity, and growth. This period, known as the golden age, will last as long as one thousand or even countless thousands of years, during which time the world will be Christianized.[2] This Christianization will mean that the majority of the world's population will become Christians, or at least will be culturally and morally Christian. However, the discourse does not paint a picture of a golden age, but quite the opposite. Christ warns of persecution and apostasy. Preterism very conveniently places all such persecution and apostasy (and other negative events) *in the past.* Therefore, they cannot interfere with the future golden age promised by postmillennialism. Gary North, another postmillennialist, expresses it this way:

> The fact is, *the vast majority of prophecies in the New Testament* refer to this crucial event [the destruction of Jerusalem in AD 70], the event which publicly identified the transition from the Old Covenant to the New Cove-

---

1 David Chilton, *Paradise Restored: A Biblical Theology of Dominion* (Tyler, TX: Dominion Press, 1994), 86.

2 David Chilton writes, "The '1,000 years' of Revelation 20 represent a vast, undefined period of time. It has already lasted almost 2,000 years and will probably go on for many more. 'Exactly how many more years?' someone asked me. 'I'll be happy to tell you,' I cheerfully replied, 'as soon as you tell me exactly how many hills are in Psalm 50'" (ibid., 199).

nant, and which also marked the triumph of rabbinic Judaism over priestly Judaism, Pharisee over Sadducee, and the synagogue system over the temple.[3]

In addition, many postmillennialists uncharitably label (Reformed) amillennialists as "pessimillennialists," as if we were pessimistic about the future. However, that we deny a future golden age—free from persecution, apostasy, and the antichrist—and that we warn that these things are coming in our future does not make us pessimistic. We believe that Christ is the Lord of history and that he has successfully gathered, defended, and preserved his church from the beginning to the end of the world. Indeed, we echo Paul's triumph, "We are killed all the day long; we are accounted as sheep for the slaughter," yet "in all these things we are more than conquerors through him that loved us" (Rom. 8:36–37). We overcome the world as Christians, not by taking over the UN, NATO, and the United States Congress, and not by massive revivals, but "by the blood of the Lamb, and by the word of [our] testimony; and [we love] not [our] lives unto the death" (Rev. 12:11).

Premillennial dispensationalists generally view the Olivet Discourse the same way they interpret the book of Revelation. Both passages, they contend, speak exclusively of the future. The events promised in Matthew 24–25 do not in any sense concern the fall of Jerusalem in AD 70. As dreadful as that was, Jesus does not speak of it here. Instead, argue many premillennial dispensationalists, the discourse concerns a *future* Jerusalem

---

3 Gary North, publisher's preface, in Kenneth L. Gentry Jr., *The Beast of Revelation* (Tyler, TX: Dominion Press, 1994), x; emphasis added. In that book, Gentry argues that the antichrist was the emperor Nero, and therefore, there is no future antichrist. This is a common view among modern postmillennialist theologians.

with a *future* temple. Everything prophesied in Matthew 24–25 is future not only to the disciples, but also to us. The signs were not for the disciples, or even for us, but for a future generation who will be alive when the Jews rebuild the temple in a restored Jewish state. That state, argue many premillennial dispensationalists, has been established—it is modern Israel—and now we await the promised temple, which will be built soon.

I will interact with these views throughout this study of the words of Christ in the Olivet Discourse.

The Reformed Amillennial Approach

What then is the relationship between Christ's words, the fall of Jerusalem in AD 70, and the future coming of Christ at the end of history? How, therefore, do we view the Olivet Discourse?

We answer—typologically.

The two events, the fall of Jerusalem and the second coming of Christ, are related in the minds of the disciples and in the mind of Christ. They are related in this way. One is a type, or picture, that foreshadows the other. In other words, AD 70 is not the end of the world, but it is a type, or picture, of the end of the world. Christ illustrates the end of the world, which is in the distant future from the disciples' perspective, with the fall of Jerusalem in AD 70, which is in the near future from the disciples' perspective.

This explains several features of the discourse.

First, it explains Matthew 24:34, "Verily I say unto you, This generation shall not pass, till all these things be fulfilled." This is, without any exaggeration, the trump card of postmillennialism. With this verse postmillennialists explain that everything—including the abomination of desolation, the great tribulation, and even the darkening of the sun and moon in verse 29—was fulfilled exhaustively in AD 70. We Reformed amillennialists, on the other hand, understand Christ's meaning differently. All these things shall happen in one generation— we do not deny that—but they shall happen in historical type. We cannot push all these things into the distant future, as the disciples were tempted to do, and as the futurist premillennial dispensationalists do. The events around AD 70 do not exhaust the fulfillment of "all these things." Jerusalem shall fall, the abomination of desolation shall be set up, and there shall be great tribulation, but these things will continue throughout the New Testament age. We can push them all neither into the past (postmillennialism) nor into the future (premillennial dispensationalism). We know this because "immediately after the tribulation of those days" (v. 29) Christ shall come, but he did *not* return immediately after the events of AD 70.

Second, the typological approach to the Olivet Discourse does justice to the disciples' double-barreled question in Matthew 24:3: "Tell us, when shall these things be? and what shall be the sign of thy coming, and of the end of the world?" The disciples had two questions, or one question with two parts. The postmillennial preterist approach addresses the first part of the question, "When shall these things be?" but neglects the second part of the question, "What shall be the sign of thy coming, and of the end of the world?" The premillennial dispensationalist futurist approach addresses the second part of the question, "What shall be the sign of thy coming, and of the end of the world?" but neglects the first part of the question, "When shall these things be?" The (Reformed) amillennial typological approach answers both questions, or both parts of the disciples' double-barreled question.

Third, the typological approach to the Olivet Discourse provides an explanation for the Jewish flavor of Christ's presentation. Jesus addresses Jewish disciples in a Jewish city concerning the future of the Jewish nation. That is why in Matthew 24 he speaks of the "holy place" (v. 15), the mountains beyond Judea (v. 16), the flat roofs of Palestine (v. 17), and prohibitions concerning Sabbath travel (v. 20). Several Reformed amillennial commentators explain the significance of this:

> In describing the brief period of great tribulation at the close of history, ending with the final judgment, Jesus is painting in colors borrowed from the destruction of Jerusalem by the Romans.[4]

> Jesus was on the Mount of Olives speaking as God's final prophet, using the temple and the city of Jerusalem as graphic visual aids. Jesus spoke not only directly about God's coming judgment on the city and the temple but also to the church awaiting the great consummation and the end of the present age many years hence.[5]

> Jesus is proclaiming events in the distant future in close connection with events in the near future. The destruction of Jerusalem which lies in the near future is a type of the end of the world; hence the intermingling. The passage, therefore, deals neither exclusively with the destruction of Jerusalem nor exclusively with the end of

---

4   William Hendrickson, *New Testament Commentary: Exposition of the Gospel according to Matthew* (Grand Rapids, MI: Baker Book House, 1973), 847.
5   Kim Riddlebarger, *A Case for Amillennialism: Understanding the End Times* (Grand Rapids, MI: Baker Books, 2003), 158.

the world; it deals with both—sometimes with the latter in terms of the former.[6]

This feature of prophecy in general, and of the Olivet Discourse in particular, makes these chapters a challenge for the exegete. There are two threads in Matthew 24–25. One concerns the events of AD 70. The other concerns the events of the entire New Testament age leading up to and culminating in the second coming of Christ. However, these two threads are so expertly woven together that we find it difficult to unravel them. Indeed, we should not expect to be able to unravel them. Christ has woven them together for a reason. Matthew Henry writes,

> This prophecy, under the type of Jerusalem's destruction, looks as far forward as the general judgment; and, as is usual in prophecies, some passages are more applicable to the type, and others to the antitype; and toward the close, as usual, it points more particularly to the latter.[7]

Jesus, in the Olivet Discourse, is speaking as a prophet. Indeed, he is, as the Heidelberg Catechism teaches, "our chief Prophet and Teacher."[8] One of the outstanding features of biblical prophecy is prophetic perspective, in which one event, the second advent, is described in terms of two distinct events, in this case the destruction of Jerusalem in AD 70 and the end of the world. In addition, we need to bear in mind the "two ages"

---

6 Anthony A. Hoekema, *The Bible and the Future* (Grand Rapids, MI: Wm. B. Eerdmans Publishing Company, 1979), 149.

7 Matthew Henry, *Matthew Henry's Commentary on the Whole Bible*, vol. 5, *Matthew to John* (Old Tappen, NJ: Fleming H. Revell Company, n.d.), 5:347.

8 Heidelberg Catechism A 31, in Philip Schaff, ed., *The Creeds of Christendom with a History and Critical Notes*, 6th ed., 3 vols. (New York: Harper and Row, 1931; repr., Grand Rapids, MI: Baker Books, 2007), 3:317.

view of the New Testament—this age and the age to come. Many postmillennialists wrongly see "this age" as the pre-AD 70 Jewish age and "the age to come" as the post-AD 70 church age. Rather, this age is the New Testament age (the period of time from the first to the second advent), and the age to come is the age of eternity.

Let us then sit at the feet of the Master, as he instructs us about those things that must come to pass. Let us not fear, for these things concern our salvation.

Part One

THE
SIGNS
OF
CHRIST'S
COMING

Chapter 1

♦

THE DISCIPLES' QUESTIONS ABOUT THE END

And Jesus went out, and departed from the temple: and his disciples came to him for to shew him the buildings of the temple. And Jesus said unto them, See ye not all these things? verily I say unto you, There shall not be left here one stone upon another, that shall not be thrown down. And as he sat upon the mount of Olives, the disciples came unto him privately, saying, Tell us, when shall these things be? and what shall be the sign of thy coming, and of the end of the world?—Matthew 24:1–3

Christ is coming. Do you hear his footsteps? Ever since he ascended to his Father in order to prepare a place in heaven for his church, he has been on the way back. In heaven, he is not simply sitting idly at the right hand of God, waiting for the signal to return, but he is actively moving all of history toward that certain end. The history of the New Testament is the preparation for his return. The first coming was necessary so that he could set in motion events that bring about his second coming (Heb. 9:28). That coming will be sudden and unexpected for the wicked and for the professing church that is spiritually asleep. Therefore, we must be found watching and waiting.

Christ's disciples were interested in Christ's coming. They knew he had come as the Messiah; they knew he was the king of God's kingdom; and they knew that he would come again, but the details were fuzzy in their minds, so they asked him in Matthew 24:3, "Tell us, when shall these things be? and what shall be the sign of thy coming, and of the end of the world?" They asked for a sign, but Christ surpassed their expectations by giving them not merely one sign, but *many* signs of his coming. These signs, which would begin to take place already in that generation, continue throughout the New Testament age and intensify just before the end.

The Occasion

The disciples do not ask their question out of the blue. In the context of Matthew 23, the disciples had just witnessed Christ angrily denouncing the unbelieving Jewish leaders. He had pronounced no fewer than eight solemn woes against them. The apostate Jews of Christ's day had followed in the footsteps of apostate Judaism. Upon them, says Christ, shall come all the righteous blood that had been shed upon the earth from Abel to Zacharias (v. 35). In the Hebrew Bible, Genesis is the first book and 2 Chronicles (not Malachi) is the last book. Since Abel's death is recorded in Genesis, and Zacharias' death is recorded in 2 Chronicles, Jesus means all the blood of martyrs that had been shed throughout the Old Testament. The persecution of God's righteous servants was their greatest sin, and the Pharisees of

Christ's day showed that they followed in their fathers' footsteps by refusing to believe in Christ and by persecuting those who believed in him. Soon they would be guilty of the worst of all crimes: the murder of the Son of God, a sin for which God's wrath would fall upon them in terrifying intensity. The cross, on which Christ would die, would be proof of their opposition to God, as well as the great display of God's justice and mercy to his elect church.

Jesus commands the Pharisees to fill up the measure of their fathers (Matt. 23:32). In the history of the world, several cups must be filled. The first is the cup of iniquity. Sin, which has developed from a seed planted in the fall of man, has brought forth a bitter harvest. Various peoples have filled up their cups in history, but now it would be the Jews' time. Followed by the cup of iniquity is the cup of God's wrath: God will not pour out the fullness of his wrath until the wicked have filled the cup of their sins (see Gen. 15:16). Once her cup has been filled, God will destroy Jerusalem for her sins. He did that especially in AD 70 by means of the Roman invasion.

This greatest woe upon Jerusalem is something they welcomed. Christ will abandon them: "I say unto you, Ye shall not see me henceforth, till ye shall say, Blessed is he that cometh in the name of the Lord" (Matt. 23:39). That is really the desolation of Israel, for Christ leaves them.

Israel existed as a nation because God would keep his covenantal promises to Abraham, Isaac, Jacob, and then David, but with the coming of Christ and Israel's rejection of him, God had no further use for that nation. Remember his chilling warning in Matthew 21:43: "The kingdom of God shall be taken from you, and given to a nation bringing forth the fruits thereof." That new nation is the church of believing Jews and Gentiles in the New Testament (1 Pet. 2:9).

The temple, once called the house of God, was also abandoned. It had become an empty shell of mere formalistic religion. The worship of that place foreshadowed and prepared for Christ. Now that Christ had come the temple had fulfilled its purpose. For Christ to leave any people or any church is for that people and church to be desolate—a wasteland, a desert, a lifeless, empty shell. Accordingly, Christ's actions match his words. He leaves the temple and never returns. The woes of Matthew 23 are the last words Christ speaks in his last visit to the temple. Often he had taught there, but now he wipes the dust off his feet. The Jews heard God's word, but they rejected it. Accordingly, chapter 24 begins, "Jesus went out, and departed from the temple" (v. 1).

One can only imagine what troubling thoughts rushed through the disciples' minds as their beloved Master spoke such words to the religious leaders. As if to stop Christ in his tracks and maybe even to make him reconsider his judgment against the temple, the disciples call his attention to the grandeur of the temple buildings. You can almost hear them say, "Lord, look at the temple. Surely, you do not think all *this* could be left desolate, do you?" Mark 13:1 records their words: "Master, see what manner of stones and what buildings are here!"

Most of Christ's disciples were Galileans (Judas Iscariot was a notable exception) who did not enjoy many opportunities to see the temple. They were understandably impressed by it. In fact, there was no greater structure in Jerusalem than the temple; it dominated the city. From whichever direction the pilgrims came, the temple could be seen. The temple was the glory of Jerusalem. It was the reason pilgrims flocked there. It was the center of Israel's worship. It was her boast. "We have the temple, and God dwells with us," they enthused. So long as the temple stood, Israel felt safe, indeed indestructible, but now Christ warns that the temple will be destroyed and desolate.

The temple in question was not the first in Israel's history. The first had been built from stone cut from the quarries and wood from the cedars of Lebanon, covered over with gold, in the glory days of Solomon. The Babylonians had destroyed *that* temple. Zerubbabel built the second temple after the Babylonian captivity. That temple was not as impressive as the first, but it was still a great structure. Antiochus Epiphanes (c. 215–164 BC) defiled it in the intertestamentary period. We will learn more about that wicked king when we study the meaning of the abomination of desolation (Matt. 24:15).

Herod the Great (c. 74–4 BC) built the temple that stood in Jerusalem during Christ's earthly ministry. He had spared no expense in making it the most impressive edifice in Jerusalem. Huge marble blocks, pure gold, and Corinthian brass were used in its design. The disciples call to Christ's attention the beautiful buildings of Herod's temple. "It was adorned with goodly stones and gifts" (Luke 21:5). Alfred Edersheim describes the glory of the temple that the disciples beheld:

> Alone, and isolated in its grandeur, stood the Temple Mount. Terrace upon terrace its courts rose, til, high above the city, within the enclosure of marble cloisters, cedar-roofed and richly ornamented, the Temple itself stood out a mass of snowy marble and of gold, glittering in the sunlight against the half-encircling green background of Olivet. In all his wanderings the Jew had not seen a city like his own Jerusalem. Not Antioch in Asia, not even imperial Rome herself, excelled it in architectural splendor. Nor has there been, either in ancient or modern times, a sacred building equal to the Temple, whether for situation or magnificence; nor yet have there been festive throngs like those joyous hundreds

of thousands who, with their hymns of praise, crowded towards the city on the eve of a Passover...

[The] eight side gates, as we may call them, were all two-leaved, wide, high, with superstructures and chambers supported by two pillars, and covered with gold and silver plating. But far more magnificent than any of them was the ninth or *eastern* gate, which formed the principal entrance into the Temple. The ascent to it was from the terrace by twelve easy steps. The gate itself was made of dazzling Corinthian brass, most richly ornamented; and so massive were its double doors that it needed the united strength of twenty men to open and close them. This was the "Beautiful Gate."[1]

Christ is not impressed by architecture. Yes, the temple was splendid to behold, but it was a hindrance. The people trusted in it; they gloried in it. Their attitude was as it had been in Jeremiah's day:

4. Trust ye not in lying words, saying, The temple of the LORD, The temple of the LORD, the Temple of the LORD, are these.
5. For if ye throughly amend your ways and your doings; if ye throughly execute judgment between a man and his neighbour;
6. If ye oppress not the stranger, the fatherless, and the widow, and shed not innocent blood in this place, neither walk after other gods to your hurt:

---

1 Alfred Edersheim, *The Temple: Its Ministry and Services as They Were at the Time of Jesus Christ* (Grand Rapids, MI: Wm. B. Eerdmans Publishing Company; repr., 1982), 28, 47.

7. Then will I cause you to dwell in this place, in the land that I gave to your fathers, for ever and ever.
8. Behold, ye trust in lying words, that cannot profit.
9. Will ye steal, murder, and commit adultery, and swear falsely, and burn incense unto Baal, and walk after other gods whom ye know not;
10. And come and stand before me in this house, which is called by my name, and say, We are delivered to do all these abominations?
11. Is this house, which is called by my name, become a den of robbers in your eyes? Behold, even I have seen it, saith the LORD. (Jer. 7:4–11)

"Your house is left unto you desolate" might be open to misinterpretation, but Christ's blunt response is not. Every stone would be thrown down. This speaks of a violent, sudden, and complete destruction, which literally occurred some forty years later. Christ's prophecy is not that the temple would simply fall into disrepair. Rather, it would be thrown down, so that one stone would not be left upon another.[2]

Let us be clear that the temple Christ meant was the one the disciples were now admiring: "there shall not be left *here* one stone." I emphasize this because in this book, as was explained in the introduction, we must interact with two erroneous but popular views of eschatology, premillennial dispensationalism and postmillennialism.

Premillennial dispensationalism understands Matthew 24 in terms of the distant future, a view often called futurism. For the

---

2 Some have argued that Christ's prophecy was not fulfilled, because the Wailing Wall still exists in Jerusalem today. However, the Wailing Wall was not part of the temple proper but was part of an extension to the temple site constructed by Herod the Great.

premillennial dispensationalist, Christ's words really have nothing to do with AD 70. The premillennial dispensational scheme imagines that Christ is speaking of a rebuilt temple sometime in our future. *That* temple will be destroyed and in that temple antichrist will sit. This is necessary for the premillennial dispensational scheme because all of the horrors described in Matthew 24—especially the great tribulation—must not fall on the church, which will have escaped in the rapture. We will examine the subject of the rapture in later chapters. For now, let us understand that premillennial dispensationalism expects a *different* temple in the future.

Furthermore, premillennial dispensationalism is committed to the notion that Israel will build their temple again. It is necessary for their scheme, because all Old Testament prophecies concerning the temple must be fulfilled literally, a view that will be refuted later in this book.

The premillennial dispensationalists teach that the next thing on God's agenda is the rapture of the church. One day—it could be any moment—Christ will return invisibly and secretly and take all Christians to be with him, so that all Christians will disappear from the earth. Strictly speaking, that rapture comes without any signs, and there is no need to look for signs. When the disciples asked for signs of Christ's coming, they meant signs for Christ's coming at the end of the world, signs that have nothing to do with the disciples and have nothing to do with the church, which will be caught up in the rapture. The tribulation described here has nothing to do with us, therefore. This pertains only to a future time after the rapture when the antichrist will persecute those "left behind." But that explanation cannot be correct either. Why would Jesus answer his disciples' questions with irrelevant information about the distant future? That would be to mock them. Besides, the chapter makes clear that Christ's contemporaries are meant. *These* things! *These* buildings! There shall not be left *here*!

Therefore, Matthew 24 clearly speaks of the temple of that day, the temple whose buildings the disciples admired and the temple that Christ had just left. Yet how inconceivable and unbelievable Christ's prophecy must have seemed to the disciples! This glorious temple destroyed? Who or what could or would destroy the Jews' temple? It had taken forty-six years to build it (John 2:20). Could it really be destroyed so utterly that no stone would be left on another? Would the Romans, the world power of that day, destroy it? The Romans had always been indulgent about the Jews' temple, and there was no open war between Rome and Jerusalem. Moreover, Christ would be sacrificed by Pilate to ensure a continuation of such peace:

47. Then gathered the chief priests and the Pharisees a council, and said, What do we? for this man doeth many miracles.
48. If we let him thus alone, all men will believe on him: and the Romans shall come and take away both our place and nation.
49. And one of them, named Caiaphas, being the high priest that same year, said unto them, Ye know nothing at all,
50. Nor consider that it is expedient for us, that one man should die for the people, and that the whole nation perish not.
51. And this spake he not of himself: but being high priest that year, he prophesied that Jesus should die for that nation;
52. And not for that nation only, but that also he should gather together in one the children of God that were scattered abroad. (John 11:47–52)

Indeed, to speak against the temple in this way was blasphemous to the ears of a pious Jew. Remember how the Jews reacted to the accusation that Stephen had spoken *against* the temple (Acts 6:13). Yet the disciples believed Christ and were concerned to know more. They did not contradict Christ, but they needed further instruction, which Christ is pleased to give.

The Significance

Such an earth-shattering prediction implies more than the end of bricks and mortar in Jerusalem. It implies the end of Jerusalem, and with it, the end of the nation of Israel. It also implies the judgment of Almighty God, for how could Israel be destroyed except God do it (Amos 3:3)? Had God not done this in the past? Would he do it again? It implies the coming of Christ to judge.

Because of this, and because the disciples know that Jesus speaks the truth of God, they ask him some urgent follow-up questions.

First, *when* shall these things be? How will they, the disciples, be able to recognize that these things are about to happen? The disciples, who understand the need to be ready, urgently seek an explanation.

Second, what shall be the sign of Christ's *coming*? That word, the Greek word *parousia*, means a presence or an arrival, usually the arrival of a great king or other dignitary. It refers to Christ's future, visible coming at the end of history.

Third, what shall be the *sign*? That word *sign* often means a miracle, something spectacular in the world, in the church, and in history by which we will see and know that the coming of Christ is near. The disciples wanted to be able to watch for the coming of their Lord.

Fourth, what shall be the sign *of the end of the world?* In the minds of the disciples the end of the temple and of Jerusalem were intimately connected to the end of the world and the second coming of Christ. In fact, it is very possible that the two things were one event in the minds of the disciples.

These questions are very significant. To understand them is a key to the entire Olivet Discourse. Are the disciples asking a question *only* about the fall of Jerusalem? If so, Jesus has nothing to say about his second coming, except that he is coming in judgment upon Jerusalem to destroy it. Then everything in the chapter has reference to the history of AD 70, and the chapter has nothing to do with us. Are the disciples asking a question *only* about the end of the world, *only* about the distant future? If so, Jesus has nothing to say about the temple that was standing at *that* time, and he means some future temple yet to be built. Then the chapter has no reference to the events of AD 70, and the chapter has nothing to do with the disciples of Christ's day. We take it to be both—the disciples are asking about *both* the fall of Jerusalem *and* the end of the world with the second coming of Christ. Christ answers both questions but one question in light of the other.

In taking this view we stand against another popular view of eschatology, or view of the last things, namely, postmillennialism. Postmillennialism teaches that Christ will return after a long period of earthly peace and prosperity of the church, when the majority of mankind will be converted or at least subdued under Christian governments, and believers will have dominion in the earth. But Matthew 24 speaks of the opposite—wars, famines, earthquakes, the love of many growing cold, and persecution for the church. The solution of postmillennialism is to push all of those things into the past so that they all marked the end of the Jewish age in AD 70. Wars, famines, and earthquakes do happen today, but these are not signs for us, and these things will gradually become less frequent. The coming of Jesus Christ referred to in Matthew 24 is his coming in judgment upon Jerusalem, not that he comes personally but that he sends judgments and in that sense "comes." Besides this, "the end of the world" in verse 3 is literally the "end of the age," which means, says the postmillennialist, the end of the Jewish age, the end of the Old Testament system of Jewish temple worship. This view is often called preterism, which, as was explained in the introduction, is a name that comes from the Latin word for the past.[3]

Such an interpretation of the disciples' question is flawed for the following reasons.

First, the coming of Christ will be such a visible coming that the entire world will see him (Matt. 24:27). That coming is preceded not by spiritual prosperity, but by wickedness and unbelief as in the days of Noah (v. 37).

Second, the end of the age or world in Matthew 24 is not the end of the Jewish age, which supposedly ended in AD 70, but the end of the world, or the end of this physical creation, or the end of history. That is clear from an examination of that phrase "the end of the world." The same phrase is used in Matthew 13:38–40: "The field is the world; the good seed are the children of the kingdom; but the tares are the children of the wicked one; the enemy that sowed them is the devil; the harvest is *the end of the world*; and the reapers are the angels. As therefore the tares are gathered and burned in the fire; so shall it be in *the end of this world*" (emphasis added). The phrase is

---

3   Gary De Mar in his *Last Days Madness: Obsession of the Modern Church* (Atlanta, GA: American Vision Inc., 1997) argues, "These questions are related to the destruction of the temple and the Old Covenant redemptive system, *and nothing else*" (43, emphasis added).

also used in Matthew 28:19–20: "Go ye therefore, and teach all nations, baptizing them in the name of the Father, and of the Son, and of the Holy Ghost: teaching them to observe all things whatsoever I have commanded you: and, lo, I am with you alway, even unto *the end of the world*. Amen" (emphasis added).[4]

Elsewhere, Christ teaches us that the history of the world is not divided into the Jewish age and the Christian age, but this present age and the age to come, the age of eternity: "Jesus answering said unto them, The children of this world marry, and are given in marriage: but they which shall be accounted worthy to obtain that world, and the resurrection from the dead, neither marry, nor are given in marriage" (Luke 20:34–35).

Nevertheless, the postmillennialists have what they believe to be proof for their assertion that all the signs of Matthew 24 have been fulfilled in the past. They appeal to verse 34. They see that verse as the key to the entire passage. Everything, they say, must be fulfilled in one generation.

But this does not mean that everything in this chapter will be fulfilled exhaustively in AD 70, although postmillennialists have written books trying to prove that everything fits. The verse means this: everything will happen as a type of the end of the world in the destruction of Jerusalem. Nevertheless, that will not exhaust its fulfillment. All the things predicted here will happen within one generation. The disciples must not be tempted to push these things far off into the distant future—so that they do not experience any of them. Nevertheless, they will not be exhaustively fulfilled in one generation. They will continue right up to the coming of the Son of man.

This is also Calvin's interpretation of the Olivet Discourse:

---

4   The word *world* or *age* is the Greek word *aioon*, from which the English word *aeon* is derived.

Though Christ employs a general expression, yet he does not extend the discourses to all the miseries which would befall the Church, but merely informs them, that before a single *generation* shall have been completed, they will learn by experience the truth of what he has said. For within fifty years the city was destroyed and the temple was rased, the whole country was reduced to a hideous desert, and the obstinacy of the world rose up against God. Nay more, their rage was inflamed to exterminate the doctrine of salvation, false teachers arose to corrupt the pure gospel by their impostures, religion sustained amazing shocks, and the whole company of the godly was miserably distressed. Now though the same evils were perpetrated in uninterrupted succession for many ages afterwards, yet what Christ said was true, that, before the close of a single *generation,* believers would feel in reality, and by undoubted experience, the truth of his prediction; for the apostles endured the same things which we see in the present day. And yet it was not the design of Christ to promise to his followers that their calamities would be terminated within a short time, (for then he would have contradicted himself, having previously warned them that *the end was not yet;*) but, in order to encourage them to perseverance, he expressly foretold that those things related to their own age. The meaning therefore is: "This prophecy does not relate to evils that are distant, and which posterity will see after the lapse of many centuries, but which are now hanging over you, and ready to fall in one mass, so that there is no part of it which the present *generation* will not experience." So then, while our Lord heaps upon a single *generation* every kind of calamities, he does not by any means exempt future ages from the same kind of sufferings, but only enjoins the disciples to be prepared for enduring them all with firmness.[5]

Matthew 24, then, is *the* chapter that treats in detail the signs of Christ's coming. They are signs that Christ's disciples would begin to see within a generation, but signs that would continue until the end of the world. They are signs that make it clear to the child of God who has spiritual discernment that Christ is coming. These things point to his coming and they are the way in which he comes. They are necessary for his coming. Our calling is to observe these signs, to watch for them, and to pray when we see them.

Do the disciples' questions burn in your heart also? Listen to Christ's answer, then read on!

---

5   John Calvin, *Commentary on a Harmony of the Evangelists*, trans. William Pringle (Grand Rapids, MI: Baker Book House, repr., 1979), 3:151–52.

Chapter 2

✦

DECEIVERS COMING IN CHRIST'S NAME

And Jesus answered and said unto them, Take heed that no
man deceive you. For many shall come in my name, saying,
I am Christ; and shall deceive many.—Matthew 24:4–5

As we read Christ's answer to his disciples' questions, we
need to bear a few things in mind. Christ as a prophet
describes two events, which are the destruction of Jerusalem in
AD 70 and his second coming at the end of the world, and he
describes one event in the light of the other.

This twofold prophesying is called *prophetic foreshortening*. It
has often been described thus: a man is far away from a range
of mountains. From his perspective there is one great mountain,
which he describes as one. But when he approaches that mountain range, he notices that what he thought was one mountain is
actually two mountains with a wide valley between them. That is
the *prophetic perspective*, a common literary feature of the prophets.

The Old Testament prophets described the fall of Babylon as if it were the fall of the world (Isa. 13–14); they described the outpouring of the Spirit as if it happened at the same time as the sun losing her light and the moon darkening (Joel 2:28–32). Jesus does the same. He describes the end of the world using the fall of Jerusalem as a type.

We know that this approach is correct because of the questions that the disciples asked Christ at the beginning. The disciples were interested in *more* than the destruction of Jerusalem. They did ask about that, and Christ did answer that question, but they asked about more. They asked for signs of Christ's coming *and* of the end of the world. Postmillennialism, as we have seen, interprets that phrase "end of the world" to mean "the end of the Jewish age," but this phrase is used in scripture to refer to the time of the final coming of Christ and the final judgment at the end of history.

Before the end many signs must be manifest, signs that Christ is ruling; signs that Christ is coming; signs that Christ is on his way. We consider in this chapter the sign of deceivers coming in Christ's name.

Their Coming

Three times in Matthew 24, Christ warns of false teachers. First, in verse 11, he warns of false prophets; second, in verse 24, he warns of false Christs doing great signs and wonders; and third, in verse 5, he warns of the coming of deceivers in his own name.

Deception is a huge theme in the scriptures. Almost all the New Testament epistles contain warnings against it, and here the word appears twice. We should therefore be very clear what it is.

First, consider deception from the perspective of the deceiver. To deceive is to seduce, to entice, to lure, to lead astray, or to cause to err. In 2 Kings 21:9 we read that wicked King Manasseh seduced Israel to do evil by leading them to worship other gods and to adopt the ways of the heathen. In Proverbs 1:10 we read, "My son, if sinners entice thee, consent thou not." In Micah 3:5, Jehovah speaks against "the false prophets that make my people err, that bite with their teeth, and cry, Peace." Specifically, a deceiver deliberately seeks to draw God's people away from him into the paths of sin and false worship. In the Old Testament, such seducers would say to Israel, "Come, let us worship this other god, whom our fathers did not worship." Israel's calling was to reject the deceiver and stone him to death (Deut. 13:6–11). Jeroboam, the son of Nebat, was a deceiver who made Israel to sin by saying, "Let us worship Jehovah through the golden calves, which I have set up at Dan and Bethel" (1 Kings 12:28–30). The New Testament age is filled with deceivers too, from the heretics in the early church to the heretics of our day, all seeking a following for themselves.

Deceivers have various motives, none of them good. Do not think of them as honest purveyors of what they think is the truth. Consider them rather as distributers of spiritual poison, deliberate enemies of the truth. Some deceivers are motivated by covetousness, greed, and the love of money. This is certainly the motivation behind the so-called prosperity gospel. Peter writes, "Through covetousness shall they with feigned words make merchandise of you" (2 Pet. 2:3). Other deceivers are motivated by power. They desire to have a large following, to be popular with the people. This is certainly the motivation behind the megachurch movement and the Roman popes. Paul warns, "Of your own selves shall men arise, speaking perverse things, to draw away disciples after them" (Acts 20:30). Other deceivers are motivated by pride. They desire to make a name for themselves as great teachers. Such men and women love novelty and to be able to say that God revealed something to them that no one else knows.

Paul summarizes the motivation of deceivers and warns against them:

14. That we henceforth be no more children, tossed to and fro, and carried about with every wind of doctrine, by the sleight of men, and cunning craftiness, whereby they lie in wait to deceive;
15. But speaking the truth in love, may grow up into him in all things, which is the head, even Christ. (Eph. 4:14–15)

3. I fear, lest by any means, as the serpent beguiled Eve through his subtilty, so minds should be corrupted from the simplicity that is in Christ.
4. For if he that cometh preacheth another Jesus, whom we have not preached, or if ye receive another spirit, which ye have not received, or another gospel, which ye have not accepted, ye might well bear with him.

13. For such are false apostles, deceitful workers, transforming themselves into the apostles of Christ.
14. And no marvel; for Satan himself is transformed into an angel of light.
15. Therefore it is no great thing if his ministers also be transformed as the ministers of righteousness; whose end shall be according to their works. (2 Cor. 11:3–4, 13–15)

Second, we examine the subject of deception from the perspective of the one deceived. To be deceived is to wander or to go astray, to be drawn away from the truth, to err, or to become bewitched or mesmerized by a plausible false teacher. The guilt for deception lies primarily with the deceiver. However, the one deceived must also bear some responsibility: he is usually the wandering, unstable, unlearned type, a person not grounded in the truth and therefore tossed about by every wind of doctrine. In addition, those bewitched by deceivers are often drawn away by their own lusts: the deceiver offers financial rewards, an easier life, and a less strict form of Christianity. That is what the people want, and they readily receive it. Deception is a judgment of God upon one who knew the truth but did not love the truth. The truth of God's word was not important to the apostate, and God suffered him to be deceived and to lose the truth he once professed.

That deception was a serious issue in the churches is reflected in many of the epistles. Over and over again the apostles write, "Be not deceived" (see 1 Cor. 3:18; 6:9; 15:33; Gal. 6:7; Eph. 5:6; 2 Thess. 2:3; 1 John 3:7). Here Christ says the same thing: "Take heed that no man deceive you" (Matt. 24:4). Deceivers are subtle, dishonest, underhand, and crafty, and they ensnare many. Besides, we have within ourselves the capacity to be deceived because our flesh desires what the deceiver offers, and Satan knows exactly which bait to use. In fact, says Christ in Matthew 24:24, deceivers will be so convincing that they will almost succeed in deceiving the very elect of God.

Both deceivers and the deceived will be found throughout the period of time leading up to the return of the Lord Jesus Christ. Many deceivers will come, not just one, not just one or two, but many, and increasingly so as the day of the Lord approaches. These deceivers will have an alluring, enticing, seductive message, a message of peace and prosperity, a message that gains them a following. The true church will be vexed with false teachers of every conceivable kind so that she must constantly battle for the truth, and at times the battle for the truth will be so fierce that it will appear that the truth is forever lost.

This, of course, has been the history of the church. False teachers opposed the apostles. One need only mention the Judaizers. Heretics such as Arius, Pelagius, and many others opposed the early church. False teachers multiplied in the Middle Ages. Heretics from both Rome and the Anabaptists vexed the reformers. To this day the church must battle false teachers on every side. Expect therefore to see, to meet, and to be sorely tempted by many false teachers, and do not be surprised when many follow such deceivers. Christ has warned us beforehand.

Why does Christ make a point of warning the disciples about this? Because the disciples were ill prepared for it. They were expecting the kingdom of Christ to be something much different. They were expecting the knowledge of God to fill the earth from sea to sea, and every man to know the Lord from the least to the greatest (Hab. 2:14; Jer. 31:33–34). They were *not prepared* for a battle for the truth. The disciples expected the kingdom of Christ to be one of outward splendor. They expected Christ to win the hearts of most, if not all, of the Jews and to destroy his enemies. But this was not to be: yes, Christ's kingdom is glorious, but glorious in a spiritual way. The church is not glorious in superior numbers. The church's glory is not her dominion in the earth. With the coming of Christ to suffer, die, rise again, and ascend into heaven, the devil has only become more enraged because he knows his time is short, so he exerts more effort to deceive the world and destroy the church through heresy (Rev. 12:12, 17). The coming of deceivers is in the providence of God part of the devil's last desperate attempt to bring about his own kingdom, and he will succeed for a time when the great deceiver who is the antichrist comes to power.

Postmillennialists today make the same mistake and are ill prepared for the future. They have a vision, not of increased deception and increased attacks by the devil, but of the end of deception or, at the very least, a sharp decrease in it. The presence of many deceivers who deceive many is incompatible with the postmillennial dream of a golden age, so they push the deceivers of Matthew 24 into the pre-AD 70 period. Nevertheless, Paul writes in 2 Timothy 3:13, "Evil men and seducers shall wax worse and worse, deceiving and being deceived."

Here is a sign that Christ is at the right hand of God, moving all things to his second coming: there is an increase in deceivers in the world and especially in the church world. We must not think that the presence of heretics who deceive many is outside Christ's control. Certainly, such deceivers do not take God or Christ by surprise, for he prophesies of their coming. "Many shall come" in his name, he says (Matt. 24:5).

Moreover, Christ exercises more than simple foreknowledge: the deceivers are in his hand, and he uses them for his sovereign and good purposes (Job 12:16). He uses them to stir up the church to develop the truth, to chastise the church for her unfaithfulness, and as a means to bring about the destruction of the reprobate. This must always be our comfort when we experience the reality of deceivers in the New Testament age. Christ knows about this; he forewarned us, and he is sovereign over it. Every heretic, every cult leader, every new heterodox movement is another footstep as Christ makes his way to us, to take us to himself. We must not be alarmed. If Christ had not forewarned us, we might have had reason to be alarmed. You can hear the objection: "We thought everything would be easy. We thought the church would preach, that men would submit to Christ, and the church would take the kingdoms of this world to be the kingdom of Christ." Christ does not give us false hope: "Do not be deceived," says the Lord, "for my kingdom is coming in the way of struggle, fighting for the truth, and contending with many deceivers." That is God's good and wise purpose.

Their Character

The deceivers in Matthew 24:5 are to be distinguished from those in verse 11 (false prophets) and in verses 24 and 26 (false christs and false prophets doing signs and wonders). The deceivers in verse 5 come in Christ's name ("many shall come in my name").

To come in the name of Christ is to come claiming his authority, and to come upon the basis of the revelation of Christ's person and work. That is what a name is in scripture. The apostles came preaching in the name of Christ, because they had seen the risen Lord Jesus and they represented him. Every true preacher today preaches in the name of Christ, "for we preach not ourselves," our opinions and theories, but the doctrine of Christ as recorded in the inspired scriptures (2 Cor. 4:5). Since it is an awesome responsibility to preach in the name of Christ, we must never preach anything in his name that he does not authorize us to preach. When preaching is faithful to the name of Christ, all of us must believe and obey it. Deceivers, then, come with a semblance of Christianity behind them, because they must at least appear to be plausible.

Deceivers do not wear horns and breathe sulphur: they are well dressed and often wear suits; or to appeal to the youth, they wear trendy, fashionable clothes and cool glasses and sit on stools. They display a wonderful smile and probably evince a friendly personality. Deceivers come with the right kind of words, quoting scripture, claiming Christian experience, and often claiming to have an office in the church. Deceivers on the surface sound orthodox: they may even speak of sin, forgiveness, justification, or grace, but they have twisted definitions of what these terms mean. This makes them dangerous.

Moreover, some of these deceivers claim to be Christ, "saying, I am Christ" (v. 5). Christ is the anointed and approved servant of God, the prophet, priest, and king of heaven. Christ is the eternal Son of God made flesh, who as our chief prophet and teacher reveals to us the will of God concerning our salvation. Christ is the eternal Son of God made flesh, who as our only high priest brings us into fellowship with God by dying on the cross for our sins and interceding for us in heaven. Christ is the eternal Son of God made flesh, who as our eternal king rules us by his grace and Holy Spirit and subdues all his and our enemies unto himself.

Deceivers who come in Christ's name, saying, "I am Christ," make claims that they can do what Christ does for his people. Christ reveals God to his people; these deceivers claim to have enlightenment, secret knowledge of the things of God, and they promise to reveal these things to their followers. Cult leaders are known for this kind of approach. Deceivers who claim to know the future, so-called prophecy experts, gain a following in this way. Christ brings his people into fellowship with God and prays for his people; these deceivers claim to have unique access to God, promising solutions to all of life's problems and great blessings. They promise instant success in prayer because they are especially close to God and can also bring you close, usually for a fee. Christ rules over his people through grace; these deceivers offer victory over poverty, sickness, and suffering; they claim to speak for God and to have heavenly authority through a special anointing of the Holy Spirit. These deceivers will be successful. There will be a market for their brand of spiritual poison. Christ warns that they "shall deceive many." Not a few—not one or two, not all—but many!

Deceivers coming in the name of Christ were common in the ancient world. The book of Acts mentions some examples:

36. Before these days rose up Theudas, boasting himself to be somebody; to whom a number of men, about four hundred, joined themselves: who was slain; and all, as many as obeyed him, were scattered, and brought to nought.

37. After this man rose up Judas of Galilee in the days of the taxing, and drew away much people after him: he also perished; and all, even as many as obeyed him, were dispersed. (Acts 5:36–37)

"There was a certain man, called Simon, which beforetime in the same city used sorcery, and bewitched the people of Samaria, giving out that himself was some great one: to whom they all gave heed, from the least to the greatest, saying, This man is the great power of God" (Acts 8:9–10).

"Art not thou that Egyptian, which before these days madest an uproar, and leddest out into the wilderness four thousand men that were murderers" (Acts 21:38)?

In the early church, men like Montanus (second century) appeared, who claimed to be the Paraclete, the Holy Spirit; and Mani (third century), who also claimed to be the Paraclete. Today we see all kinds of people who claim to have a so-called anointing, but who bring false gospels. In the future we will see a man who is able to give earthly peace and prosperity to the world. He will be the antichrist, the culmination of all deception.

Such deception is plausible to those who seek an earthly, carnal kingdom. Such deceivers are only successful when they can convince people to look away from the spiritual blessings of salvation purchased on the cross to the satisfaction of their earthly needs. Finally, when a man will appear on the scene of history, one who will claim to be able to solve the problems of this world, bring about the end of war and famine, and solve the economic woes of our day, he will be hailed as the savior that mankind needs. His diabolical nature will be seen in this: he will offer blessings without the cross of Christ and peace without the forgiveness of sins.

Our Calling

Christ's warning concerning a multitude of deceivers in the last days must lead us to constant vigilance. Too many in the church are asleep and are guilty of presumption: "Oh, I will never be deceived. I am a Christian!" But Christ means us to take this warning seriously: "Take heed that no man deceive *you*" (Matt. 24:4, emphasis added). Christ does not say, "Take heed that no man deceive your neighbor, your friend, or your spouse, or the weaker members of the church." All that is true. But remember this: "Take heed that no man deceive *you*." You will be no use to your fellows if you are deceived. There is no point looking outside at the other churches: look at yourself and take heed that no man deceive *you*.

Do not immediately assume that you know so much theology that you could never be deceived. Watch and pray for the deception will be severe. Christ warns us that this deception could come from anywhere. "Take heed that *no man* deceive you" (emphasis added). That is an indefinite pronoun: it means literally "anyone," "a certain one." The deceiver could be a wide-eyed, self-proclaimed prophet, or he could be a sober-minded biblical scholar; he could be a friendly preacher or an affable priest. Take heed that no man, no matter who he is, how nice he appears, and how popular he might be, deceive you!

This is always the calling of the church, to watch and pray and to avoid deception from every quarter. That comes out in the tense of "take heed." It is present tense in the Greek. The force of Christ's command is this: take heed and keep on taking heed that no man deceive you. Deceivers do not give up, and Satan does not give up sending them.

The calling of the church in light of all this is twofold: first, to sound the warning to her members and to anyone who will listen; and second, to heed the warning herself. The church today needs preaching that exposes the lie and faithfully sets forth the truth. The preacher today has a sacred calling to be antithetical. He must not be vague, but sharp in making distinctions, in presenting the truth against the dark background of the lie. The preacher today has a sacred calling to be polemical, that is, to engage in theological and spiritual warfare, to expose and refute the lie. The people must hear warnings! The preacher today must be specific in his preaching: he must not say, "There are false teachers and deceivers in the world, but I am not going to tell you who the false teachers are and what they teach, nor am I going to explain to you what the Bible says against their lies." Although it might appear impolite and uncharitable, faithful preaching must expose false teachers *by name.*

Many today believe that heretics exist only in the abstract, as if they were not living, breathing individuals. Antithetical, polemical preaching will make the church deeply unpopular and the preacher will be tempted to blunt his sword, but he must not, he may not, do so, because "many shall come in [Christ's] name...and shall deceive many" (Matt. 24:5).

Take heed that Rome does not deceive you. For priests will come, claiming to be followers of the same Christ. They shall invite you to ecumenical services. Many shall participate, and you will be maligned as a bigot if you resist their ecumenical charms. Take heed that the interfaith movement does not deceive you. For smiling clergy will come and tell you that all religions are equal and invite you for dialogue and shall deceive many, and you will be excluded if you refuse. Take heed that the Pentecostals and charismatics do not deceive you. For excitable people will come claiming tongues and prophesies and shall entice you to believe in their so-called spirit, deceiving many. Heed the warning and watch and pray. Attend the preaching and support the minister who faithfully seeks to blow the trumpet when he sees the deceivers coming, even when some of the people do not take kindly to the warnings. Study the scriptures, arm yourself with the truth, and grow in the knowledge of God's word. Then, by the grace of God, you will not be enticed away from the truth.

Chapter 3

♦

TURMOIL
IN NATURE AND
AMONG THE NATIONS

And ye shall hear of wars and rumours of wars: see that
ye be not troubled: for all these things must come to pass,
but the end is not yet. For nation shall rise against nation,
and kingdom against kingdom: and there shall be famines, and pestilences, and earthquakes, in divers places.
All these are the beginning of sorrows.—Matthew 24:6–8

The signs in Matthew 24 are not listed neatly according
to their significance or importance. The most important
sign is the worldwide preaching of the gospel (v. 14), but Christ
mentions something else first—the coming of deceivers. He
warns about them first because of the immediate danger to the
disciples. They could be deceived, and Christ wanted to warn
them.

I dare say that when people talk about the end times, the
most dramatic signs receive the most attention. Sensationalist

preachers like to scare their audiences with lurid details about wars, famines, pestilences, and earthquakes. These are the stuff of novels and movies. Perhaps one word characterizes Christ's description of the entire New Testament age in this text: turmoil. Let us consider this turmoil soberly, and let us receive the comfort that Christ gives us.

The Meaning of the Turmoil

Christ prophesies that turmoil and unrest (not peace and tranquility) will characterize the New Testament age. He lists four disasters: war, famine, pestilence, and earthquake. To that Luke adds, "fearful sights and great signs…from heaven" (Luke 21:11) and "upon the earth distress of nations, with perplexity; the sea and the waves roaring" (v. 25). The disciples will begin to experience them, but these things will continue throughout the New Testament age.

Look briefly at the four things Christ prophesies.

First, war is the expression of man's hatred for his fellow man, his "inhumanity to man," and consists in conflict between nations or even among people groups within one nation. People suffer in war; even in the best wars there are many casualties, and often men's cruelty and greed come to terrifying expressions. No one who has lived through warfare can forget it—the noise, the stench of death, the screaming of the injured, and the groaning of the dying. War can be worldwide (there have been two world wars in recent history), or localized, or even a civil war within one nation. The term *war* includes civil unrest, widespread rioting on the streets, and all the violence involved in those events. Some of the wars will be close and others far away (rumors). Some we will witness firsthand; in others we will be participants. Others (rumors) will be reported to us via the media. War comes from the evil, covetous heart of man. Nation rises against nation and kingdom against kingdom, because one people wants to enlarge its borders at the expense of its neighbor or because one people group wants to annihilate another people group.

Second, *famine* can mean either intense hunger, subsistence living, or widespread starvation. Famine is often the result of war, because in war food production is severely reduced: either food production becomes impossible or the enemy destroys or plunders the food supply. We have all seen the devastation of famine: television screens have shown haunting images of starving children in Africa. The prodigal son experienced "a mighty famine," so that he exclaims, "How many hired servants of my father's have bread enough and to spare, and I perish with hunger [famine]" (Luke 15:14, 17). Paul experienced famine also, for he was "in weariness and painfulness, in watchings often, in hunger [famine] and thirst, in fastings often, in cold and nakedness" (2 Cor. 11:27). In Acts 11:28, Agabus prophesied a great dearth (famine), which took place during the reign of Claudius Caesar.

The third event that Christ prophesies is pestilence, the spread of disease, often to epidemic proportions. Pestilence often follows war and famine. With rotting corpses lying on the fields and in the towns and a lack of food, disease often spreads, killing huge numbers of people. Pestilence or plague usually carries away the weak and vulnerable, and if there is poverty or lack of medicine, the death toll can be enormous. History records many pestilences: think, for example, of the Black Death in the Middle Ages, which wiped out one-third of Europe's population; and of the recent scourges of AIDS, bird flu, swine flu, SARS, Ebola, and the like. Modern medicine has not ended the risk of pestilences.

Fourth, adding to the misery caused by war, famine, and pestilence, the Lord speaks of earthquakes, which will be "in

33

divers places." An earthquake is the violent shaking of the earth, bringing terrible destruction in its wake. When a quake occurs under the sea, the result can be a tsunami, a terrible tidal wave that brings destruction. Man is helpless before an earthquake, and even a modest earthquake can bring about the death of thousands of people. God sends such earthquakes to remind us that this earth will not last forever:

25. See that ye refuse not him that speaketh. For if they escaped not who refused him that spake on earth, much more shall not we escape, if we turn away from him that speaketh from heaven:

26. Whose voice then shook the earth: but now he hath promised, saying, Yet once more I shake not the earth only, but also heaven.

27. And this word, Yet once more, signifieth the removing of those things that are shaken, as of things that are made, that those things which cannot be shaken may remain.

28. Wherefore we receiving a kingdom which cannot be moved, let us have grace, whereby we may serve God acceptably with reverence and godly fear:

29. For our God is a consuming fire. (Heb. 12:25–29)

The disciples will see these four things (war, famine, pestilence, and earthquake). These will be signs for the disciples that Christ is ruling at the right hand of God and executing judgment in the world.

We know this from Revelation 5–6. In those chapters, Christ receives a book (really a scroll), sealed with seven seals. That book or scroll contains God's counsel, God's plan for the whole of New Testament history. Because of Christ's work of redemption, he is worthy to receive and open the book, which he receives at his ascension and begins to open immediately and progressively through the New Testament age.

In Revelation 6, when Christ opens the seals, one by one terrible things are unleashed upon the earth, especially with respect to the second, third, and fourth seals. When Christ opens the second seal, he sends war and bloodshed upon the earth. Christ takes peace away from the earth so that mankind becomes drenched in blood and is plunged into the misery of war. When Christ opens the third and fourth seals, he unleashes famine and social inequality upon the earth, followed by death in all its forms: "to kill with sword and with hunger [famine], and with death, and with the beasts of the earth" (v. 8). The third seal is important, because it shows us that economic turmoil, the gap between rich and poor, is also sent upon the earth by Christ. The basic measure of grain for one day, "a measure of wheat for a penny, and three measures of barley for a penny" (v. 6), will cost a day's wages (that is, subsistence living, living hand to mouth); but the luxuries of life, "the oil and the wine," will still be enjoyed by the rich.

These events are signs for the disciples and signs for the church of all ages. Every time war breaks out, or famine, pestilence, or earthquakes strike, we are to remember that Christ is at the right hand of God. He sent that. War, famine, pestilence, and earthquake are signs that Christ is coming. Every one of those events is a footstep of Christ as he makes his way to be with his church.

In addition, these events are judgments of God upon the world. They are reminders to the wicked that God rules, that God is just, and that God is angry with the ungodly. Expect, therefore, to see these things. Expect turmoil among the nations and in nature. Expect even the earth to shake. God is angry, God is just, and Christ is coming.

We must not misunderstand these signs. Many have been the so-called prophecy experts who have looked at the number of earthquakes and other disasters, counted the wars and other tumultuous events, and concluded that "the end is very near." But that is *not* what these signs are: you cannot count earthquakes, wars, and other upheavals and make predictions. In fact, says Christ, "The end is not yet." The presence of war is a sign that the end is *not* yet. Rather, "all these are the beginning [not the end, not almost the end, but the *beginning*] of sorrows" (Matt. 24: 6, 8).

To avoid confusion about the significance of wars, famines, pestilences, and earthquakes as signs of the coming of Christ, we need to be clear what signs are. The signs, called precursory signs (signs that run before), are not mere signposts that indicate how far you are from a destination. Let me illustrate. If you intend to drive from Limerick to Dublin, Ireland, you get on the M7 motorway or freeway. A roadway sign will say, "Dublin 198 km." As you progress along the road in the right direction, the sign will change to "Dublin 100 km," "Dublin 75 km," and so on. The road sign is merely a marker indicating direction and distance, nothing more. But the precursory signs that indicate Christ's coming are more than that.

Consider rather a thunderstorm. You do not see a mechanical sign, "Thunderstorm in six hours." Nevertheless, there are all kinds of signs that a thunderstorm is coming. You notice an almost palpable change in the atmosphere. Scientists have observed that animals can sense a thunderstorm. There is warm, muggy weather; the skies darken; lightning flashes in the distance; and you hear peals of thunder. All of these changes are due to the approach of the thunderstorm itself. They are part of the storm, and they bring it on. In fact, they are necessary for the thunderstorm to show itself.

The coming of Christ is like that thunderstorm. You cannot interpret the signs (false prophets, wars, famines, pestilences, and earthquakes) to mean that the coming of Christ is two thousand years away, or two hundred years away, or ten years away, or a month away. By observing the signs, we can know that Christ is definitely coming, just as you can know by the atmospheric changes, the darkening of the skies, and the muggy weather that a storm is coming. All these signs are exactly what we should expect because Christ is ruling at the right hand of God. We must be able to discern the coming of Christ in these things. They are signs to the disciples of the first century, and to the saints of all ages, and to us that Christ is on his way.

The wicked, however, observe the same phenomena and say, "Oh, there have always been wars, famines, pestilences, and earthquakes. By our scientific advancements we will overcome all these. By our political alliances we will end war. These things mean nothing." Instead of preparing for the coming storm, the ungodly people of this world explain away all the signs and are destroyed when the storm finally comes. The wicked will be denying the signs of the coming of Christ until the very day he rends the heavens and comes down!

The Necessity of the Turmoil

Christ reassures us in Matthew 24:6, "See that ye be not troubled: for all these things must come to pass." All these things are contained in the book with the seven seals, a book written by God, a book that contains God's comprehensive will for the history of the world. These things must come to pass exactly because God has decreed them.

These things are necessary, first, because God is holy and just. Given the evil of the world, we should be surprised if these things did *not* happen. Many unbelievers object to Christianity because they imagine that a God of love could not or would not allow terrible things like war, famine, pestilence, and earthquakes to happen. Christ sees no objection! He says, "All these things must come to pass." In fact, Christ sends them! Remember that God is not simply a God of love. He is the God of absolute holiness, and he must judge sin and sinners, especially wicked mankind, Jews and Gentiles alike, who crucify his Son and daily blaspheme his name. God reminds the wicked every day that he is angry and that they must repent. He does so by inflicting upon the wicked world tokens of his wrath, such as wars, famines, pestilences, and earthquakes—and much more besides. The world seeks peace in unrighteousness, but God will not give peace without the cross and without repentance from sin.

These things are necessary, second, because the church must be gathered. While turmoil occurs in the history of the nations and in nature, the true church is busy preaching the gospel, "and then shall the end come" (v. 14). What would happen if there were no war or if there were worldwide peace among the nations? What *will* happen when the nations of the world finally come together under one head, and when one man is able to solve the social and economic problems of the world? The answer is that the world, which hates the church of Christ, will be able to concentrate on its desire to destroy the church, because it will no longer be distracted by wars and other disasters. When wars cease, *then* the church should begin to see a sign that the end is near. But when wars continue, and when we see wars and hear about wars in other places (rumors of wars), we can confidently say, "The end is *not* yet." While the Lord sends out war, famine, pestilence, and death (the last three horsemen of the apocalypse [Rev. 6:1–8]), he also sends forth the preaching of the gospel (the white horse [Rev. 19:11–16]).

When the white horse has fulfilled his course, the other horses will cease their running, but not before then.

These things must happen throughout the New Testament age, not simply in the period leading up to AD 70 (postmillennialism) and not simply in the period after the fictional future rapture (premillennial dispensationalism).

Postmillennialism dreams of earthly peace and prosperity, brought about by the success of the preaching of the gospel. Therefore, says the postmillennialist, the wars, rumors of wars, famines, pestilence, and earthquakes were signs *only* for the disciples prior to AD 70. They are not signs for us. The end spoken of in Matthew 24:6 and 14 (and verse 3) is the end of the age *for the disciples*. We should expect these things to cease, or at least to decrease. Premillennial dispensationalism dreams of a sudden rapture of the saints: the seals of Revelation 6 are opened, they say, *after* the rapture; the turmoil mentioned in the text happens *after* the rapture; and the disasters we see around us, while interesting, are not signs for us. They are signs for the saints—especially the Jews—during the great tribulation.

Thus, these two eschatological schools teach that the beginning of sorrows is really the beginning of sorrows *for the Jews*, either for the Jews prior to AD 70 (postmillennialism) or for the Jews of the future post-rapture tribulation (premillennialism). Both are wrong: these things begin to happen in the lives of the disciples and mark God's dealings with mankind throughout the New Testament age. Christ will be sending war, famine, and pestilence. And Christ will be shaking the earth with increasing frequency and intensity until he returns on the clouds of glory.

Since these things must come to pass—they are part of God's sovereign will—it is foolish for us to seek to prevent them. They are necessary for God's glory and the good of Christ's church. When you pray, "Thy kingdom come!" this means, "Lord, send wars, famines, pestilences, and earthquakes upon the earth, and Lord, send forth thy gospel and gather thy church!" Christ will not come in any other way: Christ will not come in the way of peace, in the way of the eradication of poverty, in the way of environmentalism, so that the erratic weather patterns (caused, we are told, by manmade climate change) can be counteracted.

However, that *is* the way in which antichrist comes. Antichrist brings together the nations; antichrist brings together the religions; antichrist solves the problem of the world's economy; antichrist creates prosperity and peace for all (as long as you worship him; otherwise he persecutes you and kills you!). The church's calling, then, is not to transform society, to promote recycling, to end poverty, to end social injustice, and to pray for earthly peace. These things are not wrong in themselves, but they can become a distraction from the church's actual calling.

The church has *one* calling: preach the gospel of "Christ crucified" (1 Cor. 1:23). In fact, through the church's prayers God brings turmoil upon the earth. This does not mean that we pray, "God, send an earthquake here or send famine there." We cannot be so specific. It means that we pray for God's kingdom to come and for the kingdom of Satan to be destroyed. Nor does it mean that it is wrong for us to enjoy freedom from war, famine, pestilence, and earthquakes. God does not send these things on all nations at one time, and while we have peace, we ought to use it for God's glory. Nevertheless, the fact remains that our prayers do have a role to play:

3. And another angel came and stood at the altar, having a golden censer; and there was given unto him much incense, that he should offer it with the prayers of all saints upon the golden altar which was before the throne.

4. And the smoke of the incense, which came with the prayers of the saints, ascended up before God out of the angel's hand.

5. And the angel took the censer, and filled it with fire of the altar, and cast it into the earth: and there were voices, and thunderings, and lightnings, and an earthquake. (Rev. 8:3–5)

All these things must come to pass because they are the birth pangs of a new age, the eternal age of the new creation.

The word translated as "sorrows" in Matthew 24:8 is a very specific kind of sorrow: birth pangs or labor pains. There are various kinds of pains in this world, but labor pains are unique. They are unique in their sharpness: labor pains are powerful contractions of the muscles of the womb, which serve to prepare the baby to be born. Because of their sharpness they are incapacitating. They are sudden pains. They come, especially at the beginning, without warning. A mother might know her due date, but she cannot predict when her labor pains will begin: they might be earlier or later than her due date. Labor pains also intensify, becoming more regular and closer together as the birth of the child approaches. Perhaps they begin more than ten minutes apart, but just before birth they are much closer together and much more intense.

Wars, famines, pestilences, and earthquakes and other natural disasters are the beginning of labor pains. Each war, famine, or earthquake is another contraction indicating that the birth of the new world is approaching. Therefore, we can expect that these things will bring much pain upon the world, and that the pain will be unexpected: "For when they shall say, Peace and safety, then sudden destruction cometh upon them, as travail upon a woman with child; and they shall not escape" (1 Thess.

5:3). We also expect that as the day of Christ's return approaches these pains will become more intense and more frequent, until finally there is a war to end all wars (Armageddon) and the final shaking of the heavens and the earth:

12. And I beheld when he had opened the sixth seal, and, lo, there was a great earthquake; and the sun became black as sackcloth of hair, and the moon became as blood;

13. And the stars of heaven fell unto the earth, even as a fig tree casteth her untimely figs, when she is shaken of a mighty wind.

14. And the heaven departed as a scroll when it is rolled together; and every mountain and island were moved out of their places.

15. And the kings of the earth, and the great men, and the rich men, and the chief captains, and the mighty men, and every bondman, and every free man, hid themselves in the dens and in the rocks of the mountains;

16. And said to the mountains and rocks, Fall on us, and hide us from the face of him that sitteth on the throne, and from the wrath of the Lamb. (Rev. 6:12–16)

If you ask, of what these labor pains promise the birth, we answer, the new heavens and the new earth.

Postmillennialism, as you would expect, sees these labor pains leading to a different birth. For postmillennialism, all these pains are in the past, because they were the beginning of sorrows *for Israel.* Therefore, they have no such significance for us. In fact, war, famine, pestilence, and earthquake will cease (or at least become relatively infrequent) during a coming golden age. These things gave birth to the Christian era, as the church broke free of its Jewish garb.

We object to postmillennialism because the end in view is not the end of Jerusalem, not AD 70, but the end of the world. Romans 8:22 speaks of the birth pangs of the creation: "The whole creation groaneth and travaileth in pain." This is true both before and after AD 70. It is groaning and travailing with a view to the final salvation of God's people. That is the end or goal: the consummation of the kingdom of Christ in the salvation in body and soul of all the elect to the glory of the triune God. Only when *that* goal is reached will the birth for which the creation labors in pain have occurred.

Our Comfort in the Turmoil

We must not forget one other truth about birth pangs, really the most important truth. Birth pangs are the harbingers of hope and of promised salvation. Birth pangs signal the coming of a child! Birth pangs are not pointless, fruitless, purposeless tortures, but they have a happy ending. That is why the mother is able to endure them: with each contraction or each push she says, "The baby is coming. I am almost there. Soon I will be holding a baby." Jesus said, "A woman when she is in travail hath sorrow, because her hour is come: but as soon as she is delivered of the child, she remembereth no more the anguish, for joy that a man is born into the world" (John 16:21). When the goal of creation's birth pangs is reached, we will forget the pain we suffered in this world because of the joy we will experience in the new heavens and new earth.

The result of this turmoil will be, as Luke puts it, "men's hearts failing them for fear, and for looking after those things which are coming on the earth, for the powers of heaven shall be shaken" (Luke 21:26). This must not be our attitude. Fear, of course, is a natural reaction. War, famine, pestilence, and earthquake are fearful events. We have all seen them on our television screens and been moved by them. We ought also to have compassion on those caught up in disastrous events and as much as we are able seek to help them, and especially, seek to help the church. This was the case in the early church: when a famine came upon Jerusalem, the churches of Greece and Asia Minor collected money for them, which Paul brought to the suffering saints.

When Christ says, "See that ye be not troubled," he means, "Do not be in a clamor, a tumult; do not be frightened or alarmed." Evidently, Christ expected fear to be their natural reaction, so he told them, "Make sure you are not troubled." Evidently too, Christ expected that they would go through the trouble: they would be caught up in warfare; the church would be affected by famine, by pestilence, and by earthquakes. The church will go through such things, and the church must expect to go through such things. Do not expect an easy escape route through a rapture!

But do not be troubled. Fear not because Christ is at right hand of God and these are signs of his coming. If the devil were sending wars, famines, pestilences, and earthquakes and God were not in control, we would and should be troubled, alarmed, and even terrified. None of these things can hurt us—not really, for they are tokens of God's wrath for the world, but not for the church. On Calvary, Christ has borne the wrath that we deserve. So when you see or hear of a war; when you see social unrest; when you see or hear of a famine, a plague, or an earthquake, do not listen to the unbelieving media, which ignore the coming of Christ. Instead, respond as a Christian and say, "That is a birth pang, a sign that Christ is on his way."

And lift up your heads, for your redemption draws nigh.

Chapter 4

🔥

THE CHURCH HATED BY ALL NATIONS

Then shall they deliver you up to be afflicted, and shall kill you: and ye shall be hated of all nations for my name's sake. And then shall many be offended, and shall betray one another, and shall hate one another.—Matthew 24:9–10

One of the signs of the coming of Christ is persecution, tribulation, affliction, and suffering for the people of God. Christ warns about that at length in the Olivet Discourse in Matthew 24. Christians shall be persecuted and even put to death. Later in the chapter, Christ, using the type of the destruction of Jerusalem, warns of a coming great tribulation (v. 21). Immediately after the great tribulation—of which AD 70 was a type—is the coming of Jesus Christ.

Suffering is a common theme in the Bible. In Matthew 5 Christ includes being persecuted as one of the spiritual characteristics of the citizens of his kingdom. Therefore, all Christians

45

are poor in spirit, mourn over their sins, hunger and thirst after righteousness, and are meek, merciful, pure in heart, and peace-makers. And *all* Christians are persecuted for righteousness' sake and are therefore blessed. In Acts 14:22, Paul and Barnabas tell the Christians, "We must through much tribulation enter into the kingdom of God." Paul writes, "Yea, and all that will live godly in Christ Jesus shall suffer persecution" (2 Tim. 3:12).

Because Christ is at the right hand of God, the church must be persecuted and is persecuted. That might seem strange to us. After all, should not Christ's rule guarantee our *exemption* from suffering? If Christ loved us, would he really allow his church to suffer so much while she waits for him to return? Will he really permit his church to go through the great tribulation and face the antichrist?

The postmillennialists and premillennialists both argue against future suffering for the people of God. For the post-millennialists, the suffering of the church is in the past, for the suffering prophesied in Matthew 24:9–10 happened before AD 70. Although there is and has been suffering, that will gradually disappear as the so-called golden age, so coveted by postmillen-nialism, approaches. For the premillennial dispensationalists, the suffering prophesied here in Matthew 24 belongs to the future after the rapture. We will escape it, while the Jews and the so-called tribulation saints will suffer it.

But do not be fooled! Let no man deceive you! The church has suffered, is suffering, and will continue to suffer until the end, not because Satan is in control, not because Christ does not love us, but because suffering serves the coming of Christ and the end of all things.

If your idea of victory does not fit the description of Romans 8, you need to reevaluate your understanding of victory: "Who shall separate us from the love of Christ? shall tribulation, or distress, or persecution, or famine, or nakedness, or peril, or sword? As it is written, For thy sake we are killed all the day long; we are accounted as sheep for the slaughter. Nay, in all these things we are more than conquerors through him that loved us" (Rom. 8:35–37).

In all these things!

Not through avoiding or escaping all these things!

The Meaning

Christ has a solemn word for his disciples: "Ye shall be hated of all nations" (Matt. 24:9). Hatred is an attitude of the heart, the opposite of love. One who hates dislikes someone intensely, loathes, detests, and abhors him and wills to do evil to him. The church, says Christ, will be the object of such hatred in the New Testament age.

This hatred will be directed, first, toward the eleven disciples (Judas Iscariot will not be included, although Christ has not yet revealed that). This means that all nations will hate Peter, Andrew, James, John, and the other disciples, and by extension, Paul and all believers throughout all ages until the second coming of Christ. This is not, emphatically not, a hatred that will be directed only toward the Jews, or only toward the Christians who lived prior to AD 70, or only to the "tribulation saints" after the rapture. Certainly, the Jews have suffered greatly in history, but that is not Christ's concern here. "*Ye* shall be hated" (emphasis added). This hatred will begin almost immediately after Christ is crucified, is raised from the dead, ascends into heaven, and takes his place at God's right hand.

This hatred will be the general attitude of all men and all nations throughout the New Testament age. No matter where the disciples go, they and their message will be treated with

47

scorn, and they will be hated by all. That hatred will begin in Jerusalem, continue in Samaria, and persist as the disciples travel into Asia Minor, Greece, and Europe. When the church spreads into Asia, America, and Australasia, hatred will follow her. All kinds of men from every walk of life will hate the disciples: emperors, kings, governors, the common people, the religious, and the irreligious alike will join in hating the church. Therefore, never expect to be popular, warns Jesus. Never expect crowds of adoring fans, but expect hardship, unpopularity, scorn, derision, and hatred.

How long will this attitude of hatred last? Will the people of this world ever tire of hating God's people? Perhaps, you imagine, the world will find another object for their hatred and leave the church alone. Not at all! Christ's church will be hated until the day Christ returns to deliver her from her hateful enemies. The tense of Christ's words makes clear that this will be the ongoing, continuous, uninterrupted attitude of all people: "Ye shall be being hated of all nations."

Christ's words have been fulfilled: the disciples were hated; the early church was hated by the Romans; the medieval and Reformation church were hated by the apostate Roman harlot; the modern church is hated by Communists, Islamists, and secularists. This hatred will only continue and intensify as Christ's coming draws near.

This news of universal detestation by the nations of the world was a huge shock to the disciples because this was not what they were anticipating. The disciples did not fully understand Christ's mission. They believed that he was the Messiah, and even the Son of God, and they expected a kingdom. Nevertheless, Christ's sufferings and their own sufferings were not part of their vision for the future. Christ was at this point at the height of his popularity with the common people. Two days before this, Christ had ridden into Jerusalem to the popular acclaim of "Hosanna to the Son of David." Expectations were running high that the kingdom of God was about to be established. Christ seemed to be the one with the miracle-working power to drive out the Romans and establish that kingdom. The disciples, who had been with Christ from the beginning, were expecting fame, honor, glory, prestige, and the best seats in the kingdom of God because of their close association with Christ. Universal hatred was not part of the plan.

This is not the expectation of many Christians today either. Perhaps it is not our expectation. Religion is supposed to make a person popular, to bring advantages. That is the message coming from many parts of the church. Christ came to give us health and wealth. Christians are respectable middle-class citizens. Be a Christian, and people will love you. You will have many friends.

Given this erroneous understanding of Christianity, a Christianity that costs nothing and demands nothing, there is very little interest today in these words of Christ. Deflection is a common ploy: "Surely, that applies only to the people left behind after the rapture. Surely, that is only for certain Christians in far off places. Surely, that was only for Christians in the past." But all of that is Christianity without the cross, Christianity without holiness, and a loss of the offense of the gospel. That is the nice, respectable, social Christianity that the world applauds, but it is not the Christianity of the Bible. True Christianity brings hated and opposition.

This hatred of the nations will manifest itself. It will not remain forever hidden in the hearts of men, but will come to cruel expression in affliction and tribulation. First, "they shall deliver you up" (Matt. 24:9). The Greek word means to give over someone into the power of another, to lay hold on someone and give him into the custody of another. Christ's saints will be delivered up "to be afflicted" (v. 9). That is the hostile, hateful purpose of their enemies. The enemies of the church want Christians to suffer, to experience pain and anguish, and to feel the hatred they have for the church. The word *affliction* comes from a verb that means to squeeze, to squash, or to press down upon. The aim of the afflicter is to make one's position narrow and cramped in the world. The ultimate goal of the wicked persecutors of Christ's church is to pursue after, to chase after, to hunt down every last Christian, in order to squeeze them out of the world.

Mark and Luke provide additional details about the kinds of affliction that Christians will experience. Remember that Christ is painting a picture of the future with a Jewish brush and Jewish colors. Mark 13:9 speaks of councils (the Sanhedrin), of synagogues, of beatings in the synagogues, and of appearing before various kinds of rulers to stand trial. Luke 21:12 speaks of evil men laying hands on the disciples, of persecution, of synagogues and prisons and of standing before kings. Do not be misled by the Jewish brush and colors with which Christ, as a master artist, depicts the prophecy! Christ does not mean only synagogues and the Jewish Sanhedrin. Oh yes, it will begin there! Christ also means the torture chambers of the Inquisition, the gulags of forced labor in Communist Russia, the metal crates of Eritrea, the secret police of Communist China and North Korea, the appalling persecution in the Muslim world, the future persecution of the western world, and the evils of the government of the antichrist.

Finally, the Lord adds, "They shall kill you" (v. 9). The enemies of the church stoned Stephen (Acts 7), beheaded James (Acts 12), and later killed Paul and Peter. The enemies of the church have been killing Christians ever since.

Matthew 24 does not specify who will deliver the Christians up to be afflicted, but Mark and Luke add that it will be in some cases former friends and even family members. Jesus had already warned about this: he had not come to bring peace, but to bring a sword (Matt. 10:34). The result would be opposition and enmity among friends and even families. Now he underlines it again: you will be handed over to the authorities to be afflicted and to be killed. Your friends will do it! Your parents will do it! Your brothers and sisters will do it! Your sons and daughters will do it! "Now the brother shall betray the brother to death, and the father the son; and children shall rise up against their parents, and shall cause them to be put to death" (Mark 13:12). "And ye shall be betrayed both by parents, and brethren, and kinsfolks, and friends; and some of you shall they cause to be put to death" (Luke 21:16).

What a bitter pill that will be to swallow! Surely it is bad enough to be arrested; bad enough to be treated as a criminal; bad enough to be thrown into prison, to be tortured, to be put to death. But to watch as your own family do it! To hear your nearest and dearest say, "Take him. He is a Christian. We hate him. We are not on his side." How dreadful!

All this is another sign of the coming of Christ, a sign that Christ is at the right hand of God and a sign that Christ is on his way. The hatred of the church by all nations is part of the development of sin and part of the filling up of the cup of God's wrath, both of which must take place with a view to the end of all things.

Since the fall of man, two principles have been at work in this world. The first is the principle of grace, gathering and preserving a church out of the world. The second is the principle of sin, the expression of man's enmity against God. At the same time two kingdoms are developing: the kingdom of God with

Christ as king and the kingdom of darkness with Satan as king. Satan knows that his time is short, so he is making a desperate attempt to crown himself king by setting up a man-centered, God-defying, anti-Christian kingdom. That means opposition to the church.

The opposition between these two kingdoms has intensified since the coming of Christ. His coming was not a ceasefire or a cessation of hostilities, but the declaration of war. Christ came to spoil Satan's goods. Satan knew it and tried to stop him. Christ defeated Satan at the cross, and now Satan can do only one thing: stir up the hatred of all nations against the church. Christ is out of reach, but the church is not. This is what the disciples must expect. Christ prepares them for this. This is what we must see as a sign of his coming: not worldwide peace, not popularity, not most of the world Christianized, but a church hated and almost hounded out of existence by an ungodly world.

Satan is not inactive. In the New Testament age, however, his activity is limited because Christ has bound him at the cross. Soon he will be loosed, and widespread persecution under antichrist will result. Then what Christ prophesies here will be finally and perfectly fulfilled.

Whether Satan is bound or loosed, we do not fear him. Our God, despite the roaring of Satan and the raving of ungodly men, remains in the heavens and does whatsoever he pleases for the good of his church (Ps. 115:3).

The Cause

The cause of this hatred of the church by all nations is the nations' hatred of Christ himself. "Ye shall be hated of all nations for my name's sake [on account of my name]" (Matt. 24:9). The name of Christ is the revelation of Christ, the Son of God, the prophet, priest, and king of God, the savior of his people. For a while, as long as the name "Christ" was the kind of Christ the crowds wanted, it seemed that the name of Christ was the ticket to popularity for the disciples. A Christ who heals the sick, feeds the multitudes, does miracles that astound and amaze the people—*that* Christ the people would accept. The people saw in Christ a savior from poverty, from oppression, and especially from Roman occupation. As long as Christ seemed to be that kind of Christ, crowds thronged him.

But this Christ refused to be their king, taught them that they should pay tribute to Caesar, and was arrested by the Jewish authorities and tried by the Romans. Then they understood: he is not the Christ we want. Away with him! Crucify him! Christ the earthly king pleases; Christ the crucified Lord offends. He offended the Jews who believed that a crucified Christ was blasphemy. He offended the Greeks and Romans who believed that a crucified Christ was foolishness. He offends many today. Christ the crucified savior confronted the people with their sin and their utter powerlessness to save themselves. They hated him and they hated his message.

The same is true today. A Christ who makes you healthy; a Christ who makes you wealthy; a Christ who improves society; a Christ who ends poverty, hunger, discrimination; a Christ who flatters you by giving you some part, no matter how small, in your salvation—*that* Christ people will believe in. But a Christ who is crucified; who refuses to indulge your pride and self-righteousness; and who demands holiness of life—*that* Christ will be hated, and rejected, and the promoters of that Christ will be opposed, hated, hounded, and persecuted.

The church will be hated and cruelly persecuted by all nations, simply because she belongs to and is associated with Jesus Christ ("for my name's sake" [v. 9]). The faithful church must always associate herself with this name and preach the name of Christ, even when it brings persecution. This means that the preaching of the church must always have as its content Christ, the glories of Christ, and especially the cross of Christ. The church must call the world to repent and believe in this Christ and in no other Christ. The church must not be tempted to imagine that she can win the world by watering down or changing her message. She may fill her buildings. She may attract more to her worship services. But she will betray the cause of Christ. The message of the gospel will never be popular with fallen man. It will always offend, for the nations will always hate the messengers of such a gospel.

Nevertheless, Christians must be careful that their suffering is only for the name of Christ. Christians must not suffer because of their own behavior and then piously claim to be suffering for the name of Christ. Peter writes, "If ye be reproached for the name of Christ, happy are ye; for the spirit of glory and of God resteth upon you: on their part he is evil spoken of, but on your part he is glorified. But let none of you suffer as a murderer, or as a thief, or as an evildoer, or as a busybody in other men's matters" (1 Pet. 4:14–15).

A Christian who is obnoxious, arrogant, and prideful, or a Christian who is needlessly fanatical, pursuing a cause but not promoting the gospel, cannot claim the text in support of his actions. If you are to offend unbelievers, let the offense be only the gospel itself! Let the offense not be in your offensive behavior!

The infamous Westboro Baptist Church pickets the funerals of US servicemen with hateful, offensive signs. Predictably, the world hates them, and they glory in such hatred, but they are not hated for the name of Christ. They are hated because they are nasty people. Some Christians are simply foolish in their behavior. Consider the example of the pastor who some time ago threatened to burn a Koran and brought international condemnation upon himself and disgrace upon the name of Christ. Such a man is a fool, not a martyr for Christ.

The deeper underlying reason for the hatred and consequent persecution of the church by all nations is that association with Christ always means suffering. The important biblical principle is this: suffering before glory! Christ, the head, had to suffer before he entered his glory. Therefore, we the members will have to suffer before we enter the glory prepared for us. Christ suffered for our sins. He willingly and gladly went to the cross because he loved us and looked forward to the glory that would follow. The sufferings of Christ were inflicted by both God and men: God punished Christ in strict justice for the sins of all the elect whom he represented; while men displayed their cruel hatred for Christ by spitting on him, beating him, nailing him to a cross, and leaving him to die in agony. All of that would happen in just a few days after Christ spoke these words. As a reward to Christ for his obedience unto death, Christ is exalted to the right hand of God, all power is his in heaven and on earth, and he is the head of a church gathered from all nations, tribes, and tongues.

Paul makes a very significant statement in Colossians 1:24: "[I] now rejoice in my sufferings for you, and fill up that which is behind of the afflictions of Christ in my flesh for his body's sake, which is the church." Christ has suffered everything necessary for our salvation. His redemptive sufferings have fully paid for our sins. Nevertheless, Christ's body must continue to suffer on earth in his church, not redemptive sufferings but the cruelty of men and the malice of the devil. In this way, in suffering for the name of Christ, we have fellowship with Christ in his sufferings. Paul desired this: "That I may know him, and the power of his resurrection, and the fellowship of his sufferings, being made conformable unto his death" (Phil. 3:10). That understanding of sufferings ennobles them. Elsewhere Paul writes, "[We are] always bearing about in the body the dying of the Lord Jesus, that the life also of Jesus might be made manifest in our body. For we which live are alway delivered unto death for Jesus' sake, that the life also of Jesus might be made manifest in our mortal flesh" (2 Cor. 4:10–11).

No wonder the disciples rejoiced that they were found worthy to suffer shame for the name of Jesus (Acts 5:41). It is a privilege to suffer for Jesus Christ.

Besides, suffering for Christ's name is not harmful but useful, indeed, necessary. That seems strange to us. By nature, we try to avoid suffering. Nevertheless, God is preparing us for glory exactly by bringing us through suffering:

16. For which cause we faint not; but though our outward man perish, yet the inward man is renewed day by day.
17. For our light affliction, which is but for a moment, worketh for us a far more exceeding and eternal weight of glory;
18. While we look not at the things which are seen, but at the things which are not seen: for the things which are seen are temporal; but the things which are not seen are eternal. (2 Cor. 4:16–18)

God has great plans for us, but we are not complete. We must be perfected and tried in the fires of suffering. Our Father uses the wicked for that very purpose. That is not their evil purpose, of course, but it is God's good purpose. Impatience, worldliness, pride, and many other impurities spoil our Christian lives. Suffering trains us in Christian virtues; suffering makes this world uncomfortable for us so that we long for heaven; suffering makes us dig our roots deeper into Jesus Christ. We will not grow in these virtues if God wraps us up in cotton wool and we sail through life without any opposition. As hard as it is to be hated, we need it, for our own salvation's sake.

Do not fear suffering. Do not fear the hatred of this world. Do not fear being afflicted, squeezed, or crushed, because nothing the world does can harm us. Christ tells the disciples not even to worry about what they will say (Mark 13:11). God will give us words that will testify to him, his glory, his grace, his goodness, and his power, words that the wicked will not be able to gainsay.

To be hated of all nations is nothing to fear therefore, because God loves us, Christ died for us, and the Spirit will sustain us. All nations hate the church, but the hatred of the nations is a token of the love of God. "Ye shall be hated of all nations," says Christ, but, "*I* will not hate you, and *my Father* will not hate you." Paul writes to the Philippians, "In nothing terrified by your adversaries: which is to them an evident token of perdition, but to you of salvation, and that of God. For unto you it is given in the behalf of Christ, not only to believe on him, but also to suffer for his sake" (Phil. 1:28–29).

The Effect

Persecution will have a sifting effect. "Many," says Christ, will be "offended" (Matt. 24:10). The word *offended* signifies "scandalized." It means that many will stumble and fall. Christ himself, Christ crucified, is the stumbling block, for they will fall over him. Those who are offended are professing Christians who have come to realize what following Christ actually implies. They promised themselves, or false teachers promised them, ease, but instead they experience hatred for the gospel of Christ. Their reaction is to be offended. "This was not part of the package I signed up for!" they exclaim. "If this is Christianity, I want none of it! Christ is not worth suffering and dying for!"

This will be the case, not with one or two, but with many: "Then shall *many* be offended" (v. 10, emphasis added). "Many" occurs quite a few times in Matthew 24. There are *many* deceivers; they shall deceive *many*; there shall be *many* offended; *many* false prophets shall arise; the love of *many* shall grow cold.

This is also a necessary warning for the disciples—and for us. There will be people who will appear to be enthusiastic Christians for a while, but when Christ makes too many demands on them, when their family opposes them, when society starts to squeeze them, Christ will be cast aside as an old rag. Do not be discouraged by that. Do not imagine that because of it the cause of Christ has failed in the world, but watch and pray for grace to endure. Whatever you do, do not expect a golden age or a rapture to rescue you before the suffering begins. If you do, you too will be offended when great persecution comes.

Worse than stumbling and falling are the hatred and betrayal such apostates will display. The "many" who are offended "shall betray and shall hate one another" (v. 10). Just imagine! Judas Iscariot was listening to the Olivet Discourse, and he became the first fulfillment of this awful prophecy. The very next day, Judas, who had heard these words of warning, went to the chief priests and did just that. He arranged to betray Jesus for thirty pieces of silver. Why? Judas hated Jesus and finally his mask slipped. All this talk of suffering—Christ's own suffering and then the disciples' suffering—was too much for him. Rather than follow such a Christ, he forsook him while he was still in a position to make some money out of his Master.

This has been the sad history of the church. Men and women have hated Christ so much, a Christ they once professed to love, that they betrayed him and hated his church. Some betrayed him out of cowardice and later repented. This happened in the early church. This happened to the eleven disciples: "All ye shall be offended because of me this night, for it is written, I will smite the Shepherd and the sheep of the flock shall be scattered" (Matt. 26:31). Peter's denial of Christ was most public, but the other ten also showed cowardice. Invariably in the history of the church Christ's bitterest enemies and the church's cruelest persecutors have been apostates. We must expect that. Expect that even within families and from friends. Do not be surprised when it happens, and especially do not be offended when it happens. All of it is a sign that Christ is on his way!

The comfort, however, is that "many shall be offended," but not all. Not all will fall away. Apostasy will be shocking, but some will endure (Matt. 24:13). Some—maybe even a few in comparison with the many who will stumble—will endure unto the end. Some will endure unto the end of their lives; they will die for Christ's name. Many have done so in the past, and others are doing so today as you read these pages. Some will endure even unto the end of the world: they will be enduring the hatred and persecution of the world until the very moment of Christ's return. They will endure, and they will be saved.

That endurance will glorify God and the Christ of God. Men will see that Christ is so precious that his people are willing to be delivered up, to be afflicted, and to be put to death, rather than to deny him. Then it will be seen how powerful the grace of God is: grace took sinners and made them saints; and that grace was so powerful that even the universal, Satan-inspired hatred of the whole world could not pluck them out of the Savior's hand. That is our hope: not in our strength to endure, but in Christ's grace to keep us until he comes.

Chapter 5

◊

THE COOLING
OF THE LOVE
OF MANY

And many false prophets shall rise, and shall deceive many. And because iniquity shall abound, the love of many shall wax cold. But he that shall endure unto the end, the same shall be saved.—Matthew 24:11–13

The signs given in Matthew 24 can be divided roughly into two categories. First, there are the signs in the world of nations and of nature. Included among these are wars, famines, pestilences, and earthquakes. Such events usually receive the most attention because they are the most dramatic. These are powerful indicators of God's coming judgment. Second, there are the signs in the church, such as persecution, preaching, and apostasy.

The most important sign, the worldwide preaching of the gospel, will be treated in the next chapter. However, intimately connected to that sign are the two negative signs of persecution and apostasy. The church is persecuted because she preaches the gospel, and the church is in constant danger of falling away from the truth of the gospel.

What is the greatest threat to the life of the church? It is not poverty: not that her members starve in famine or are left homeless by an earthquake. It is not even persecution: not that her members are cast into prison and put to death in cruel ways by a world that hates her. Instead, the greatest threat to the life of the church is apostasy. If the church apostatizes and loses the truth, she loses the right to be called church. Christ comes in judgment against her and takes away her golden candlestick. She becomes the false church—an empty, lifeless shell. That tragic end begins with the outstanding sign of Christ's coming, the love of many waxing cold.

The Meaning

In Matthew 24:12, Christ makes a startling prediction: "The love of many shall wax cold." This is a warning that many professing faith in Christ will lose their fervor. Either their love will fall to a low ebb, or it will disappear altogether.

The verb translated "wax cold" is only used once in the New Testament. It means to be cooled by blowing. When we have a hot meal or a hot drink, we often blow on it to cool it. That is exactly the idea here. Exposure to a cold breath of air, or a chilling icy wind, has a cooling effect. This cooling does not happen overnight, but over a matter of weeks, months, or years. At the beginning perhaps the cooling effect is barely noticeable, but it ends in cold numbness and deadness. The chilling effect of a cold, icy wind is like this: first, something is hot; then as the icy wind blows, it becomes merely warm; then the more it is exposed to the chilly blast, it becomes lukewarm; then cold; then frigid; and finally there is a danger of it freezing.

Christ does not refer to the cooling of hot coffee or of leaving a hot pie on the windowsill to be cooled down. Rather, he warns about the much more serious cooling of *love*. Specifically, this is cooling of love for Christ and of love for God in Christ. That is the clear, solemn meaning of Christ's words here. Many, warns Christ, may be fervently and passionately in love with me, but over time as the cold winds blow upon them, that love cools down until it is mere affection. If that spiritual declension is not stopped urgently, mere affection becomes a kind of distant coolness, indifference, and disinterest. Finally, a numbness or a deadness sets in, which results in spiritual hypothermia. With this cooling of love for Christ comes the cooling of love for others, for our neighbors, and especially for our fellow Christians, because we cannot love our neighbor unless we love Christ.

Every believer ought to be genuinely alarmed at the possibility that his love for Christ could be cooled, because love for Christ is the heart of all true religion. Love is the expression of genuine Christian piety. Love for Christ is more than loving what we receive from Christ, more than a speaking well of Christ, and more than admiring him. Love for Christ is to breathe after him in ardent devotion, to treasure him as precious and dear, and to delight in him as the supreme object of the desire of our hearts. That is simply the meaning of *love* in scripture. To love Christ means to desire to please him above all, to love to spend time with him, and to long to be closer to him. Love is to enjoy sweet communion with him in the covenant of grace. To love Christ is to love him exclusively, to serve him faithfully, to obey him gratefully, and to have no rivals in our affections because he is the altogether lovely Son of God and the savior of his church.

Reader, is Christ the one your soul loves? Do you express for Christ what the psalmist expressed for the Lord of hosts? "O

God, thou art my God; early will I seek thee: my soul thirsteth for thee, my flesh longeth for thee in a dry and thirsty land, where no water is. To see thy power and thy glory, so as I have seen thee in the sanctuary. Because thy lovingkindness is better than life, my lips shall praise thee" (Ps. 63:1–3).

The love of many shall wax cold! We need to use the word of God as a thermometer to take our spiritual temperature. Is our love of Christ hot, warm, or in danger of cooling?

This disease, the cooling of love, is the most serious spiritual malady we can suffer. Better to suffer poverty, disease, or persecution than to be sick with this cooling of love, which will be the case with many. This is the spiritual litmus test by which Christ measures us: do you love him; is your love for him hot and fervent? Remember his words to Peter, "Simon, son of Jonas, lovest thou me?" (John 21:15–17) and remember his withering rebuke to the church in Ephesus, "I have somewhat against thee because thou hast left thy first love" (Rev. 2:4). All service, all church attendance, all obedience, all defense of the truth, and all witnessing must flow out of love for Christ. Why do you attend church? Why do you work? Why do you keep the commandments? Is it out of fear? It must be out of love!

Listen to the words of the Belgic Confession:

We believe that this true faith, being wrought in man by the hearing of the Word of God and the operation of the Holy Ghost, doth regenerate and make him a new man, causing him to live a new life, and freeing him from the bondage of sin. Therefore it is so far from being true, that this justifying faith makes men remiss in a pious and holy life, that on the contrary without it they would never do any thing out of love to God, but only out of self-love or fear of damnation. Therefore it is impossible that this holy faith can be unfruitful in man: for we do not speak of a vain faith, but of such a faith as is called in scripture, *a faith that worketh by love*, which excites man to the practice of those works which God has commanded in his Word.[1]

We must not deceive ourselves by using the wrong thermometer to take our spiritual temperature. How can we *know* whether our love for Christ is hot, fairly warm, lukewarm, tepid, or dangerously cold?

Some imagine you can measure love for Christ by activity. Surely, if a person is active in church, active in the community, active in peacemaking, in witnessing, and in acts of kindness, *that* person loves Christ. Others imagine you can measure love by the loudness of the profession one makes. If a person proclaims loudly that he loves Christ, wears a T-shirt or badge with a Christian slogan, or gets excited in worship, surely *that* person loves Christ. Those kinds of Christians often accuse the less exuberant, emotional, bubbly type of Christian of coldness.

Nevertheless, it is better to liken the Christian life to a good marriage. The deep, passionate, heartfelt love of a couple who have been married for years is often much greater and deeper than the frothy, exuberant relationship of dating couples or newlyweds. Love is based on knowledge and the deepening of affection that grows over time. A couple who have lived together for some fifty, sixty, or even seventy years have grown to love one another deeply. Such too is the love of a mature Christian for Christ. Faced with the choice of denying Christ or suffering death, an early Christian leader called Polycarp (AD 80–167) exclaimed: "Eighty and six years I have served

---

1   Belgic Confession 24, in Schaff, *Creeds of Christendom*, 3:411.

him, and he has done me no wrong. How then can I blaspheme my King and Savior?" Surely, the love of Polycarp for Christ did not wax cold!

Love is measured by knowledge, not merely intellectual knowledge, but knowledge of Christ, his person, his perfections, and his works. One who loves Christ has not fallen in love with a sentimental fantasy of Christ. Such a person has not fallen in love with an experience, but loves Christ for who Christ is and for what he has done. Here is the test: How well do you know Christ? But more, how much do you *desire* to know Christ, and how much do you seek after Christ? How much do you love the truth where Christ reveals himself? How much do you love Christ's people, Christ's church? Let no one say that he loves Christ who is indifferent to the truth, does not care to know the truth, is willing to sell the truth for an easy life, and is not willing to obey the truth! You cannot love Christ and not love his truth. That truth must affect how you think and how you live. Moreover, love is revealed in our obedience to God in Jesus Christ: "If ye love me, keep my commandments" (John 14:15).

Decreasing love in the church for Christ *is* apostasy. It is the beginning or the root of apostasy, an outstanding sign that Christ is on his way. Apostasy is the falling away of individuals or of churches from Christ as he is revealed in the truth of God's word. Apostasy is a falling away from the truth by churches and individuals who do not love the truth. Those who love the truth do not apostatize. They will rather die than apostatize. Paul describes the process of apostasy in 2 Thessalonians 2. "Let no man deceive you by any means: for that day shall not come, except there come a falling away first" (v. 3). This concept of falling away is denoted by the word *apostasy*. Verses 10–11 identify the bitter root of this apostasy and those who will be caught up in it: "They received not the love of the truth that they might be saved, and for this cause God shall send them strong delusion that they should believe a lie."

Therefore, the question might be asked: why does a church embrace false doctrine and begin to deny cardinal doctrines of the faith? The answer is simple. They do not love the truth. The truth is not important. More important is man, man's feelings, man's preferences, and man's convenience. "The love of many [for Christ in the truth] shall wax cold."

Apostasy is falling away by professing Christians and professing Christian churches. Unbelievers do not apostatize. Atheists do not apostatize. Muslims, Hindus, and Buddhists do not apostatize. Their love does not grow cold, because in no sense did they ever love Christ. However, there are men and women who make professions. They say that they love Christ. They seem to be excited about Christianity for a while. They become members of the church, but their love grows cold. A cold, icy blast blows upon their professed love for Christ, and they leave the church, they leave the truth, and they leave Christ.

Their love waxes cold!

Christ warns that as his coming approaches, the spiritual temperature of many, even the majority of, professing Christians will dramatically decrease. Many there shall be who grow up in the sphere of the church, but their interest in Christ gradually dwindles. They do not care about doctrine, worship, truth, or holy living. Some may maintain their professions—if you ask them, they will claim to be Christians—but their lives are the same as the world. Such false professors of religion will show no interest in the practice of Christianity, in keeping God's commandments, in public worship, in prayer, or in fellowship with other Christians. Others will become members of the false church or become outspoken critics of the true church. They will adopt heresies that attack the truth of Christ. Why? Their love will wax cold.

Let us be warned! Widespread apostasy, multiple defections from the church, and a spiritual lethargy among believers are signs of the coming of Christ.

This is incompatible with what the disciples were expecting and with what postmillennialism promises. An earthly kingdom of splendor in Jerusalem with the twelve disciples as Christ's right-hand men? A golden age of peace and prosperity? No, says Christ. Do not expect that! Expect to be hated by all nations! Expect turmoil among the nations and in nature! And expect that many will depart from the truth to follow seducing spirits, false teachers, and the love of pleasure.

Postmillennialism dreams about the Christianization of the earth and massive advances of the gospel to bring about the conversion of the majority of mankind. Postmillennialism promises an earthly kingdom for at least one thousand years, during which Christ will rule through an earthly triumphant church without fear of persecution or apostasy. If you ask the postmillennialist about this text or about the many other texts in the New Testament that warn of apostasy, the answer is that the "last days" are the days between the birth of Christ and AD 70. The last days, says the postmillennialist, have come and gone. They were the last days for the Jews, but the *beginning* of days for the church. Therefore, the cooling of the love of many applies *only* to the period between Pentecost and the destruction of Jerusalem in AD 70. After that the church must expect earthly victory.

We must not be fooled. Apostasy has always been a fearful reality for Christ's church. There must be a falling away so that Christ can come. Second Thessalonians 2 tells us that the falling away prepares for the revealing of the man of sin, the antichrist himself. Antichrist promotes apostasy and is really the final development of apostasy. Apostasy is the way in which sin develops, because there is no one more wicked than the apostate, the one who knew the truth, professed to love the truth, and then fell away from that truth. When sin develops to the level of widespread apostasy from the church of Christ, the second coming is near. Remember that the first New Testament apostate was present listening to all of this! Judas Iscariot, the traitor, professed love for Jesus. Very soon, though, he would reject Jesus Christ for the love of money.

The Cause

The cold wind that blows across history and chills the love of many is abounding iniquity: "and because iniquity shall abound" (Matt. 24:12). The word "iniquity" is lawlessness. Lawlessness is to be without law or to be in opposition to law, specifically God's law. God's law is the expression of his holy will by which he declares to the creatures he has made what is pleasing and displeasing to him. Lawlessness is the expression of man's contempt for God. Man shakes his fist in God's face and says, "I will rule myself. You will not tell me how to live. I will not have God rule over me!" Lawlessness characterizes every fallen son and daughter of Adam, and lawlessness is the way of life for all unbelievers in this wicked world. Christ warns in verse 12 that lawlessness shall abound, increase, multiply, or proliferate. Paul describes the general character of human society in the last days, the days between the first and second coming of the Lord:

1. This know also, that in the last days perilous times shall come.
2. For men shall be lovers of their own selves, covetous, boasters, proud, blasphemers, disobedient to parents, unthankful, unholy,

3. Without natural affection, trucebreakers, false accusers, incontinent, fierce, despisers of those that are good,

4. Traitors, heady, highminded, lovers of pleasures more than lovers of God;

5. Having a form of godliness, but denying the power thereof: from such turn away. (2 Tim. 3:1–5)

That is sober reading. Wickedness will not be restrained. God will increasingly give men over to the lusts of their flesh. Mankind will not improve. Men will give free rein to their sins. Open, defiant, blatant lawlessness! Men casting off the yoke of God's law! Men glorying in, boasting in, and flaunting sin! What a grim picture Christ paints. Yet that is exactly how we see society developing before our eyes today as total depravity continues throughout the last days.

We are living in the "last days." The last days are not a sliver of time just before the end of the world, and they are certainly not the last days of the Jews just prior to AD 70. The "last days" is a biblical expression that denotes the entire period of time between the two comings of the Messiah. It is in the last days that God promises the gathering of believing Jews and Gentiles into one holy catholic church; it is in the last days that God promises the outpouring of the Holy Spirit; and it is in the last days that God promises to bring final judgment upon the wicked.

The prophets write of the last days (Isa. 2:1–4; Joel 2:28–32; Micah 4:1–5). Peter applies Joel's prophecy to the events of Pentecost: "This is that which was spoken by the prophet Joel; and it shall come to pass *in the last days*, saith God, I will pour out of my Spirit upon all flesh" (Acts 2:16–17, emphasis added). In the "last days," Peter includes the entire period from Pentecost

("I will pour out of my Spirit") to the second advent ("blood, and fire, and vapour of smoke" [v. 19]). In addition, the writer to the Hebrews identifies the "last days" as those days in which God sent his Son into the world: "God, who at sundry times and in divers manners spake in times past unto the fathers by the prophets, hath in these last days spoken unto us by his Son" (1:1–2). Paul urges the Corinthians to learn from the Old Testament scriptures: "All these things happened unto them for ensamples: and they are written for our admonition, upon whom the ends of the world [literally, 'ages'] are come" (1 Cor. 10:11). Not only are we in the "last days" (which have already continued for some two thousand years), we are also in the "last time" (literally, "hour"), a time characterized by the proliferation of antichrists (1 John 2:18), scoffers (2 Pet. 3:3), and mockers (Jude 18).

Add to that the false prophecy of Matthew 24:11. False prophecy is itself lawlessness, and false prophets contribute to and promote an increase in lawlessness. False prophets redefine sin. Sin is no longer the transgression of God's law. What we once considered sin is no longer sin. According to the modern false prophets, not even adultery and homosexuality are sins. False prophets soothe men. False prophets promise God's blessings without repentance, and they promise salvation *in* sin, not *from* sin. Thus false prophets seduce many away from the truth, from Christ in the truth, and from a practice of the truth.

The effect of abounding lawlessness on the church is the cooling of the love of many. Christ underlines that causal relationship in verse 12 (literally, "and on account of the multiplying of lawlessness the love of the many shall be cooled down"). Satan blows a cold, icy blast of lawlessness over the church to rob her of her ardor for Christ. As a hot apple pie exposed on a windowsill to the chilly wind will cool down rapidly, so abounding iniquity has a chilling effect on the church. As a man exposed to the wind chill of winter risks hypothermia unless he insulates himself and wraps himself in warm clothing, so a church exposed to abounding iniquity is in danger of spiritual hypothermia. Thus we see that the devil's purpose in stirring up men and women in abounding iniquity is to destroy the beloved, redeemed church of Christ. This is always Satan's purpose. The devil hates, above all things, the church of Jesus Christ, because he hates God and the Christ of God. Unable to attack Christ, he attacks the church, which is Christ's body and bride in the earth.

The chilling effect of iniquity is that for many the attraction of sin proves to be greater than any professed love for Christ. This was the case with Judas. For him money was more important than Christ. This was the case with Demas, of whom Paul writes, "Demas hath forsaken me, having loved this present world" (2 Tim. 4:10). The carnal element in the church loves sin, and for all their professed love for Christ, their love for sin prevails. The more sin has to offer, the less likelihood there is that such will stay in the church. Lawlessness is a bait that ensnares many, because lawlessness seems to offer a free, easy, pleasant life without the restraints of God's commandments.

Spiritual cooling is not just the lot of the carnal element, the hypocrite in the church. We need to beware also. There is no better way for the devil to cool our spiritual ardor than for us to expose ourselves to sin. Sinful pleasures and sinful relationships will make us feel distant from Christ, because we grieve the Holy Spirit. What we watch, what we read, and what we listen to will have an enormous effect on our ability to pray, to think holy thoughts, and to meditate on God's word. To keep up our spiritual ardor, let us do what will keep us warm, and let us avoid the chilling winds of iniquity. Watch and pray! Attend public worship frequently and faithfully to hear the preaching! Should you become cold, you will be reheated under the word of God. Neglect the means of grace and expect to become colder and colder.

8. Finally, brethren, whatsoever things are true, whatsoever things are honest, whatsoever things are just, whatsoever things are pure, whatsoever things are lovely, whatsoever things are of good report; if there be any virtue, and if there be any praise, think on these things.

9. Those things, which ye have both learned, and received, and heard, and seen in me, do: and the God of peace shall be with you. (Phil. 4:8–9)

3. But fornication, and all uncleanness, or covetousness, let it not be once named among you, as becometh saints;

4. Neither filthiness, nor foolish jesting, which are not convenient: but rather giving of thanks.

5. For this ye know, that no whoremonger, nor unclean person, nor covetous man, which is an idolater, hath any inheritance in the kingdom of Christ and of God. (Eph. 5:3–5)

The Promise

Christ adds an encouraging promise in Matthew 24:13: "He that shall endure unto the end, the same shall be saved." Endurance means to bear up under a heavy burden. The church must endure three heavy burdens until the coming of Christ.

First, there is the heavy burden of persecution. He who endures persecution unto the end, the same shall be saved.

Second, there is the heavy burden of abounding lawlessness. He who endures lawlessness and keeps his garments unspotted unto the end, through a constant washing of his garments in Christ's blood, and through a constant fleeing to Christ for refuge, the same shall be saved.

Third, there is the heavy burden of increasing apostasy, to see friends and family betray and hate one another and defect from Christ. He who endures that to the end, the same shall be saved.

Mark well! The text does not say, "He who escapes before the end, because he is carried off in a secret rapture, the same shall be saved." That we endure means that we will live *through* the times described in the text. There will be persecution, lawlessness, and apostasy. Be prepared for it. Expect it. Do not be offended when it comes. Do not say that Christ never warned you. Remember that the end in mind is not merely AD 70, but the end of the world. He who endures in the faith of Christ to the end of the world or to the end of his own life, whichever comes sooner, the same shall be saved. Apostates, those who do not endure, were never saints and were never saved (1 John 2:19).

The love of many will wax cold. Many will profess their love of Christ, but they will be lured away by the lawlessness of this world or by false prophecy or be offended by persecution. Such have no root in Jesus Christ. The chill winds of abounding lawlessness expose them for what they are. Thanks be to God that the harder the devil blows, the more we cling to Christ.

We have no strength of our own, but our strength is in Christ. He died for us. His Holy Spirit indwells us. He will preserve us. His hand will not let us go.

Chapter 6

♦

THE GOSPEL
PREACHED IN
ALL THE WORLD

And this gospel of the kingdom shall be preached in all
the world for a witness unto all nations; and then shall the
end come.—Matthew 24:14

Think of the background. The world is in a constant state
of turmoil and in opposition to the church. Wars, economic chaos, social unrest, abounding lawlessness! Earthquakes,
famines, pestilence! Persecution, apostasy, and the threat of antichrist! But here is a little gem in the midst of a chapter that
might otherwise discourage us and make us afraid. The world
might quake under our feet and Satan might roar against us,
but the gospel goes forth, conquering and to conquer. The
gospel is unstoppable. In this chapter we see *the* sign of the
second coming. We know that because it more than any other
sign determines the end. So when you hear the preaching of

the gospel and hear of mission work, do not think, *That is only preaching*, but think, *Christ is coming*.

Each sermon is a footstep closer.

The Meaning

As the world fills the cup of iniquity, as God's wrath is treasured up, and as the church fills up Christ's sufferings in his body, the gospel is preached. The text calls attention to "this gospel of the kingdom." The gospel is good news; and how we need good news against the background of Matthew 24!

The gospel is not good news that things in the world will get better, at least, not until the coming of Christ. The gospel is good news that God has performed a wonder of grace; and a few days after this speech on the Mount of Olives, that wonder of grace will take place on Calvary and in Joseph's tomb. The gospel is the good news that God in mercy has pitied our miserable estate; that he has sent his only begotten Son into the world; that Christ died for our sins, was raised from the dead, ascended into heaven, and will return at the end of history to take us to glory.

The gospel is the gospel *of the kingdom*, that is, the good news concerning the kingdom of God. The kingdom of God, or the kingdom of heaven (they are the same reality), is the spiritual rule of God in Jesus Christ by his grace and Holy Spirit in the hearts and lives of his elect people so that we serve the triune God in Jesus Christ. The kingdom has a king, the Lord Jesus Christ; the kingdom has citizens, the elect and regenerated children of God; the kingdom has borders and territory, the hearts and lives of those conquered by grace; the kingdom has a charter, the holy scriptures; the kingdom has an earthly manifestation, the church. The good news of the kingdom is this: Christ the king has come; he has inaugurated his kingdom; his kingdom is growing as more are conquered by the grace of God; and the final manifestation of the kingdom will appear at Christ's second coming.

Against this kingdom are arrayed all wicked kingdoms, but only Christ's kingdom will last forever. The kingdom of the Romans, which within forty years would destroy what was left of the kingdom of the Jews, depended on brute force, political power, and earthly wealth. Behind every human kingdom stands Satan, intent on gathering all nations together to form one final, universal, man-centered, devil-worshiping, God-defying kingdom with the antichrist at its head. But Christ's kingdom is not a kingdom of force, politics, and wealth. Despite its outward weakness, Christ's kingdom destroys all other kingdoms, especially the kingdom of darkness, by spiritual weapons, especially the preaching of the gospel of the kingdom.

36. Jesus answered, My kingdom is not of this world: if my kingdom were of this world, then would my servants fight, that I should not be delivered to the Jews: but now is my kingdom not from hence.

37. Pilate therefore said unto him, Art thou a king then? Jesus answered, Thou sayest that I am a king. To this end was I born, and for this cause came I into the world, that I should bear witness unto the truth. Every one that is of the truth heareth my voice. (John 18:36–37)

"The kingdom of God is not meat and drink; but righteousness, and peace, and joy in the Holy Ghost" (Rom. 14:17).

Therefore, the kingdom of God does not progress by armies, political intrigue, and clever philosophy—all things admired by men—*but by preaching*. "This gospel of the kingdom shall be *preached*" (Matt. 24:14, emphasis added). What shall be preached? Quite simply this: Jesus Christ is king, that is, Lord. That is the offence of the gospel. Say, "Jesus Christ is merely another great teacher," and the world will tolerate that. But declare, "Jesus Christ is universal, sovereign, and exclusive Lord," and you risk the wrath of Caesar, who says he is lord, or the wrath of modern man, who says, "I am my own master and lord." Jesus Christ is king, one vested with power and authority by virtue of his being the Son of God, one able to subdue all things unto himself. He is not a pathetic beggar or merely a nice man. He is king and Lord. We must believe and proclaim that.

Behold the mystery of the gospel! Jesus Christ is the crucified one. A crucified king! Who could have imagined it. Jesus Christ was king when he sat on the Mount of Olives, and he was king when he hung on the cross. Only through the cross could Jesus Christ establish the kingdom of God in righteousness and make us citizens of this kingdom.

To establish his kingdom, Jesus Christ at the right hand of God does not send forth tanks and rocket launchers, nor does he launch a publicity campaign to woo the voters, but he sends *preachers*. These preachers are heralds. A herald is a man commissioned by the king to proclaim his message to the people. In ancient times kings sent official heralds throughout the land. They stood in public places, unfurled their scrolls, and cried, "Thus saith the king."

That is preaching. This means, first, that preachers must be sent by King Jesus through the church:

> 14. How then shall they call on him in whom they have not believed? and how shall they believe in him of whom they have not heard? and how shall they hear without a preacher?

15. And how shall they preach, except they be sent? as it is written, How beautiful are the feet of them that preach the gospel of peace, and bring glad tidings of good things! (Rom. 10:14–15)

The Westminster Larger Catechism also teaches this:

By whom is the word of God to be preached?
The word of God is to be preached only by such as are sufficiently gifted, and also duly approved and called to that office.[1]

This means, second, that preachers must be received because of their office. To despise preaching is to despise the King who sends the preacher with the message.

This means, third, that the herald must never change the message of the King: never may he water it down or twist it. Woe to the false and unfaithful herald who dares do that! Preaching therefore is the official proclamation of the will of the King. He wills that sin be condemned and exposed, sinners be warned, and believers be comforted. He wills that his truth be taught, and above all he wills that the glorious gospel of his kingdom grounded in his cross and resurrection be preached.

This gospel of the kingdom shall be preached in "all the world." This very significant change marks the last days. In the Old Testament and even during Christ's earthly ministry, the gospel was for the Jews, and he preached almost exclusively to them. By and large the other nations in the Old Testament wandered in darkness.

The Old Testament, however, prophesied of the glorious age of the Messiah, when all nations would worship Jehovah

---

1 Westminster Larger Catechism Q&A 158, in *Westminster Confession of Faith* (Glasgow: Free Presbyterian Publications, 2009), 251.

God. Consider the following representative Old Testament passages:

9. They that dwell in the wilderness shall bow before him; and his enemies shall lick the dust.
10. The kings of Tarshish and of the isles shall bring presents: the kings of Sheba and Seba shall offer gifts.
11. Yea, all kings shall fall down before him: all nations shall serve him. (Ps. 72:9–11)

2. It shall come to pass in the last days, that the mountain of the LORD's house shall be established in the top of the mountains, and shall be exalted above the hills; and all nations shall flow unto it.
3. And many people shall go and say, Come ye, and let us go up to the mountain of the LORD, to the house of the God of Jacob; and he will teach us of his ways, and we will walk in his paths: for out of Zion shall go forth the law, and the word of the LORD from Jerusalem. (Isa. 2:2–3)

1. In the last days it shall come to pass, that the mountain of the house of the LORD shall be established in the top of the mountains, and it shall be exalted above the hills; and people shall flow unto it.
2. And many nations shall come, and say, Come, and let us go up to the mountain of the LORD, and to the house of the God of Jacob; and he will teach us of his ways, and we will walk in his paths: for the law shall go forth of Zion, and the word of the LORD from Jerusalem. (Micah 4:1–2)

"And it shall come to pass, that every one that is left of all the nations which came against Jerusalem shall even go up from year to year to worship the King, the LORD of hosts, and to keep the feast of tabernacles" (Zech. 14:16).

"From the rising of the sun even unto the going down of the same my name shall be great among the Gentiles; and in every place incense shall be offered unto my name, and a pure offering: for my name shall be great among the heathen, saith the LORD of hosts" (Mal. 1:11).

We must not understand these passages in a literalistic manner. When all nations flow into Zion exalted as the highest mountain of the earth; when distant kings come with gifts and bow down before the Messiah; when the nations come to worship Jehovah the king and keep the Feast of Tabernacles; when Jehovah's name is great among the heathen; and when incense and a pure offering are offered to him in every place, the age of the Messiah has come.

That can be proven by examining James' authoritative interpretation of Amos 9 at the Jerusalem Council. Amos 9:11 makes the following promise: "In that day will I raise up the tabernacle of David that is fallen, and close up the breaches thereof; and I will raise up his ruins, and I will build it as in the days of old." A literalistic reading of Amos 9 demands the rebuilding of the temple, the conquering of Edom (a people wiped off the face of the earth by God's righteous judgments according to Malachi 1:3–4; where are the Edomites today?), and a repopulating of Canaan by Israelites. However, that is not how James, and that is not how the New Testament, interprets Amos 9. Instead, the New Testament interprets Amos 9 to be a prophecy concerning the salvation *of the Gentiles*:

14. Simeon hath declared how God at the first did visit the Gentiles, to take out of them a people for his name.
15. *And to this agree the words of the prophets*, as it is written,

16. After this I will return, and will build again the tabernacle of David, which is fallen down; and I will build again the ruins thereof, and I will set it up:

17. That the residue of men might seek the Lord, and all the Gentiles, upon whom my name is called, saith the Lord, who doeth all these things.

18. Known unto God are all his works from the beginning of the world. (Acts 15:14–18, emphasis added)

The gathering of the Gentiles, although it was prophesied, was a new thing in the earth. The disciples and apostles found it difficult at the beginning to accept it. Peter needed a vision to persuade him of it. Even in Christ's earthly ministry the preaching of the gospel was restricted to Israel: "These twelve Jesus sent forth, and commanded them, saying, Go not into the way of the Gentiles, and into any city of the Samaritans enter ye not: But go rather to the lost sheep of the house of Israel" (Matt. 10:5–6). "[Jesus] answered and said, I am not sent but unto the lost sheep of the house of Israel" (Matt. 15:24).

Very soon, says Christ, the gospel of the kingdom of God will go to the Gentiles, that is, into all the world. The word "world" in Matthew 24:14 means the inhabited earth. Often it referred to the then-known world, the Roman Empire: "It came to pass in those days, that there went out a decree from Caesar Augustus, that all the world should be taxed" (Luke 2:1). "There stood up one of them [prophets from Jerusalem] named Agabus, and signified by the Spirit that there should be great dearth throughout all the world: which came to pass in the days of Claudius Caesar" (Acts 11:28). "They [the Jews] drew Jason and certain brethren unto the rulers of the city, crying, These that have turned the world upside down are come hither also" (17:6).

The wider meaning of "world" is the entire inhabited earth,

made up of all nations, tribes, and tongues. From this word we derive the word *ecumenical*, which means worldwide.

Christ says that this gospel of the kingdom, which declares that he, Jesus, is a universal king, will be preached throughout the Roman Empire and beyond that to every nation. That is an astounding prophecy, coming from a man who just a few days later will be hanging on a cross!

Astounding as it may seem, within a few years the gospel spread rapidly, carried by heralds to all nations. A few days after the Olivet Discourse, Christ died. His enemies thought they had heard the last of him, but he arose the third day. Forty days later he ascended into heaven, and ten days later an incredible, earth-shattering event took place—Pentecost. With the outpouring of the Holy Spirit, every nation in principle heard the gospel:

5. There were dwelling at Jerusalem Jews, devout men, out of every nation under heaven.

6. Now when this was noised abroad, the multitude came together, and were confounded, because that every man heard them speak in his own language.

7. And they were all amazed and marvelled, saying one to another, Behold, are not all these which speak Galilaeans?

8. And how hear we every man in our own tongue, wherein we were born?

9. Parthians, and Medes, and Elamites, and the dwellers in Mesopotamia, and in Judaea, and Cappadocia, in Pontus, and Asia,

10. Phrygia, and Pamphylia, in Egypt, and in the parts of Libya about Cyrene, and strangers of Rome, Jews and proselytes,

11. Cretes and Arabians, we do hear them speak in our tongues the wonderful works of God. (Acts 2:5–11)

From Jerusalem the gospel quickly spread into Samaria. When Paul was called to be an apostle, the gospel spread rapidly to the Gentiles. Finally, by the end of Paul's ministry the gospel had reached Rome and Spain (Rom. 15:24, 28). Later the gospel spread into other parts of Europe, Africa, Asia, North and South America, and Australia. In fact, the New Testament speaks in terms like these: "[The gospel] is come unto you, as it is in all the world; and bringeth forth fruit, as it doth also in you, since the day ye heard of it, and knew the grace of God in truth" (Col. 1:6). "If ye continue in the faith grounded and settled, and be not moved away from the hope of the gospel, which ye have heard, and which was preached to every creature which is under heaven; whereof I Paul am made a minister" (v. 23).

We must be clear what Christ is promising when he says, "This gospel of the kingdom shall be preached in all the world." First, the fulfillment of this is not AD 70. That is the view of many postmillennialists, who are committed to a golden age free from persecution, apostasy, and moral decline. The preaching prophesied in Matthew 24:14 stands against the dark background of those things. Therefore, *that* preaching cannot be the sign of the coming of Christ. Instead, says the postmillennialist, the "end" in Matthew 24, whether in verse 3 ("the end of the world") or in verse 6 ("the end is not yet") or in verse 14 ("and then shall the end come") is AD 70, the end of the Jews, the temple, Jerusalem, and Israel as a nation.

However, that cannot be the meaning. "End," as I have demonstrated, does not refer to AD 70. The preaching of the gospel to the ends of the Roman Empire is the beginning only *in principle*, but not in reality. The end in view is the second coming of Christ on the clouds of heaven. When the preaching of the gospel has accomplished God's purpose, then, and only then, will the end come.

Second, the fulfillment of Matthew 24:14 is not that every person will hear the gospel. That has never happened, and that will never happen. It is not even God's will for that to happen. Countless millions of people have lived and died, even in the New Testament age, without hearing the gospel. It is not even true that every tribe and island has to hear the gospel. Just as we cannot be certain exactly what constitutes a "kind," when Genesis says that God made plants and animals to reproduce after their kind, so we cannot know for sure what constitutes a tribe or nation. Does God mean by "nation" or "tribe" our ideas of geographical borders? Does he mean race? Does he mean cultural distinctions? God means people of all types scattered throughout the world since the Tower of Babel. God knows where his people are scattered, and he will use the preaching of the gospel by the church as the instrument in his hand to gather the elect from all nations by his word and Holy Spirit.

The Heidelberg Catechism explains:

> What dost thou believe concerning the *Holy Catholic Church*?
>
> That out of the whole human race, from the beginning to the end of the world, the Son of God, by his Spirit and Word, gathers, defends, and preserves for himself unto everlasting life, a chosen communion in the unity of true faith; and that I am, and forever shall remain, a living member of the same.[2]

Here is the beauty of the text. The gospel will be unstoppable. It will go forth conquering and to conquer as the first horse and rider in Revelation 6. The little church preaching this gospel of the kingdom will be hated by all nations, and many of her

---

2   Heidelberg Catechism Q&A 54, in Schaff, *Creeds of Christiendom*, 3:324–25.

preachers will be imprisoned and put to death, but "this gospel of the kingdom shall be preached in all the world." The world will be in disarray with one war after another, economic turmoil, and abounding iniquity. The very earth will shake under our feet at times, but "this gospel of the kingdom shall be preached in all the world." The church will seem to shrink, the love of many will grow cold, there will be departure from Christ and his truth, but "this gospel of the kingdom shall be preached in all the world." What a gloriously encouraging promise for the church!

The Effect

By the worldwide preaching of the gospel of the kingdom, God gives a witness or a testimony to all nations. A testimony is an authoritative witness that leaves the hearer without excuse. The early church witnessed directly of Jesus, because the apostles sent to preach him were "eyewitnesses of his majesty" (2 Pet. 1:16). All the apostles had seen the risen, glorified Jesus Christ and had been personally commissioned by him to be his witnesses. The truth concerning Jesus was passed on to faithful men, who taught faithful men after them, and the truth was recorded for all ages in holy scripture (2 Tim. 2:2; 2 Pet. 1:19–21). "Witness" has a second meaning: martyr. Many of the witnesses of Christ testified of him and became martyrs. Peter, Paul, James, and many others died as martyrs.

God's witness or testimony is something that must, upon pain of eternal punishment, be believed. God does not merely invite you to believe in the testimony of his Son; God does not encourage you that it might be a good idea to believe the gospel; God certainly does not beg and plead with you to trust Jesus. Rather, he *commands* you. God has declared that Jesus Christ is his Son and the one approved, anointed, and equipped to be his king. He declared this at his baptism; he declared it at his resurrection and at Pentecost; and now he declares it in the preaching. One who does not believe in Jesus Christ calls God a liar: "He that believeth on the Son of God hath the witness in himself: he that believeth not God hath made him a liar; because he believeth not the record that God gave of his Son" (1 John 5:10). Thus the preaching of the gospel is a testimony, not a chance of salvation, or an offer, or a take-it-or-leave-it proposition.

Many people imagine that when God sends the gospel to people, he is offering them salvation. So popular is this view that it is not only the Arminian position, but many professing Calvinists promote it as well. Such believe that in the preaching God expresses an earnest desire, even longing, to save all men. Others believe that God, to be fair, is obligated to give everyone a chance at salvation and then leaves them a free will to accept or reject it. Nevertheless, Christ does not say that this gospel of the kingdom shall be preached in all the world as an *offer* to all nations, or as a *chance of salvation* to all nations, but as a *witness* unto all nations.

In fact, when the testimony of the gospel comes to the reprobate, they are hardened under it and left without excuse. The reprobate despise a spiritual savior, a spiritual king, and a spiritual kingdom. They despise the cross and the forgiveness of sins, and they want no part of it. Thus the gospel was a great stumbling block to the Jews and utter foolishness to the Gentiles (1 Cor. 1:23). When they heard it, they were stirred up to hate it, and multitudes rejected it, but it was still a testimony to them. When Christ returns, every nation will have heard that Jesus Christ is king and Lord, every nation will have been confronted with the truth of God, and every nation will have rejected it in favor of the earthly, carnal kingdom of Satan and antichrist. That is no failure of the gospel, for out of every nation God saves an elect remnant. Man's sin will be exposed, man will be ripe for judgment, and Christ will come. All of this serves God's purpose with the gospel.

That is not the most important or even the main effect of the preaching of the gospel. The gospel is *good* news, and by it God gathers many into the kingdom and church of Christ. The preaching of the gospel of the kingdom is the way the King comes. The gospel must be preached and will be preached in all the world to all nations, because God's elect people are in all the world in all nations. If God had so decreed, he could have had all his elect born and live in one place at one period in history, but that was not God's purpose. God wills a worldwide, history-long preaching of the gospel so that in every place and in every time the name of Christ is glorified when people of every nation, tribe, and tongue believe in him and rejoice in his gracious rule. In every place and in every period of history, there are citizens of King Jesus, some not yet born, some not yet converted, who will hear the preaching and be saved. The Reformed Christian makes this confession about the church:

> We believe and profess one catholic or universal Church, which is a holy congregation and assembly of true Christian believers, expecting all their salvation in Jesus Christ, being washed by his blood, sanctified and sealed by the Holy Ghost.
>
> This Church hath been from the beginning of the world, and will be to the end thereof; which is evident from this, that Christ is an eternal king, which, without subjects, can not be. And this holy Church is preserved or supported by God against the rage of the whole world; though she sometimes (for a while) appear very small, and in the eyes of men, to be reduced to nothing:

as during the perilous reign of Ahab, when nevertheless *the Lord reserved unto him seven thousand men, who had not bowed their knees to Baal.*

Furthermore, this holy Church is not confined, bound, or limited to a certain place or to certain persons, but is spread and dispersed over the whole world; and yet is joined and united with heart and will, by the power of faith, in one and the same spirit.[3]

Therefore, the church must preach. The church must promote preaching, as well as train and send preachers and missionaries. The one great calling of the church is to hold up the truth of the kingdom of Christ before the world so that the elect will hear and believe. Pray for pastors and missionaries! Support them! In this way the kingdom comes. In this way Christ comes.

This truth explains the devil's opposition to preaching. This gospel of the kingdom, when preached by heralds, destroys the devil's kingdom, which is why the devil fears preaching and seeks to stop preaching. The devil really does not care how many worship bands a church has, how many puppet shows, how many flower shows, or how many bake-offs. Satan does not care whether a church has political clout, so that her ministers have direct access to the White House, nor does he care about the grandeur of her architecture. He cares about preaching. The devil loves to see professing Christians clapping their hands, swaying to the music, or falling over, and he loves to see them involved in social work, but he hates to see them listening to, believing, and obeying preaching.

Therefore, the devil will do his utmost to make sure that we do not preach. He will make the ministers discouraged and the

---

3   Belgic Confession 27, in ibid., 3:416.

members bored. The evil one will whisper, "Preaching has no power. Why hear preaching?" That is because the devil knows the preaching of the gospel of the kingdom is the power of God unto salvation to everyone who believes (Rom. 1:16)! Any church, therefore, that downplays preaching or opposes preaching altogether is playing into the devil's hands. The elect will not be gathered by any other means except preaching, and that is why Christ, from our perspective, delays his coming. Without preaching, the devil's kingdom is at peace; without preaching, the elect who are not yet born or who are not yet saved cannot be saved. The devil knows this more than we do. Nevertheless, the devil cannot prevent the preaching. Churches might apostatize and become nothing but entertainment centers, but Christ will call, equip, and send heralds, and there will be preaching until he comes.

The Goal

Concerning the preaching of the gospel, Christ says, "Then shall the end come" (Matt. 24:14). "End" is *telos* in the Greek, which means a goal or a mark at which one aims. *Teleological* comes from that Greek word. God is the God of the beginning and of the end, and all things are moving toward his definite goal or end.

Unbelief has no purpose for the beginning or for the ending of all things. Why should life have started on this planet? What is the purpose for the life of a slug? Does a slug have any more importance or less importance than your life? Unbelief has no answer. Moreover, how will the world end? Will it continue for millions of years? Will the human species be wiped out by a nuclear war or a meteor from outer space, or will the world just peter out? Will it end with a bang or a whimper? Finally, when we are all dead (and according to unbelief there is nothing for us beyond death except to be eaten by worms), what was the point of it all? Unbelief has no answer.

Listen to the hopelessness of atheism:

> In a universe of blind physical forces and genetic replication, some people are going to get hurt, other people are going to get lucky, and you won't find any rhyme or reason in it, nor any justice. The universe that we observe has precisely the properties we should expect if there is, at bottom, no design, no purpose, no evil, and no good, nothing but blind, pitiless indifference.[4]

> That Man is the product of causes which had no prevision of the end they were achieving; that his origin, his growth, his hopes and fears, his loves and his beliefs, are but the outcome of accidental collocations of atoms; that no fire, no heroism, no intensity of thought and feeling, can preserve an individual life beyond the grave; that all the labours of the ages, all the devotion, all the inspiration, all the noonday brightness of human genius, are destined to extinction in the vast death of the solar system, and that the whole temple of Man's achievement must inevitably be buried beneath the debris of a universe in ruins—all these things, if not quite beyond dispute, are yet so nearly certain, that no philosophy which rejects them can hope to stand. Only within the scaffolding of these truths, only on the firm foundation of unyielding despair, can the soul's habitation henceforth be safely built.[5]

---

4   Richard Dawkins, *River Out of Eden: A Darwinian View of Life* (London: Wiedenfeld & Nicholson, 1995), 131–32.

5   Bertrand Russell, "A Free Man's Worship," in Bertrand Russell, *Mysticism*

But God has a goal. God, in all things, is aiming at something, and he created all things and directs all of history with a view to that goal. God created all things for his glory, and with a view to Jesus Christ, who is the center and purpose of history (Col. 1:16). All things are not merely trundling along. God is directing all things to the final consummation of his kingdom and covenant. To accomplish that, he is saving for himself a church, elected from every nation, tribe, and tongue, for his Son Jesus Christ. God's glory is the goal; Jesus Christ is the focus; the gathering of the church is the means. Everything else in history is subordinate to that.

Only about worldwide preaching does Christ say, "And then shall the end come." There will be wars and rumors of wars, but the end is not yet! There will be famines, widespread starvation, and connected to that economic turmoil, but the end is not yet! There will be rioting and mob violence in the streets, but the end is not yet! There will be pestilences, epidemics, terrible upheavals in nature, storms, hurricanes, earthquakes, and eruptions. But these are only the *beginning* of sorrows! There will be terrible persecution of the church and shocking departure from the truth by much of the church. Error and false prophets will abound, but the end is not yet! Mankind will descend into deep depravity so that lawlessness will abound, but the end is not yet!

The gospel shall be preached in all the world; all the elect shall hear, believe, and be saved. Only *then* will the end come.

Do not fear, therefore. Frightening things are ahead, but the gospel is victorious. And nothing will stop God from saving his own by the preaching of the gospel.

---

and Logic and Other Essays (London: George Allen & Unwin, 1917), 48.

Chapter 7

###

THE ABOMINATION
OF
DESOLATION

When ye therefore shall see the abomination of desolation, spoken of by Daniel the prophet, stand in the holy place, (whoso readeth, let him understand:) Then let them which be in Judaea flee into the mountains: Let him which is on the housetop not come down to take any thing out of his house: Neither let him which is in the field return back to take his clothes. And woe unto them that are with child, and to them that give suck in those days! But pray ye that your flight be not in the winter, neither on the sabbath day.—Matthew 24:15–20

Christ gave five main signs that characterize the entire history of the New Testament age. These are signs indicating that he is at the right hand of God and that he is on the way back to execute judgment. By these signs Christ comes, for they are part of his coming. These five signs are the rise of false prophets; economic, social, and natural turmoil (among nations and in nature); persecution; apostasy; and worldwide gospel preaching. These signs will intensify as the second coming of our Lord approaches.

Having explained these signs, Jesus returns to the subject with which Matthew 24 began, the destruction of the temple and the fall of Jerusalem. Remember that Christ's prediction that the temple would be utterly destroyed triggered two questions from the disciples. Jesus has been concentrating on the second question: "What shall be the sign of thy coming and of the end of the world?" But now he returns to the first question: "Tell us, when shall these things [the destruction of the temple] be?" (v. 3). Remember that Jesus does not separate the fall of Jerusalem and his coming. He *blends* them, using one as a type or a picture of the other.

Christ's method of teaching is not surprising and is common practice among the prophets. The flood was a type or picture of the final judgment at Christ's coming. "Likewise also as it was in the days of Lot; they did eat, they drank, they bought, they sold, they planted, they builded; but the same day that Lot went out of Sodom it rained fire and brimstone from heaven, and destroyed them all" (Luke 17:28–29).

Other examples could be given. The ten plagues in Exodus were a picture of the final judgment, as were the fall of Babylon and the fall of other mighty nations in the Old Testament (Isa. 13–14). In a similar way the fall of Jerusalem in AD 70 is a type of the final judgment. However, the fall of Jerusalem does not *exhaust* the prophecy of Matthew 24, because prophecies can have a double or even a triple fulfillment, as is clear from the prophecy of Daniel. Therefore, the abomination of desolation concerns both the destruction of Jerusalem in AD 70 *and our future.*

Jesus commands us to read the prophecy of Daniel: "Whoso readeth, let him understand" (Matt. 24:15). To that prophecy we now turn.

The Prophecy

Christ refers the disciples to a prophecy of Daniel concerning the "abomination of desolation," which is mentioned three times in the book of Daniel: "He shall confirm the covenant with many for one week: and in the midst of the week he shall cause the sacrifice and the oblation to cease, and for the overspreading of abominations he shall make it desolate, even until the consummation, and that determined shall be poured upon the desolate" (9:27). "Arms shall stand on his part, and they shall pollute the sanctuary of strength, and shall take away the daily sacrifice, and they shall place the abomination that maketh desolate" (11:31). "From the time that the daily sacrifice shall be taken away, and the abomination that maketh desolate set up, there shall be a thousand two hundred and ninety days" (12:11).

The most notable of these prophecies is in Daniel 9, the prophecy of the seventy weeks. Because of the importance of this passage for eschatology, we will study this passage in considerable detail.

Almost seventy years prior, Daniel had been taken captive to Babylon, and Nebuchadnezzar's armies had destroyed Jerusalem and the temple. As Daniel prays, he is now an old man, probably at least eighty years old. This aged saint has been studying the prophecy of Jeremiah, and from it he understands that the Babylonian captivity will last for seventy years. Because that time is almost fulfilled, Daniel approaches God in earnest, heartfelt prayer, beseeching God to remember his covenantal mercies, to forgive Israel's sins, and to restore his people to the Promised Land:

18. O my God, incline thine ear, and hear; open thine eyes, and behold our desolations, and the city which is called by thy name: for we do not present our supplications before thee for our righteousnesses, but for thy great mercies.

19. O Lord, hear; O Lord, forgive; O Lord, hearken and do; defer not, for thine own sake, O my God: for thy city and thy people are called by thy name. (9:18–19)

God sends the archangel Gabriel to encourage and comfort Daniel, thus answering his prayer in the form of prophecy: "Seventy weeks are determined upon thy people and upon thy holy city, to finish the transgression, and to make an end of sins, and to make reconciliation for iniquity, and to bring in everlasting righteousness, and to seal up the vision and prophecy, and to anoint the most Holy" (v. 24).

This is a difficult portion of God's word, and it has been seized upon by the premillennial dispensationalists who view Daniel 9 as a key text in their entire system. In it they find proof of the coming of Christ, the temporary rejection of Israel, the antichrist, and the great tribulation with the abomination of desolation. But do their claims stand up to scrutiny, and is dispensationalism what Christ had in mind when he directed the disciples' attention to Daniel's prophecy?

We should notice, first, that although dispensationalists claim to be consistently literal in their interpretation of the Old Testament, they are not. Dispensationalists often criticize Reformed amillennialists for supposedly spiritualizing the Old Testament. Dispensationalists pride themselves on taking all Old Testament prophecies literally, or literalistically. However, their treatment of Daniel 9 is far from consistent.

The dispensationalists insist that this is a prophecy not of seventy weeks, but of four hundred ninety years. Daniel 9 speaks of seventy weeks, divided into three periods of time: seven weeks (v. 25); then sixty-two weeks (v. 25); and finally, one week (v. 27):

25. Know therefore and understand, that from the going forth of the commandment to restore and to build Jerusalem unto the Messiah the Prince shall be seven weeks, and threescore and two weeks: the street shall be built again, and the wall, even in troublous times.

26. And after threescore and two weeks shall Messiah be cut off, but not for himself: and the people of the prince that shall come shall destroy the city and the sanctuary; and the end thereof shall be with a flood, and unto the end of the war desolations are determined.

27. And he shall confirm the covenant with many for one week: and in the midst of the week he shall cause the sacrifice and the oblation to cease, and for the overspreading of abominations he shall make it desolate, even until the consummation, and that determined shall be poured upon the desolate.

The total seventy is seven plus sixty-two plus one. The dispensationalists interpret this as four hundred ninety years, because a week supposedly equals a week of years (seven years). Seventy times seven years equals 490 years.

Did you notice the sleight of hand? Seventy weeks equals seventy weeks of years? How is *that* a literal interpretation? Where in scripture does a week equal seven years? A literal interpretation would be 490 days. There is no other passage in scripture where a week equals seven years. "Week" in Daniel 9 is literally "seven." In Deuteronomy 16:9 it means literally seven weeks: "Seven weeks [literally, 'seven sevens'] shalt thou number unto thee: begin to number the seven weeks [literally, 'seven sevens'] from such time as thou beginnest to put the sickle to the corn." Daniel 9 is a prophecy of seventy sevens, but the dispensationalists without good cause make that seventy times seven years.

Second, and even more seriously, dispensationalists claim that the seventieth week does not follow immediately after the sixty-ninth week. In fact, the seventieth week is still *future* to us.

Here is the dispensationalist reading. There are seven weeks (the period of time to rebuild Jerusalem after the captivity). Following that first period, there are sixty-two weeks (the period of time to the first coming of Christ). The total is sixty-nine weeks, which equal 483 years. However, at the end of the sixty-ninth week, something unexpected happened. The so-called prophetic clock stopped ticking! It stopped ticking because the Jews rejected Christ. That clock will stay on pause until the rapture, after which God will restart his prophetic stopwatch and continue his program *with the Jews.* In the meantime, between week sixty-nine and week seventy, there is a gap, a parenthesis, during which time God saves the Gentiles. Thus, according to dispensationalism, we are presently living between the sixty-ninth and the seventieth weeks of Daniel 9. The entire church age, from Pentecost to the future rapture, is a parenthesis, a pause, between these two prophetic weeks.

Is *that* a literal reading of Daniel 9? Can you see any gap of over two thousand years between the sixty-ninth and seventieth weeks? Do you see God prophesying an interruption to his "program" between the sixty-ninth and seventieth weeks? Was this unexpected? Verse 24 promises to Daniel, "Seventy weeks are determined." Determined means preordained.

Perhaps an illustration will help. Imagine that I borrow one thousand dollars from you, and I promise to pay you back in seventy weeks. After sixty-nine weeks I come to you with the excuse, "I forgot to mention, between weeks sixty-nine and seventy, there is a gap of one hundred years. I will pay you back in one week, but that week will begin after one hundred years from now." What would you think of me? You would rightly call me a con man or a swindler!

This leaves the dispensationalist in a quandary. Either God knew that his program would be interrupted, and he misled Daniel, or God did not know and is therefore not omniscient concerning the future.

Third, the dispensationalists read several additional theories into Daniel 9. The dispensationalists claim that at the end of the sixty-ninth week the age of the Gentiles or the church age began. At the end of that age, the rapture will take place. Christ will return secretly and all New Testament Christians will disappear. Not in Daniel 9!

Also, after the New Testament church is safely out of the way, antichrist will ascend to prominence ("the people of the prince that shall come" [v. 26]). At first, he will appear to be Israel's friend, and then he will permit Israel to rebuild her temple. He will even enter into a political alliance with Israel ("he shall confirm the covenant with many for one week" [v. 27]). Halfway through the week antichrist will betray Israel, unleash upon her the great tribulation, defile her temple, and slaughter her people. This great tribulation will continue for three and a half years, after which Christ will return from heaven, destroy antichrist, and rule for one thousand years. According to dispensationalism, the temple in Matthew 24 that shall be destroyed is a *future* rebuilt temple—not the temple that stood in the days of Jesus and the apostles. However, the very idea that the Jews will rebuild their temple is fraught with difficulty and is not something any Christian should expect or desire.

Where is all that to be found in the text? All of that is read into the text from outside!

The key to Matthew 24:15 is that term "the abomination of desolation, spoken of by Daniel the prophet," mentioned in Daniel 9:27: "He shall confirm the covenant with many for one week: and in the midst of the week he shall cause the sacrifice and the oblation to cease, and for the overspreading of abominations he shall make it desolate, even until the consummation, and that determined shall be poured upon the desolate." The Hebrew could be translated as, "He shall cause to cease sacrifice and offering and upon a wing of desolating abominations and until the completion, and those things that have been determined shall pour forth upon the desolating one."

What does all this mean? First, someone will cause sacrifice to cease. The dispensationalists argue that this is antichrist. I will argue later that it is Christ who causes sacrifice to cease by his death on the cross. Second, abominable things will come upon the city of Jerusalem. Third, the one who desolates the city (the antichrist) will be destroyed.

The abominable and desolating things that the antichrist will bring are described in Daniel 11–12, especially 11:31: "Arms shall stand on his part, and they shall pollute the sanctuary of strength, and shall take away the daily sacrifice, and they shall place the abomination that maketh desolate."

In those two chapters, Daniel receives a detailed prophecy concerning a king who will bring desolation to Jerusalem. Chapter 11 begins with a prophecy of the end of the kingdom of Persia. The last king of Persia will attack the kingdom of Greece or Macedonia (v. 2). The king of Macedonia will defeat the larger Persian kingdom, but he shall be cut off and his kingdom divided, not to his descendants but between four. This is none other than Alexander the Great, who died in 323 BC, after which his sons were murdered and his kingdom was divided among his four most powerful generals. Much of chapter 11 describes the power struggle between two empires, Egypt and Syria, known as the king of the south and the king of the north. Finally, a "vile person" stands up and "obtains the kingdom by flatteries" (v. 21). This is Antiochus IV Epiphanes (who reigned from 175 to 164 BC), the evil tyrant responsible for the abomination of desolation (11:31; 12:11).

The "abomination of desolation" means literally "the detestable thing that desolates." *Abomination* means a detestable, revolting, disgusting, vile thing. This is a common reference to idolatry in the Old Testament: "Ye have seen their abominations, and their idols, wood and stone, silver and gold, which were among them" (Deut. 29:17). "Then did Solomon build an high place for Chemosh, the abomination of Moab, in the hill that is before Jerusalem, and for Molech, the abomination of the children of Ammon" (1 Kings 11:7).

Every pious Jew held any form of idolatry in abomination. It was detestable, disgusting, revolting, and vile in the sight of God, and therefore a horror for any Jew. The phrase "of desolation" means the abomination shall have a desolating effect. To make desolate is to lay waste, make into a desert, or destroy. The abomination of desolation will make the temple desolate, so that the true worship of God will be impossible there. God's people will be driven out of their place of worship, God's public worship will be terminated, and God's people will suffer terribly when the abomination of desolation is set up.

The Fulfillments

The prophecies of Daniel admit of more than one fulfillment. That is clear from Christ's words, "When ye therefore shall *see* the abomination of desolation spoken of by Daniel the prophet" (Matt. 24:15; emphasis added). This prophecy is fulfilled in the Old Testament. Nevertheless, Christ's disciples will *see* it happen again. Moreover, it will happen again in our future. Thus scripture teaches three fulfillments: by Antiochus Epiphanes, by the Romans, and by the antichrist just prior to Christ's second coming.

The prophecy of Daniel 9 was fulfilled at the coming of Christ. Let us examine what this prophecy really means. We do not interpret this prophecy literally (seventy sevens) or, as the dispensationalists do, as four hundred ninety years. Daniel receives a vision.

Visions contain symbolism, especially symbolic numbers. Seventy sevens is a highly symbolic number made up of seven times seven times ten. Seven is the number of God's covenant (the seventh day, etc.) and ten is the number of completeness (the ten commandments, the ten plagues, etc.). Daniel's vision refers to the perfection of the covenant according to God's counsel.

When we read of seventy weeks or seventy sevens in Daniel 9, we do not take out our calculators and do some number crunching. Daniel was not number crunching: he was studying Jeremiah, and he read about seventy years—seventy *actual* years: "This whole land shall be a desolation, and an astonishment; and these nations shall serve the king of Babylon seventy years. And it shall come to pass, when seventy years are accomplished, that I will punish the king of Babylon, and that nation, saith the Lord, for their iniquity, and the land of the Chaldeans, and will make it perpetual desolations" (Jer. 25:11–12). "Thus saith the Lord, That after seventy years be accomplished at Babylon I will visit you, and perform my good word toward you, in causing you to return to this place" (29:10).

In Daniel 9, we do not read of years, but of sevens. It was not Daniel's or anyone else's calling to add these numbers to calculate the date of Christ's coming. Daniel 9 does not feed our curiosity but assures us that God's determined plan to confirm his covenant is on track and even Israel's sins, over which Daniel had been lamenting, will not annul God's promises.

Daniel 9 perfectly accords with Christ's incarnation, death, and resurrection. Verse 24 promises that Christ will do six things, and he has fulfilled them all: "Seventy weeks are determined upon thy people and upon thy holy city, [1] to finish the transgression, and [2] to make an end of sins, and [3] to make reconciliation for iniquity, and [4] to bring in everlasting righteousness, and [5] to seal up the vision and prophecy, and [6] to anoint the most Holy."

Christ dealt with sin. The three verbs "to finish," "to make an end," and "to make reconciliation" apply to his atonement; and the threefold "transgression," "sin," and "iniquity" refer to the sin of God's people. In addition, Christ brought in "everlasting righteousness," which refers to justification. Furthermore, Christ sealed up the vision and prophecy. To seal means to put a stamp of approval on something and to stop or close something. Christ did that, for he placed a stamp of approval on all Old Testament prophecy by fulfilling it all. In so doing, he stopped it, ended it, or completed it. We expect no more prophecy in the New Testament age. Christ anointed the Most Holy, not by entering the physical temple, but by his resurrection and ascension he entered the heavenly sanctuary: "It was therefore necessary that the patterns of things in the heavens should be purified with these; but the heavenly things themselves with better sacrifices than these. For Christ is not entered into the holy places made with hands, which are the figures of the true; but into heaven itself, now to appear in the presence of God for us" (Heb. 9:23–24).

By his death on the cross, Christ confirmed the covenant and caused sacrifice and oblation to cease (Dan. 9:27). The "he" of Daniel 9:27 is not antichrist, but Christ. Dispensationalism could not be more wrong here! Antichrist fulfills the covenant with Israel for seven years? Antichrist breaks the covenant with Israel after three and a half years? How foreign to the truth of scripture! How dishonoring to Christ, the head of the covenant!

Daniel 10–12 was fulfilled especially in Antiochus IV Epiphanes, but not even he exhausted the prophecy. Antiochus IV Epiphanes was a wicked Syrian king who exalted himself above the God of Israel. Antiochus sought to Hellenize his kingdom, which means he imposed Greek culture upon his subjects. Many of the Jews adopted Greek culture, but the more strict Jews opposed it, which was the origin of the movement of the Pharisees. Antiochus imposed a corrupt high priest upon Israel; he had a Greek gymnasium built in Jerusalem; and he renamed Jerusalem Antioch after himself. Antiochus had coins minted with his image on them. So arrogant was Antiochus that he called himself Epiphanes, which means the manifestation of God. Thus Antiochus proclaimed himself to be God. In fact, he reflected exactly what 2 Thessalonians 2:4 describes, and he was a type of the antichrist: "Who opposeth and exalteth himself above all that is called God, or that is worshipped; so that he as God sitteth in the temple of God, shewing himself that he is God."

The abomination of desolation itself took place when Antiochus Epiphanes defiled the temple in 167 BC. In that year a rumor reached Jerusalem that Antiochus had been killed in battle. Consequently, many of the Jews rebelled against his rule. However, Antiochus was very much alive, and in great fury he came to Jerusalem to punish the Jews. His desire was to exterminate Judaism altogether. He prohibited circumcision,

Sabbath observance, and Jewish food laws upon pain of death. He also set up pagan altars throughout the land. Finally, he set up a statue to Zeus in the Jewish temple, sacrificed pigs on the altar of burnt offering, and forced the Jews to eat pork. Those who refused were mercilessly slaughtered in the cruelest possible ways. The result was a terrible bloodbath.

Imagine the horror! Swine flesh upon the altar, the same altar that was typical of Christ's blood of atonement! The worship of God was impossible because the abomination of Antiochus Epiphanes made the temple desolate. The temple remained desolate until the Maccabees cleansed it in 165 BC, an event so significant that it is still celebrated in the Jewish festival Hanukkah, called the Feast of the Dedication in John 10:22. Antiochus died in 164 BC and went to his own place.

The horrible history of Antiochus Epiphanes lived in the consciousness of the Jews, but, warns Jesus on the Mount of Olives, a few days before his arrest, trial, and death, there is another fulfillment coming. "When *ye* therefore shall *see* the abomination of desolation spoken of by Daniel the prophet stand in the holy place" (Matt. 24:15, emphasis added). Christ's disciples would witness in a few years the abomination of desolation spoken of by Daniel the prophet. They must be prepared for that awful event.

The second abomination of desolation occurred in the period leading up to AD 70, when Jerusalem and the temple were defiled and destroyed by the Romans. Around that time, a Roman general named Titus came to squash a Jewish uprising. The Jews had been troublesome to the Romans, for they were constantly rebelling and they had a class of freedom fighters in their midst called the Zealots. One of Christ's disciples, Simon, now repentant, had belonged to the Zealots.

The history prior to AD 70 was tumultuous. When Pilate

was governor, the Jews reacted with horror at the idea of Rome's soldiers carrying their idolatrous standards bearing the Roman eagle into Jerusalem. In AD 40 Emperor Caligula ordered a statute of himself to be erected in the temple, but he died in AD 41 before his orders could be carried out. Between AD 66 and AD 70 the Great Jewish Revolt took place. After a prolonged siege, Rome conquered Jerusalem, entered the city, and defiled the temple. Not one stone was left standing upon another, just as Jesus had warned.

The Christians did not imagine, as the Zealots did, that God would not allow the Romans to conquer Jerusalem and that he would spare her at the last minute. In fact, Daniel 9:26 prophesies of this destruction: "The people of the prince that shall come shall destroy the city and the sanctuary."

Postmillennialism has its own peculiar interpretations of this abomination of desolation prophecy. The postmillennialists insist that AD 70 exhausted the prophecy, and they point to the words "when *ye* shall see." There is, they say, no *future* abomination of desolation.

The premillennial dispensationalists contend that Christ's prophecy will be fulfilled in a future Jerusalem, a future temple, and the future seventieth week after the rapture of the church. God is about to restart his stopwatch. The Jews will build their temple. Later, antichrist will break his alliance with the Jews and defile their rebuilt temple again. This explains the obsession of dispensationalism with the political development of the state of Israel. Excitedly, the dispensationalists look to Israel, because they believe that events there will soon trigger the rapture of the church and the beginning of Daniel's seventieth week. Post-millennialism and premillennial dispensationalism have this in common—they both *deny* that the *church* will see the abomination of desolation.

Reformed amillennialism looks for a future fulfillment of this prophecy because of Matthew 24:29–31: "Immediately after the tribulation of those days…" The tribulation triggered by the abomination of desolation will be followed *immediately* by the second coming of Jesus Christ. That did not happen in AD 70. Moreover, 2 Thessalonians 2:3–4 must be fulfilled before the end: "Let no man deceive you by any means: for that day shall not come, except there come a falling away first, and that man of sin be revealed, the son of perdition; who opposeth and exalteth himself above all that is called God, or that is worshipped; so that he as God sitteth in the temple of God, shewing himself that he is God."

That did not happen in AD 70. The man of sin has not yet appeared. When he does appear, he will defile the temple of God, which is the true church of Jesus Christ.

We expect another abomination of desolation in the future when antichrist shall rule. But this will not be an abomination of desolation that only affects the Jews and that happens after a rapture of the church into heaven, nor one that will literally occur in a rebuilt Jewish temple.

Not only is the rebuilding of a temple in Jerusalem *not* prophesied in scripture, but such an event would be undesirable for the Christian church. Premillennial dispensationalism eagerly expects the Jews to rebuild their temple. However, if such an event took place, it would simply be another proof of Jewish apostasy and a confirmation of their rejection of Jesus Christ. What was the function of the temple but to offer sacrifices? What would be the function of a rebuilt Jewish temple, especially if the prophecies of Ezekiel 40–48, for example, were literally fulfilled? To offer sacrifices—after the one sacrifice of Jesus Christ on the cross! The whole of the New Testament, and especially the epistle to the Hebrews, is against such an idea.

Besides that, God is building a temple in the New Testament age. The church is the temple of God. One by one, God is gathering, by his word and Holy Spirit, stones for his temple. By the power of regeneration, he makes us "lively [living] stones":

4. To whom coming, as unto a living stone, disallowed indeed of men, but chosen of God, and precious,

5. Ye also, as lively stones, are built up a spiritual house, an holy priesthood, to offer up spiritual sacrifices, acceptable to God by Jesus Christ.

6. Wherefore also it is contained in the scripture, Behold, I lay in Sion a chief corner stone, elect, precious: and he that believeth on him shall not be confounded.

7. Unto you therefore which believe he is precious: but unto them which be disobedient, the stone which the builders disallowed, the same is made the head of the corner,

8. And a stone of stumbling, and a rock of offence, even to them which stumble at the word, being disobedient: whereunto also they were appointed.

9. But ye are a chosen generation, a royal priesthood, an holy nation, a peculiar people; that ye should shew forth the praises of him who hath called you out of darkness into his marvellous light:

10. Which in time past were not a people, but are now the people of God: which had not obtained mercy, but now have obtained mercy. (1 Pet. 2:4–10)

It ought not escape our attention that Peter applies Isaiah 28:16, Exodus 19:5–6, and Hosea 1:10 and 2:23 to the gathering of Jews and Gentiles into the New Testament church. Those passages will not be fulfilled literally in a future Jewish kingdom during an earthly millennium.

Paul also teaches explicitly that the New Testament church made up of elect Jews and Gentiles is the temple of God. Of a future rebuilt temple in Jerusalem the New Testament knows *nothing.* "Know ye not that ye are the temple of God, and that the Spirit of God dwelleth in you? If any man defile the temple of God, him shall God destroy; for the temple of God is holy, which temple ye are" (1 Cor. 3:16–17). "What? know ye not that your body is the temple of the Holy Ghost which is in you, which ye have of God, and ye are not your own" (6:19)? "What agreement hath the temple of God with idols? for ye are the temple of the living God; as God hath said, I will dwell in them, and walk in them; and I will be their God, and they shall be my people" (2 Cor. 6:16).

19. Now therefore ye are no more strangers and foreigners, but fellow-citizens with the saints, and of the household of God;

20. And are built upon the foundation of the apostles and prophets, Jesus Christ himself being the chief corner stone;

21. In whom all the building fitly framed together groweth unto an holy temple in the Lord:

22. In whom ye also are builded together for an habitation of God through the Spirit. (Eph. 2:19–22)

Therefore, when Paul prophesies that "the man of sin...sitteth in the temple of God, shewing himself that he is God" (2 Thess. 2:3–4), he cannot mean the physical temple in Jerusalem, whether in AD 70 or in our future. He must mean the *church.*

Sometime in our future, a man will rise from the troubled nations of the world, and he will do something no other man has ever been able to accomplish. For a time, he will unite all nations under one head. In the past, there have been types of antichrist, men or groups of men, who ruled vast kingdoms: Nebuchadnezzar, Alexander the Great, Antiochus IV Epiphanes, and the Roman emperors were all types of antichrist. Nevertheless, for the last two thousand years, the devil has been unable to unite the nations under one head. This is because Satan is bound by Christ in his death on the cross, so that Satan cannot deceive all the nations at one time to persecute the church, so that the church is free to preach the gospel: "When a strong man armed keepeth his palace, his goods are in peace: but when a stronger than he shall come upon him, and overcome him, he taketh from him all his armour wherein he trusted, and divideth his spoils" (Luke 11:21–22).

The "binding of Satan" is a concept prominent in Revelation 20, which is the only place in the Bible where one thousand years (the millennium) are mentioned. As might be expected, there is controversy over that passage also. Rather than give a detailed explanation of the various views, I will briefly set forth the Reformed amillennial exegesis of Revelation 20.

First, the events described in Revelation 20 do not take place *after* the events described in Revelation 19, which is a vision of the coming of Christ in judgment. Revelation 20 is a new vision, in which the Spirit describes the same period of history (the New Testament age) from a different angle. Second, Revelation 20 is a vision ("And I saw" [v. 1]) and is therefore not to be taken literally or literalistically. The number one thousand, the chain, the key, and the bottomless pit are symbols. Third, the binding of Satan is strictly circumscribed, which is clear from Satan's activity as soon as he is released: "Satan shall be loosed out of his prison, and shall go out to deceive the nations…to gather them together to battle" (vv. 7–8). It is not that Satan is bound from *any* evil influence during the one thousand years, but that he cannot muster all the nations together against the church. During the one thousand years the church is gathered, God's people are persecuted, and Satan is bound.

While these events are taking place, something else is taking place in heaven. The saints are reigning with Christ. Verse 4 says that John saw "thrones," but the thrones in the book of Revelation are not on earth but in heaven (Rev. 4:2; 5:1; 6:16). Those who reign are called merely "souls": "And I saw the souls of them that were beheaded for the witness of Jesus" (20:4). John sees disembodied souls, which can only refer to the intermediate state of the soul between death and the final resurrection. The intermediate state of glory, during which God's people reign with him in heaven, is called "the first resurrection" (vv. 5–6). The second resurrection is the resurrection of the body at the second advent. (The wicked do not participate in the first resurrection, and their resurrection on the last day is to corruption and damnation).

Both events happen at the same time: during the thousand years Satan is bound and he cannot establish his anti-Christian kingdom to destroy the church, so that the church is free to preach the gospel to the ends of the earth; and at the same time, the same one thousand years, in heaven the souls of God's people reign with Christ.

The passage therefore has nothing at all to do with a reign of Christians or Jews on the earth for a literal thousand years. The millennium of Revelation 20 is a long, indeterminate period of time, from the first to the second coming of Christ, or the New Testament age, or the last days.

When the church has finished her work of preaching the gospel to all nations, antichrist will rise. The nations will see in him a savior, one who will end war, economic hardship, and even religious division. Although there is world peace, economic prosperity, and religious harmony in antichrist's kingdom, there is one thing antichrist will oppose: Christianity. Antichrist will oppose Christ. He will also seek to replace Christ. His kingdom will be a kingdom of man, really the worship of man with the devil behind man. Antichrist will corrupt the worship of the church.

There will be churches under antichrist, but they will adopt his anti-Christian policies to avoid persecution. The false church will embrace him. In essence they already have. In Revelation 13 we read of antichrist's making an image and forcing all to worship it. *This* will be the abomination of desolation.

By that defiling of the church, which is called the temple of the Holy Spirit, antichrist will make the public worship of God impossible. He will take away the preaching of Christ crucified and replace it with an abominable, desolating counterfeit. The true church will be driven into desolation and will only be able to continue to meet in small isolated pockets. The abomination of desolation will trigger one final tribulation followed immediately by the coming of Christ, who will destroy antichrist with the spirit of his mouth, thus conclusively placing the man of sin on earth at Christ's return:

4. Who opposeth and exalteth himself above all that is called God, or that is worshipped; so that he as God sitteth in the temple of God, shewing himself that he is God.
8. And then shall that Wicked be revealed, whom the Lord shall consume with the spirit of his mouth, and shall destroy with the brightness of his coming:
9. Even him, whose coming is after the working of Satan with all power and signs and lying wonders. (2 Thess. 2:4, 8–9)

The Calling

Christ has one word for his church—whether just before AD 70 or when the antichrist sets up his final desecration of God's church. Flee! Do not stand and fight. Do not stockpile weapons to resist the antichristian kingdom. Do not organize political resistance against the beast. Flee!

Christ's command is typically Jewish, to a Jewish audience. He speaks of "them which be in Judea" (Matt. 24:16). In Luke 21:21, he adds, "Let them which are in Judea flee to the mountains; and let them which are in the midst of it depart out; and let not them that are in the countries enter thereinto." In addition, he speaks of the flat-roofed houses of Palestine, of the Palestinian winter, and of the outwardly strict Sabbath observance in Israel, which made travel difficult.

This warning to flee out of Jerusalem and Judea was necessary: when Rome's armies advanced around AD 70, many Jews fled *into* the city, and because the siege took place around Passover, the city was overcrowded. Those who fled *into* the city perished. Those who fled *from* the city and from Judea survived.

The call to flee is urgent. The slightest hesitation could be fatal. There will be no time to pack—get off your housetop and run; leave the field with only the clothes on your back and make for the hills. Do not look back. Think of Lot's flight from Sodom. It will be especially difficult for pregnant and nursing mothers: "Woe unto them that are with child, and to them that give suck in those days!" (Matt. 24:19). If the day of flight is in winter or on the Sabbath it will make travel difficult, so, says Jesus, pray that the day you flee be not on such days!

This topic might be discouraging and might even make us frightened. The idea of fleeing from antichrist is not a pleasant one. Remember, however, that Christ does not tell us these things to terrify us, but to forewarn us. We rest in this knowledge: the Lord has determined all these things for his glory and for the good of his church. Even the complex numbers are comforting to us, even if we never fully decipher them. We know antichrist's time is fixed in God's counsel and that it is short. Antichrist must rage and defile the church to show his great wickedness, so that Christ can show his power in destroying him.

When we see the abomination of desolation standing in the holy place, we flee. When the true gospel is everywhere replaced by a satanic counterfeit, in which the beast is worshiped, we flee. We flee because the true gospel can no longer be preached. We flee with the few believers we can find. We do not seek for a rapture to snatch us away. We do not pretend it has all happened in the past, lest we are unprepared. We listen to Christ and flee. The abomination of desolation is another heavy footstep of Jesus by which he comes to us.

Come Lord Jesus, come quickly!

Chapter 8

THE GREAT
TRIBULATION

For then shall be great tribulation, such as was not since
the beginning of the world to this time, no, nor ever shall
be. And except those days should be shortened, there
should no flesh be saved: but for the elect's sake those days
shall be shortened.—Matthew 24:21–22

The abomination of desolation is antichrist's final desecration of the church. Christ describes the abomination of
desolation in terms of the destruction of the Jerusalem temple.
Daniel had prophesied *that* abomination of desolation, and we
saw it had at least a twofold historical fulfillment. First, in 167
BC Antiochus Epiphanes offered pigs upon the altar to Zeus.
That was a desolating abomination! Second, in AD 70 the
Romans defiled and destroyed the temple. Another desolating abomination! However, AD 70 was only a type or picture
of something much worse, of antichrist's sitting in the temple
of God declaring he is God: "Let no man deceive you by any
means: for that day shall not come, except there come a falling

away first, and that man of sin be revealed, the son of perdition; who opposeth and exalteth himself above all that is called God, or that is worshipped; so that he as God sitteth in the temple of God, shewing himself that he is God" (2 Thess. 2:3–4).

Antichrist will not sit in a rebuilt Jewish temple, but in the visible church of the New Testament. Antichrist's setting up the final abomination of desolation will mark the end of the church's official witness and the beginning of a final period of persecution leading up to the second coming. The church will not be able through her official ministry to preach the gospel. Antichrist will have universal dominion, and true Christianity will be outlawed worldwide. The only religion permitted will be the religion of the worship of the image of the beast. That falsehood will be promoted by the false church that will cooperate with antichrist:

11. And I beheld another beast coming up out of the earth; and he had two horns like a lamb, and he spake as a dragon.
12. And he exerciseth all the power of the first beast before him, and causeth the earth and them which dwell therein to worship the first beast, whose deadly wound was healed.
13. And he doeth great wonders, so that he maketh fire come down from heaven on the earth in the sight of men,
14. And deceiveth them that dwell on the earth by the means of those miracles which he had power to do in the sight of the beast; saying to them that dwell on the earth, that they should make an image to the beast, which had the wound by a sword, and did live.
15. And he had power to give life unto the image of the beast, that the image of the beast should both speak,

and cause that as many as would not worship the image of the beast should be killed.

16. And he causeth all, both small and great, rich and poor, free and bond, to receive a mark in their right hand, or in their foreheads:

17. And that no man might buy or sell, save he that had the mark, or the name of the beast, or the number of his name. (Rev. 13:11–17)

That final period is known as the great tribulation, a period of unprecedented suffering, trial, and persecution for the true church. Nevertheless, we must not fear, because this too is part of the coming of Christ and is under the sovereign control of our Savior. Christ will not return to a christianized earth, but to a small, despised, almost annihilated group of believers, when evil is at its height. No tribulation, not even great—not even *the* great—tribulation will be able to separate us from the love of God that is in Christ Jesus our Lord (Rom. 8:35–39).

Dreadful

Tribulation is suffering, especially suffering of the church, which makes her place narrow in this world. Jesus has already spoken of tribulation as a characteristic of the end times in Matthew 24:9. Now in verses 21 and 22 Christ speaks of one final, dreadful period of tribulation, which immediately precedes the second coming of our Lord. This tribulation is unparalleled by anything ever seen in history and nothing after it will equal it (v. 22). This tribulation is described in terms of the destruction of Jerusalem and the temple in AD 70.

Here is another example in the Olivet Discourse where Jesus moves quickly from AD 70 to the end of the world, blending the two events. Although one is a picture of the other, the great tribulation is *not* AD 70. That is the error of the postmillennialists. Calvin writes:

> *The tribulation of those days* is improperly interpreted by some commentators to mean the destruction of Jerusalem; for, on the contrary, it is a general recapitulation of all the evils of which Christ had previously spoken. To encourage his followers to patience, he employs this argument, that the *tribulations* will at length have a happy and joyful result.
>
> Let our ears therefore be awake to the sound of the *angel's trumpet*, which will then sound, not only to strike the reprobate with the dread of death, but to arouse the elect to a second life; that is, to the call to the enjoyment of life those whom the Lord now quickens by the voice of his Gospel; for it is a sign of infidelity to be afraid when the Son of God comes in person for our salvation.[1]

A future great tribulation for the church is the opposite of the postmillennial dream, so the great tribulation must be relegated to the past. The best candidate is the destruction of Jerusalem in AD 70. Postmillennialists appeal especially to the parallel passage in Luke, which explains the tribulation of those days in terms of God's vengeance upon Israel:

> 22. For these be the days of vengeance, that all things which are written may be fulfilled.
>
> 23. But woe unto them that are with child, and to them

---

1   Calvin, *Commentary on a Harmony of the Evangelists*, 3:146, 149.

that give suck, in those days! for there shall be great
distress in the land, and wrath upon this people.

24. And they shall fall by the edge of the sword, and
shall be led away captive into all nations: and Jerusalem shall be trodden down of the Gentiles, until the
times of the Gentiles be fulfilled. (Luke 21:22–24)

Nevertheless, as horrific as AD 70 was, it was only a picture
of something worse; it was not the final fulfillment of the great
tribulation of this passage.

The error of the premillennial dispensationalists is connected to their rapture theory and their interpretation of
Daniel's seventieth week (see chapter 7). For premillennial dispensationalism the tribulation will be a literal seven-year period,
according to its misunderstanding of Daniel's seventieth week.
During these seven years antichrist will come to power immediately after the rapture of the church. Halfway through the
seven years of tribulation, there will be three and a half years of
the *great* tribulation when antichrist will be at the height of his
power, will break his peace treaty with Israel, and will persecute
the Jews in Jerusalem and defile the (rebuilt) temple. The great
tribulation will end with the battle of Armageddon and the second coming of Christ to set up a thousand-year reign on earth
in Jerusalem. During this whole tribulation period, the church
will be in heaven.

The error of the premillennial dispensationalist and postmillennialist is that they make the great tribulation *something
only the Jews will face*. For the postmillennialist the great tribulation happened in the past. The Jews have faced it already. The
great tribulation was exhausted by the events of AD 70. For the
postmillennialist, especially the more radical postmillennialist,
AD 70 is the defining date, the end of the age.

Postmillennialists are fascinated by the Jewish historian Josephus (37–100 AD), who describes the events of AD 70 in considerable detail:

> They [the deserters] were first whipped, and then tormented with all sorts of tortures, before they died, and were then crucified before the wall of the city. This miserable procedure made Titus [the Roman general] greatly to pity them, while they caught every day five hundred Jews; nay, some days they caught more: yet it did not appear to be safe for him to let those that were taken by force go their way...The main reason why he did not forbid that cruelty was this, that he hoped the Jews might perhaps yield at that sight, out of fear lest they might themselves afterwards be liable to the same cruel treatment. So the soldiers, out of the wrath and hatred they bore the Jews, nailed those they caught, one after one way, and another after another, to the crosses, by way of jest, when their multitude was so great, that room was wanting [lacking] for the crosses, and crosses wanting for the bodies.[2]

> There ran away to Titus many of the eminent citizens, and told him the entire number of the poor that were dead, and that no fewer than six hundred thousand were thrown out at the gates, though still the number of the rest could not be discovered; and they told him further, that when they were no longer able to carry out the dead bodies of the poor, they laid their corpses on

---

2   Flavius Josephus, "The Jewish War," 5.11.1, in *The New Complete Works of Josephus*, revised and expanded edition, trans. William Whiston (Grand Rapids, MI: Kregel Publications, 1999), 873–74.

heaps in very large houses, and shut them up therein; as also that a medimnus of wheat was sold for a talent; and that when, a while afterward, it was not possible to gather herbs, by reason the city was all walled about, some persons were driven to that terrible distress as to search the common sewers and old dunghills of cattle, and to eat the dung which they got there; and what they of old could not endure so much as to see they now used for food.[3]

Historian Philip Schaff explains how the temple of Jerusalem came to be destroyed:

Titus...intended at first to save that magnificent work of architecture [the temple], as a trophy of victory, and perhaps from some superstitious fear; and when the flames threatened to reach the Holy of Holies he forced his way through flame and smoke, over the dead and dying, to arrest the fire. But the destruction was determined by a higher decree. His own soldiers, roused to madness by the stubborn resistance, and greedy of the golden treasures, could not be restrained from the work of destruction. At first the halls around the temple were set on fire. Then a firebrand was hurled through the golden gate. When the flames arose the Jews raised a hideous yell and tried to put out the fire... The legions vied with each other in feeding the flames, and made the unhappy people feel the full force of their unchained rage...The shout of victory and the jubilee of the legions sounded through the wailings of the people, now surrounded with fire and sword, upon the

---

3   Josephus, "The Jewish War," 5.13.7, in ibid., 880.

mountain, and throughout the city. The echo from all the mountains around…increased the deafening roar. Yet the misery itself was more terrible than this disorder. The hill on which the temple stood was seething hot, and seemed enveloped to its base in one sheet of flame. The blood was larger in quantity than the fire, and those that were slain were more in number than those that slew them. The ground was nowhere visible. All was covered with corpses; over these heaps the soldiers pursued the fugitives.

The Romans planted their eagles on the shapeless ruins, over against the eastern gate, [and] offered their sacrifices to them.[4]

There is no doubt that AD 70 was a particularly horrific judgment upon Israel. It ended their nation, destroyed their temple, and scattered the Jews throughout the world. The Roman general Titus besieged Jerusalem. The city was overcrowded with Passover pilgrims, whom the Romans allowed to enter but not to leave. The Jewish Zealots within the city destroyed the food supply and murdered high-ranking Jews. Starvation, disease, and cruelty of the worst kind spread through the city, until finally the Romans broke through the defenses. In the standoff, the temple went up in flames and the Romans tore down the building to reach the gold that melted in the inferno. Josephus estimates that over a million Jews died and ninety-seven thousand were sold into slavery.

That is only a picture or a historical type of the end. The postmillennial interpretation sees Matthew 24 fulfilled in the

---

4   Philip Schaff, *History of the Christian Church*, vol. 1, *Apostolic Christianity AD 1–100* (Charles Scribner's Sons, 1910; repr., Grand Rapids, MI: Wm. B. Eerdmans Publishing Company, 1966), 397–98.

temple *then standing*. Premillennial dispensationalists insist all this will take place in a *future* temple.

Premillennial dispensationalists are very excited that Israel exists again as a sovereign state, and they keep their eyes glued to the television to see what is happening between the Israelis and the Palestinians. The premillennial dispensationalists expect that soon the Jews will be able to rebuild their temple on or around the site of the Dome of the Rock, a site holy to Muslims and Jews. Around the time of the rebuilding of Jerusalem's new temple, antichrist will arise, and during the great tribulation antichrist will sit in *that* temple and eventually destroy it, thus, they say, fulfilling Matthew 24 and 2 Thessalonians.

Notwithstanding, none of that is the great tribulation. The great tribulation is the final period of suffering before Christ's second coming. Three things must take place at the end of history: the rise and temporary triumph of antichrist, the last and most dreadful persecution of the church, and the outpouring of God's wrath upon a world ripened in sin. The antichrist did not appear in the past; he will appear in the future.

The final antichrist will be the last in a number of attempts by the devil to establish a worldwide antichristian kingdom. Satan's first attempt in history was Nimrod and the kingdom of Babel. God destroyed Satan's and Nimrod's hopes by confusing the languages and scattering the people across the earth (Gen. 11). In the Old Testament, kingdoms have arisen that have come ever closer to reaching worldwide dominion: Egypt, Assyria, Babylon, Medio-Persia, Greece, and Rome. All those kingdoms have sought to destroy the true church. All those kingdoms have perished.

In the New Testament the spirit of antichrist and the mystery of iniquity have been at work: "Ye know what withholdeth that he might be revealed in his time. For the mystery of iniquity doth already work: only he who now letteth will let, until he be taken out of the way. And then shall that Wicked be revealed, whom the Lord shall consume with the spirit of his mouth, and shall destroy with the brightness of his coming" (2 Thess. 2:6–8). "Every spirit that confesseth not that Jesus Christ is come in the flesh is not of God: and this is that spirit of antichrist, whereof ye have heard that it should come; and even now already is it in the world" (1 John 4:3).

God has restrained the devil from achieving his goal of a worldwide government and one world religion against the church, because the gospel must be preached. Then, and only then, when the gospel has finished its course, will the end come.

At the end of history, the devil will achieve what he heretofore has not been able to achieve. According to Revelation 13 one government will arise, ruled by one man possessed or inspired by the devil, uniting all nations, peoples, cultures, and religions under one head. That man will be antichrist. He will unleash great tribulation upon the church. His kingdom will have a twofold unity as depicted in Revelation 13 as two beasts, one from the sea and the other from the earth. These two beasts are the fulfillment (a composite) of the beasts of Daniel 7: the leopard, the bear, and the lion.

The unity will be, first, political. Antichrist will achieve what the EU, the UN, NATO, and all other international organizations have failed to accomplish—a worldwide government (Rev. 13:7). Second, the unity will be religious. Antichrist (the beast from the sea), by means of the false prophet (the beast from the earth), will achieve what the World Council of Churches and other groups have failed to bring about: one world religion. Antichrist will be welcomed as the savior of mankind, "and all the world [will] wonder after [marvel at] the beast" (v. 3).

It is possible that the present world order will collapse into chaos, and out of the ashes a man will arise who will seem to have the solution to all the world's problems: he will be able to end war between the nations, bring about disarmament, solve food shortages, and fulfill all man's dreams. If a man can give them that, the people will give him everything: their allegiance, their loyalty, even their worship. Antichrist will control every-thing: the economy, the military, law enforcement, and the media. The antichrist will be hailed as the savior, the messiah, and even the god of the world. There will be one religion, the religion of antichrist, the worship of the image of the beast.

Although antichrist will appear to be the savior of mankind, he will be evil, because he will seek to replace Christ and will oppose him. The antichristian system is based on a lie: man is God; man can save himself; and man has no need of God's grace revealed in the cross of Christ. We see that in the number 666 of Revelation 13:18. Many are fascinated by this number, and they approach it as if it were a mathematical riddle. The number 666 simply means the kingdom of man, which always falls short of seven, the number of God's covenant.

Revelation 13:18 says, "It is the number of a man," which has led some to seek to identify the man. The number 666 does not enable us to identify one particular man, for that is not its function. It is not a cryptic representation of Nero, Napoleon, Hitler, or any other historical figure. The Greek should be trans-lated, "It is the number of *man*," indicating the character of the beast—the beast's kingdom is the apotheosis of man, or the deification of man. In the beast's kingdom, there is no place for God, for Christ, or for his church, for man is the measure of all things, and to man be the glory forever!

The kingdom of antichrist cannot continue for long because it is not built upon righteousness grounded in the cross of Christ, but in the achievements of man without God. For a time, antichrist will hold sway. Satan will seem to triumph, which means a time of great tribulation for the true church that refuses to deny Christ. Through antichrist, Satan's fury will fall upon the followers of Christ. Revelation 13 teaches that the beast will make war against the saints and overcome them (v. 7); all those who will not worship the image of the beast will be killed (v. 15). Moreover, he will corrupt the church's worship by bringing his image into the church, the abomination of desolation, and he will force all men to worship him. Any church that will not comply will be shut down; any individual who will not comply will be arrested, imprisoned, and killed. These activities of antichrist will make it impossible for the church to meet for public worship, will silence the public preaching of the gospel, and will put a stop to the church's witness, because antichrist will control television, radio, and even the Internet.

Therefore, while the world rejoices in her new leader, hailed as the savior of the world, the true church will be afflicted in the great tribulation. Christians will not be able to buy and sell; they will not be able to have jobs or feed their families. The world ruled by antichrist will increasingly squeeze them. Christians will be public enemy number one, because they will not fit into antichrist's supposedly tolerant, pluralistic, man-centered, God-defying world. The increasing antichristian agenda of intolerance in the western world is a harbinger of this. The whole world will say, "The beast, antichrist, is lord," but the Christians will say, "Not so! Jesus is Lord. Man is a wicked, totally depraved sinner. Only Christ can save by the blood of the cross." Christians will overcome "by the blood of the Lamb, and by the word of their testimony; and they loved not their lives unto the death" (Rev. 12:11). Pressure will be enormous to deny Christ, and many will deny him; the church will be purged of her hypocrites, and there will be many martyrs.

Unparalleled

The great tribulation is unparalleled, which means that it is without equal in history. Christ warns of great (literally, "mega") tribulation, not merely "tribulation." There have been periods of tribulation in history, but the great tribulation under the final manifestation of antichrist will be the worst. It will be worse than the persecution under the Egyptians when all the baby boys were cast into the Nile River. It will be worse than the Assyrian or Babylonian captivities. It will surpass the cruelties of Antiochus Epiphanes. It will exceed the tribulation of AD 70. It will make the persecutions of Christians under Nero, Domitian, or others pale in significance. It will be more grievous than the Inquisition, and even than the persecution today by the Communists and Muslims.

It will be worse because it will be worldwide, concentrated, and masterminded by the Man of Sin himself. This does not necessarily mean it will be worse because man will have devised new and awful forms of torture hitherto unknown to God's people. It will be worse especially because of its *extent*.

Christ makes this unparalleled nature of the great tribulation very clear when he says, "Then shall be great tribulation, such as was not since the beginning of the world to this time, no, nor ever shall be" (Matt. 24:21). So dreadful and widespread is the great tribulation that it almost leads to the annihilation of all flesh ("there should no flesh be saved" [v. 22]). That cannot be said of AD 70, which was a local war.

Are you ready for that? We must be faithful in small things, watching and praying that we will be faithful in that day. But we must not fear. Christ will provide sufficient grace to endure the persecution when it comes.

At the same time the great tribulation will mean unparalleled suffering and wrath for the ungodly world. As antichrist in his satanic fury heats up the furnace of his wrath, God pours out his wrath upon the world, which rejects his Son and persecutes his children. That is the message of Revelation, the last book of the Bible, given for our comfort and edification.

Because of the unparalleled horror of the great tribulation, many Christians, such as the premillennial dispensationalists, believe that the church will not be on earth during this period. Others, such as the postmillennialists, believe that the great tribulation took place in the past.

Consider the rapture popularized in the Left Behind series of books and movies. Reformed Christians must not underestimate the appeal of this teaching. According to the rapture theory (the pretribulational rapture), at any moment Christ could return. When he does, no one will see him, because it will be a secret, invisible coming for his church. At that moment millions will disappear, having been taken to heaven. At the same time the dead in Christ will be taken from their graves. The disappearance of millions of Christians, missing from airplanes, cars, and every walk of life, will cause chaos. In the midst of this terrible upheaval, antichrist will take control.

The main text to which premillennial dispensationalists appeal for their doctrine of the rapture is 1 Thessalonians 4:15–18:

15. For this we say unto you by the word of the Lord, that we which are alive and remain unto the coming of the Lord shall not prevent them which are asleep.
16. For the Lord himself shall descend from heaven with a shout, with the voice of the archangel, and with the trump of God: and the dead in Christ shall rise first:

17. Then we which are alive and remain shall be caught up together with them in the clouds, to meet the Lord in the air: and so shall we ever be with the Lord.

18. Wherefore comfort one another with these words.

The premillennial dispensationalists could hardly have chosen a *worse* text by which to attempt to substantiate their doctrine of the rapture! First, Christ comes personally: "The Lord himself shall descend from heaven" (v. 16). Second, Christ's coming is very loud, possibly the loudest event in human history, the very opposite of a secret, silent rapture. Notice in verse 16 the word "shout," which refers to the rousing cry of a military general summoning his troops. One does not rally the soldiers with a whisper! It will be a cry to wake the dead, for Jesus says, "Marvel not at this: for the hour is coming in the which all that are in the graves shall hear his voice" (John 5:28). "All" in this verse refers to both the righteous and the wicked at the same time. Moreover, Jesus will be accompanied by the archangel. First Thessalonians 4:16 mentions "the voice of the archangel," possibly Gabriel or Michael. Other passages indicate that a multitude of the heavenly host will accompany Jesus (2 Thess. 1:7–8). In addition, Christ's coming will be heralded by the blast of a trumpet, namely "the trump of God" (1 Thess. 4:16). The trumpet in scripture is not a silent instrument. It was designed to give a long, loud, clear sound (Ex. 19:19). Elsewhere in scripture, the resurrection of the dead is accompanied by a trumpet (Matt. 24:31; 1 Cor. 15:51–52).

Moreover, the context of 1 Thessalonians 4 makes the premillennial dispensational theory of a rapture *impossible*, for chapter 4 is followed by chapter 5. These two chapters describe the same event, the same second coming of Jesus Christ. According to the word of God, Jesus returns for two reasons:

to save his people (chap. 4) and to punish the wicked (chap. 5). The Thessalonians were confused, troubled, and ignorant about the second coming of the Lord. Although they firmly believed that Jesus would return, and they waited for him (1:10), they were concerned about those who had fallen asleep (4:13–15). By "asleep" Paul means dead, and specifically he means the Christian dead. When a Christian dies, he falls asleep, that is, according to the body, not according to the soul. The soul of the believer is with Jesus, consciously enjoying heavenly glory, but the body sleeps in the grave until the resurrection. The Thessalonians wondered whether Christians who had already died might *miss* the second coming. Should, then, believers not sorrow "as others which have no hope" (v. 13)?

In answer to the Thessalonians' anxious questions, Paul gives an explanation of the events as well as a clarification of our participation in those events.

First, Christ will bring the souls of all departed saints with him when he returns. These souls have not perished, and they will not miss the glory of that day. They will come *with Jesus* (v. 14). Second, there will be some Christians alive when Jesus returns (vv. 15, 17). These believers shall not die ("we shall not all sleep" [1 Cor. 15:51]). Instead, they shall be instantaneously and gloriously changed (vv. 51–54). Third, the saints who are alive at the coming of the Lord shall not "prevent" the departed saints. "Prevent" in verse 15 means to precede or to come before.

Here, then, is the order. Christ descends; dead Christians are raised in the body and reunited with their souls, which are descending with Jesus from heaven. Then the saints who are alive at the second coming will be transformed, body and soul, and will be caught up (raptured) to meet Jesus in the air. Thus *all* the saints (from Adam, Eve, and Abel to the last martyr, to the last saint of history) will meet Christ in the air. What an event that will be! No wonder Paul can conclude, "And so shall we ever be with the Lord. Wherefore comfort one another with these words" (vv. 17–18).

Premillennial dispensationalism even teaches that we shall be with the Lord for seven years—while the great tribulation occurs on earth—after which time Christ shall leave his bride in heaven in order to reign over a reconstituted kingdom *of Jews* in Jerusalem for one thousand years!

Thus we understand "first" in verse 16 ("the dead in Christ shall rise *first*"). Premillennial dispensationalism teaches that the saints of the church age will be resurrected some seven years *before* the resurrection of other categories of saints (for there will be, according to premillennial dispensationalism, another resurrection of the so-called tribulation saints seven years later, at the end of the great tribulation, just prior to the millennium), and some one thousand and seven years before the resurrection of the wicked, who will be resurrected after the great tribulation and after the millennium. Premillennial dispensationalism is needlessly and unbiblically complex, with several comings, resurrections, and judgments! Paul's obvious meaning in verse 16, however, is that the dead in Christ will rise before those saints who are alive at the second coming, albeit *on the same day, even in the same hour.*

In 1 Thessalonians 5 Paul describes the effect of *the same second coming of Christ* on the wicked. The figure that Paul uses is a thief, which Christ also uses in Matthew 24:43. Many premillennial dispensationalists seize on that word "thief," and they teach that as a thief sneaks into a house to steal a person's valuables, so Christ will enter the world in a secret rapture to snatch away the Christians.

That interpretation is impossible, however. First, according to 1 Thessalonians 5:3, Christ's coming as a thief will bring sudden destruction on the wicked and unbelieving. The secret rapture theory has sudden destruction coming on the wicked *at a different time*, seven years later! It is simply impossible to find two separate second comings of Christ separated by some seven years in these chapters of God's word. In fact, Paul indicates no change of subject whatsoever where he writes, "Of the times and the seasons, brethren, ye have no need that I write unto you. For yourselves know perfectly that the day of the Lord so cometh as a thief in the night" (vv. 1–2). The "times," "seasons," and "day" described in 1 Thessalonians 5 are the same as they are described in chapter 4!

Moreover, the rapture theory does not fit Matthew 24. Verse 15 declares that "ye [i.e., the apostles and therefore Christians] shall see the abomination of desolation." Verse 16 says that Christians must flee and pray for a favorable time for fleeing. Christ does not give any indication that the Christians will have disappeared from the earth before the great tribulation begins. Christ promises in verse 22 that the great tribulation will be shortened "for the elect's sake." Why should this be so if the elect have been taken by the rapture some three and a half years earlier? Verse 24 says that the false prophets who will arise at that time will be so deceptive that, if it were possible, they would deceive the elect. Why should this be, if the elect have been taken away in the rapture before the period described occurs?

Despite these objections the premillennial dispensationalists muster a number of arguments to explain why the church will not experience the great tribulation.

First, there is a very common emotional argument: "Christ would not beat up on his bride." This is the idea that it would be cruel to make the church endure the great tribulation. However, this does not answer the question why God made his church go through persecution in other ages. Why did God not rapture away the Christians in Nero's day when they were crucified, set alight as candles in his garden parties, and thrown to the lions? Why did God not rapture the many tortured and burned by the Inquisition, and the many today languishing in prison or worse? To bring his church through persecution is not a kind of "wife beating."

Second, there are a few exegetical arguments, which are so embarrassingly weak that a Reformed Christian can briefly dispatch them. The first is from 1 Thessalonians 5:9: "God hath not appointed us to wrath." We must understand, however, that the great tribulation is not God's pouring his wrath *upon the church*. Rather, in the great tribulation God pours his wrath upon the wicked world, while antichrist unleashes his fury against the church. The church can be present during such a period, just as Israel (the Old Testament church) was present when God poured out his wrath during the ten plagues of Egypt.

The second argument is from Revelation 3:10: "Because thou hast kept the word of my patience, I also will keep thee from the hour of temptation, which shall come upon all the world, to try them that dwell upon the earth." The fact that the church in Philadelphia has kept the word of Christ's "patience" indicates that they have suffered persecution. They have suffered it *patiently*. Contextually, there is nothing here to link this promise to the great tribulation. In addition, to be kept from the hour of temptation does not mean to escape a period of time called the great tribulation. The church of Philadelphia was not taken away in any rapture. John 17:15 indicates that God keeps his church from evil without taking them *out of* the world, but by preserving them *in* the world: "I pray not that thou shouldest take them out of the world, but that thou shouldest keep them from the evil [one]." To "keep from" is the same Greek verb and preposition in both John 17:15 and Revelation 3:10.

The third argument is from Revelation 7:13–14: "One of

the elders answered, saying unto me, What are these which are arrayed in white robes? and whence came they? And I said unto him, Sir, thou knowest. And he said to me, These are they which came out of great tribulation, and have washed their robes, and made them white in the blood of the Lamb." These saints came out of great tribulation by entering it, enduring it, and coming out the other end with their robes washed in the blood of Christ. They did not escape it in any rapture. In fact, the book of Revelation makes it clear that the church will be present during the whole period of antichrist and the great tribulation.

Some premillennial dispensationalists argue that the word *church* does not appear in the book of Revelation between chapters 3:22 and 22:16. Therefore, she must have been removed from the earth. Exegetically, that is a very poor argument, an argument from silence. The word *saints* appears in Revelation. The saints are the church. The claim that these are a special class of saints, the so-called tribulation saints, people converted during the tribulation but after the rapture, is farfetched.

The following passages indicate the presence of Christians: "White robes were given unto every one of them; and it was said unto them, that they should rest yet for a little season, until their fellow-servants also and their brethren, that should be killed as they were, should be fulfilled" (Rev. 6:11). "It was given unto him to make war with the saints, and to overcome them: and power was given him over all kindreds, and tongues, and nations" (13:7). "I saw the woman drunken with the blood of the saints, and with the blood of the martyrs of Jesus: and when I saw her, I wondered with great admiration" (17:6).

Those persecuted by antichrist will be Christians, not Jews and not so-called left-behind Christians. The peace treaty with Israel, the rebuilt temple, and the secret pretribulational rapture of Christians are all *fiction*.

Therefore, let us understand that Christ warns us that just prior to the end the church shall face the worst persecution she has ever known in terms of its widespread nature. But we must not fear, because it shall be shortened.

Shortened

Antichrist will seem to triumph for a time. But for the elect's sake, whom God has chosen, God will cut antichrist short. The books of Daniel and Revelation teach us this by means of the symbol of horns.

A horn is a symbol of power, for the animal's power is in his horn. The beast, the devil, antichrist, and the antichristian harlot have ten horns: "I saw in the night visions, and behold a fourth beast, dreadful and terrible, and strong exceedingly; and it had great iron teeth: it devoured and brake in pieces, and stamped the residue with the feet of it: and it was diverse from all the beasts that were before it; and it had ten horns" (Dan. 7:7). "There appeared another wonder in heaven; and behold a great red dragon, having seven heads and ten horns, and seven crowns upon his heads" (Rev. 12:3). "I stood upon the sand of the sea, and saw a beast rise up out of the sea, having seven heads and ten horns, and upon his horns ten crowns, and upon his heads the name of blasphemy" (13:1). "He carried me away in the spirit into the wilderness: and I saw a woman sit upon a scarlet coloured beast, full of names of blasphemy, having seven heads and ten horns" (17:3).

This signifies that these enemies of God have complete power, because ten is the number of completeness. This, however, does not indicate absolute or unlimited power. The power of ten horns means power *strictly limited by God's sovereign decree*. Therefore, the devil and his allies receive only as much power as God is pleased to give them. Christ does not have ten horns, but seven horns: "I beheld, and, lo, in the midst of the throne and of the four beasts, and in the midst of the elders, stood a Lamb as it had been slain, having seven horns and seven eyes, which are the seven Spirits of God sent forth into all the earth" (Rev. 5:6).

We must be very clear. Although mathematically seven is inferior to ten, seven is not inferior to ten in terms of the number of horns. It is better. Only Christ can have seven horns, because only Christ has the power and authority *to establish the everlasting kingdom and covenant of God*. For this reason, the beast, the devil, the antichrist, and the antichristian harlot always strive to get rid of ten and reach the ideal number of seven: "I considered the horns, and, behold, there came up among them another little horn, before whom there were three of the first horns plucked up by the roots: and, behold, in this horn were eyes like the eyes of man, and a mouth speaking great things" (Dan. 7:8).

The beast plucked up three of its ten horns. Why? To reach seven! Moreover, in Revelation 12:3, 13:1, and 17:3, he has seven heads but still a strictly limited number of horns, that is, ten horns.

Another way the Bible promises a shortening of antichrist's days is with that intriguing phrase "a time, times, and half a time" in both Daniel and Revelation. For example, Daniel 7:25 prophesies the following about antichrist: "He shall speak great words against the most High, and shall wear out the saints of the most High, and think to change times and laws: and they shall be given into his hand *until a time and times and the dividing of time*" (emphasis added). "A time, and times, and half [or the dividing of] a time" is three and a half years (12:14). The same time period is "forty and two months" (11:2–3) or "a thousand two hundred and threescore days" (1,260 days [11:23; 12:6; 13:5]). All of these time periods appear in Revelation 11–13, which describe the war between antichrist and Satan (the dragon and the beast) and the church (the woman and the two witnesses) during the New Testament age.

The point of those numbers is not to determine the length of the great tribulation. The premillennial dispensationalist posits a great tribulation *of exactly three and a half years*. The issue is much simpler. The antichristian kingdom will rise ("time"), it will reach its zenith ("times"), and then it will be cut short ("half a time" or "the dividing of time").

From antichrist's perspective, the days will be shortened. Victory will seem to be at the antichrist's fingertips; the devil will be promising himself victory; and the godless world will seem to triumph. Christ's church will be almost crushed. A moment's more delay and no flesh could be saved. The elect will be crying out, "Come, Lord Jesus." Suddenly, Christ will appear in order to snatch the kingdom from Satan and the antichrist:

7. And to you who are troubled rest with us, when the Lord Jesus shall be revealed from heaven with his mighty angels,

8. In flaming fire taking vengeance on them that know not God, and that obey not the gospel of our Lord Jesus Christ:

9. Who shall be punished with everlasting destruction from the presence of the Lord, and from the glory of his power;

10. When he shall come to be glorified in his saints, and to be admired in all them that believe (because our testimony among you was believed) in that day. (2 Thess. 1:7–10)

8. And then shall that Wicked be revealed, whom the Lord shall consume with the spirit of his mouth, and shall destroy with the brightness of his coming:

9. Even him, whose coming is after the working of Satan with all power and signs and lying wonders,

10. And with all deceivableness of unrighteousness in them that perish; because they received not the love of the truth, that they might be saved. (2 Thess. 2:8–10)

Those days must be shortened, because only Christ is king. Notice what happens immediately after the great tribulation. Christ the king returns in glory. God has authorized only one everlasting and eternal kingdom: his own! Man attempts to build a counterfeit kingdom to God's kingdom and fails. Man must fail and be seen to fail because man is unrighteous. No kingdom based upon man may endure forever: not Babylon, Greece, Rome, or antichrist's kingdom. "In the days of these kings shall the God of heaven set up a kingdom, which shall never be destroyed: and the kingdom shall not be left to other people, but it shall break in pieces and consume all these kingdoms, and it shall stand for ever" (Dan. 2:44).

13. I saw in the night visions, and, behold, one like the Son of man came with the clouds of heaven, and came to the Ancient of days, and they brought him near before him.

14. And there was given him dominion, and glory, and a kingdom, that all people, nations, and languages, should serve him: his dominion is an everlasting dominion, which shall not pass away, and his kingdom that which shall not be destroyed. (7:13–14)

"The seventh angel sounded; and there were great voices in heaven, saying, The kingdoms of this world are become the kingdoms of our Lord, and of his Christ; and he shall reign for ever and ever" (Rev. 11:15).

In Daniel and Revelation, Christ, not antichrist, is the king. We suffer for Christ. In Daniel 7, Christ is the Son of man who receives the kingdom from the Ancient of days. Christ is the lamb who has been slain and is worthy to establish the kingdom (Rev. 5). Why and how? Because Christ is righteous, and therefore he is the only worthy king. He is the eternal Son of God and also the Son of man, the only perfect, sinless man in human flesh.

But we, the elect, are sinners. How are *we* in the kingdom? He died on the cross to bring us into his eternal, everlasting kingdom of righteousness. Moreover, Christ gives grace to endure the great tribulation. His grace will be magnified. Then there will be no more tribulation; no more sorrow, pain, or sin; and then God will wipe away all tears from our eyes.

Christ has received his kingdom and we will reign with him forever.

And not even the great tribulation can separate us from his love.

✦

Chapter 9

FALSE REPORTS
OF CHRIST'S
COMING

Then if any man shall say unto you, Lo, here is Christ, or there; believe it not. For there shall arise false Christs, and false prophets, and shall shew great signs and wonders; insomuch that, if it were possible, they shall deceive the very elect. Behold, I have told you before. Wherefore if they shall say unto you, Behold, he is in the desert; go not forth: behold, he is in the secret chambers; believe it not. For as the lightning cometh out of the east, and shineth even unto the west; so shall also the coming of the Son of man be. For wheresoever the carcase is, there will the eagles be gathered together.—Matthew 24:23–28

Three times in the Olivet Discourse (Matt. 24–25), Christ warns of deceivers. Clearly, this is foremost on his mind when he prepares his disciples for the future. The danger of deception is a weighty issue throughout the New Testament age until Christ's coming. Christ would not have us to be naïve, but prepared: "Behold, I have told you before" (24:25). Forewarned is forearmed! The sad fact is that so many Christians are just that—naïve. They imagine that if a person comes wearing a smile and appearing to be nice, he must be a true teacher. There will be false teachers in every period until the coming of Christ. We must expect it. The only defense against deception is to be firmly grounded in the truth. Know the truth and you will be able to detect and avoid a counterfeit. Ultimately, as Christ beautifully explains, the defense against deception is election.

These three warnings (vv. 4–5, 11, 23–28) are not meaningless repetition, but necessary emphasis. False teachers will come in various guises and with various messages and methodologies. Sometimes, they will come claiming the authority and revelation of Christ ("in my name" [vv. 4–5]). At other times they will come with damnable doctrines, which will contribute to the cooling of the love of many (v. 11). In the text that we consider in this chapter, these false Christs or counterfeit Messiahs will come with false reports about the coming of Christ, and they will lead many away after them. Only a proper understanding of who Christ is, what Christ has done, and how Christ shall come will preserve us from such deception.

The Reports

One of the signs of Christ's coming is the appearance of false Christs. Our Lord mentioned false prophets before, but now Christ speaks of false "Christs" or pseudo-Messiahs. A false Christ is someone who claims to be Christ and offers a substitute salvation in place of the salvation accomplished by the true Christ. *The* false Christ will be the antichrist, the head of a worldwide politically and religiously unified organization.

He will be the last in a long succession of many such men. We saw in Revelation 13 that the beast from the sea is the political aspect of antichrist, while the beast from the earth is the religious aspect of antichrist. Aided and abetted by the seductive world—the whore from Revelation 17—these two beasts deceive the whole world.

The antichristian kingdom will be successful because it offers what carnal, unbelieving man wants—financial prosperity, freedom from war—and will deliver the world (at least for a while) from all of its ills. Moreover, before the antichrist comes there must be many antichrists (1 John 2:18). The spirit of antichrist has been in the world from the beginning of the New Testament age. That spirit is the devilish spirit that corrupts the truth, infiltrates the church with heresy, and seeks to destroy God's children. Every new attack upon the truth is really an attack on Christ. You simply cannot love Christ and not love his truth. Every attack on Christ by means of attacking his truth is preparing for the antichrist, who will say, boldly and unashamedly, "You do not need Christ. You can have salvation in me. There is no heaven or hell. Believe in the kingdom of man!" That is the philosophy of secular humanism.

The false Christs in Matthew 24 are supported by false prophets who point out to the gullible where they can find Christ: "Lo, here is Christ, or there" (v. 23) and "Behold, he is in the desert" or "Behold, he is in the secret chambers" (v. 26). In every age since Christ spoke those words, there have been men and women foolish enough to predict the second coming of Christ and people foolish enough to believe them.

William Miller (1782–1849) and his followers gathered in 1844 to await the second coming of Christ. Many had quit their jobs and sold their businesses. When Christ failed to return, they were disappointed. The Jehovah's Witnesses prophesied that the second coming would occur in 1914. When Christ did not arrive as predicted, they declared that Christ had returned invisibly to set up a spiritual kingdom. More recently we have seen Harold Camping (1921–2013), who asserted that the second coming would probably take place in 1994. Later, he caused a worldwide sensation by predicting May 2011 as the rapture and October 21, 2011, as the end of the world.

Even in the apostolic age, some heretics taught that Christ was just about to come. Paul addressed this error in 2 Thessalonians 2. Some in Thessalonica, excited by the imminent coming of Christ, had ceased working, had become busybodies, and idly waited for the coming of Christ. Paul told them that they must work, and if any was unwilling to work, the church must not support him in his idleness: "When we were with you, this we commanded you, that if any would not work, neither should he eat. For we hear that there are some which walk among you disorderly, working not at all, but are busybodies. Now them that are such we command and exhort by our Lord Jesus Christ, that with quietness they work, and eat their own bread" (3:10–12).

It is not the calling of Christians to sit on a hill, gaze into the sky with a telescope, and wait for the coming of Christ, but to be busy until the Lord comes. Christ's parables at the end of Matthew 24 and in Matthew 25 warn us against that.

Men like William Miller, Harold Camping, and the Jehovah's Witnesses are, perhaps unwittingly, a fulfillment of prophecy and a sign of Christ's coming. Harold Camping was as much a sign of the coming of Christ as is an earthquake, a war, or persecution of the church. When Camping plastered the world with billboards, he was a sign of the coming of Christ, for our Lord prophesied that there would be men like him, and that many would follow after them and their evil ideas. Therefore, when you see and hear of false prophets, be of good cheer.

Christ is on his way. Many will be deceived. The reprobate will be hardened and blinded. Fear not, for this all serves Christ's coming. Christ's call to his people in a climate of false Christs is clear. Do not believe it; do not give credence for a moment; do not even go to check it out to satisfy your curiosity: "Believe it not," "Go not forth," "Believe it not!"

Many people are gullible and will believe anything they are told, if it seems to come from a credible Bible teacher. Some people are attracted to the idea that they could have access to knowledge that is hidden from the uninitiated, so they follow a false teacher to a secret location. Perhaps the false teacher will try to lead you into the desert, to a secluded area, where he will show you his secrets. Another false teacher will try to lead you into a secret chamber, where he will show you what he and only he has discovered in scripture. Beware of novelty or new ideas that no one else has ever discovered.

Novel ideas are born of pride and lead to disastrous deception. Heretics have pedaled novelty in the past and will do it again. James Arminius (1560–1609) held secret meetings with his students, where he taught them doctrine contrary to the Reformed faith. As a professor in the college, he appeared to be orthodox, but behind the scenes he was undermining the truth. Harold Camping seduced people away from the churches and convinced many that he had unique insights into scripture. An orthodox man, however, is honest and open in all his teachings. He does not say, "Lo, here is Christ or Lo, there!" nor does he say, "Behold, he is in the desert, or behold, he is in the secret places."

Christ says about these credible heretics masquerading as Bible teachers, be skeptical and refuse to believe them. Someone who has the audacity to predict the second coming is so far removed from orthodoxy that he should be viewed as a dangerous crank. Jesus says in unmistakable language that no one knows the day of his return (Matt. 24:36). Besides, the second coming will be so obvious that you will not need to rush into the desert or look in secret chambers in case you miss Jesus. When he comes every eye will see him (Rev. 1); none will be able to avoid seeing him; and the wicked will try to flee from him by calling for the rocks and mountains to fall upon them (Rev. 6).

Their Appeal

It is very easy to imagine that in the final days of the great tribulation, such false teachers could be very appealing. When life is so difficult, people will grasp at any message of hope, no matter how tenuous. That was the case in the period between Christ's ascension and AD 70. After Christ came but did not bring the deliverance the Jews wanted, messianic expectations among the Jews increased. John the Baptist caused excitement. Many thought when he came preaching the kingdom of God that he could be the Christ, but then Herod beheaded him. Jesus of Nazareth caused even greater excitement, because he performed miracles that no man had ever done—he even raised the dead—yet he did not resist when Pilate condemned him to be crucified. Therefore, the unbelieving Jews expected another Christ.

The apostles preached Jesus of Nazareth as the Christ, but the Jews rejected the gospel, because a crucified Messiah was a stumbling block to them. Because the Jews refused to believe in the gospel of salvation through God's crucified and risen Son, God in judgment sent "them strong delusion, that they should believe a lie: that they all might be damned who believed not the truth, but had pleasure in unrighteousness" (2 Thess. 2:11–12).

Part of that strong delusion was the multiplication of false Christs, or would-be Messiahs, that is, men who promised God's deliverance from the Romans. Many of these men gained for themselves a following, but they and their followers miserably perished. We read of Theudas (Acts 5:36–37) and "that Egyptian" (21:38), whom we mentioned earlier.

Josephus, the historian, reports that during Jerusalem's siege false prophets arose, promising that God would deliver Jerusalem from the Romans. Those false prophets and Christs were responsible for the destruction of the Jews.

This will be the case in our time also, and increasingly so, as the day approaches. The more miserable people become, the more they will look for a savior, any savior, and antichrist will fulfill their expectations. The greater the tribulation in the last days, the more professing Christians will be tempted to look for deliverance, and the more susceptible they will be to temptations from false teachers.

What is particularly dangerous about these false Christs is that they will claim the ability to do miracles and will convince many by means of such lying wonders. Thus another sign of the coming of Christ is the presence, development, and increase of miracles by the false church in promotion of their false doctrines.

The true church after the apostolic age does not perform miracles. Miracles are always given to confirm new revelation from God, but after the sixty-six books of the Bible were written, there is no further revelation. In 2 Corinthians 12:12 Paul says, "Truly the signs of an apostle were wrought among you in all patience, in signs, and wonders, and mighty deeds." Clearly, then, miracles are associated with the apostolic office and the apostolic age.[1] Hebrews 2:4 says, "God also bearing them witness, both

---

1 In the book of Acts, the only ones recorded as performing miracles are the apostles (2:43; 4:33; 5:12; 9:34, 40; 13:11; 14:3, 10; 15:12; 19:11; 28:5, 8–9), Stephen and Phillip, who were directly commissioned by apostles (6:8; 8:6, 13), and Ananias, who was directly appointed by Jesus himself (9:17). It was

with signs and wonders, and with divers miracles, and gifts of the Holy Ghost." The point is that in the New Testament age, we do not expect to do miracles, and we do not run after those who claim that the true church is able to perform miracles.

However, after the apostolic age, the false church, false religion, and finally the antichrist will perform lying signs and wonders. Second Thessalonians 2:9 speaks of the antichrist, "whose coming is after the working of Satan with all power and signs and lying wonders." These are literally "wonders of the lie," miracles performed in service of the lie, which impress and amaze the unwary. That has been the case throughout the history and development of the false church: the Montanists (late second century), the Roman Catholic Church through the Middle Ages, the charismatic movement, the Word of Faith movement, and others have promoted miracles to give credence to their false doctrines.

Antichrist will have the seducing power of the devil himself, and no man in his own strength will be able to resist his charms:

13. And he doeth great wonders, so that he maketh fire come down from heaven on the earth in the sight of men,
14. And deceiveth them that dwell on the earth by the means of those miracles which he had power to do in the sight of the beast; saying to them that dwell on the earth, that they should make an image to the beast, which had the wound by a sword, and did live. (Rev. 13:13–14)

However, these miracles will not convince God's elect. *They* will not be deceived. The deception in the days of antichrist

---

not common in the early church for all the believers to perform miracles. The working of miracles was connected to the apostolic office.

will be severe, so severe that everyone will be amazed at what the beast can do. The only way a person can be preserved from deception is by the power of God. Christ indicates that in Matthew 24:24: "If it were possible, they shall deceive the very elect." Theoretically, says Christ, the elect could be deceived, in that they, as all men, are susceptible to deception and as easily deceived as anyone else. Nevertheless, fatal deception of the elect is *impossible,* because God's decree of election *must stand.* God's election cannot be overturned, and none for whom Christ died can perish.[2] If the elect are *deceivable* of themselves, how much more will the reprobate be *deceived*! Therefore, "Take heed," Jesus says, "that no man deceive you" (v. 4). Know the truth and do not expose yourself or your family to the lie. Instead, be sure you belong to a true church and test everything you hear by scripture!

Their Falsity

The falsity of false Christs is clear because they cannot bring about the deliverance that only the true Christ has brought. At best they offer temporary, carnal deliverance. Those who listen to false Christs perish. In the Jewish rebellion of AD 67–70, the false Christs promised deliverance from the Romans. Multitudes followed such deceivers into the desert or into secret hideaways, but the Romans captured them and slaughtered them. As the Roman legions finally entered Jerusalem, the people holed up in the temple and expected their Messiah to intervene, but Israel's messianic hopes came to nothing because they had rejected the true Christ. In fact, the destruction of Jerusalem in AD 70 was God's judgment on Christ-rejecting Israel.

---

2 Canons 5.8, in Schaff, *Creeds of Christendom,* 3:594.

Antichrist will promise deliverance from earthly woes. For a short time he will have his little season: world peace, universal prosperity, and undoubtedly great advances in medicine and technology. Notwithstanding his temporal triumph, antichrist's kingdom based on a false peace cannot last. God will break it up, and it will perish in ignominious defeat. Finally, the beast, the false prophet, all those who worshiped antichrist, and all those whose names are not written in the Lamb's book of life will perish in hell (Rev. 13:8; 17:8).

The deliverance that Christ gives is the forgiveness of sins in his blood. Our greatest need is not earthly peace, but the pardon of our sins. Antichrist, false Christs, and false prophets reject that, boasting that man has the power by his efforts to attain salvation. Only the gospel says, "Man is sinful. Man is so sinful that he can do nothing good. With man it is hopeless. Look to the grace of God." The grace of God only comes through Jesus Christ. Modern antichristian religious pluralism and tolerance cannot bring salvation. Only Christ can and does. Christ brings salvation only through his substitutionary death on the cross. Christ paid fully for the sins of all the elect, so that now God has nothing against anyone for whom Christ died. God is satisfied. Sin is covered. We are heirs of eternal life.

Moreover, such prophets cannot be the true Christ, despite their amazing powers of deception, because Christ's coming will be an awesome, visible event seen by the whole world, as he comes in judgment upon an utterly corrupt world to deliver his beleaguered saints and bring them to glory. Christ gives a reason in Matthew 24:27 why we must not believe the one who invites us to look for a secret appearance of Christ: "as the lightning cometh out of the east, and shineth even unto the west; so shall also the coming of the Son of man be." When there is a thunderstorm with lightning, the lightning flashes across the sky so that everybody sees it. "So shall the coming of the Son of man be." A lightning storm is awesome and frightening. No one says, "Come into the desert or into a secret place to see the lightning." It flashes from east to west.

The idea is clearly that the coming of Christ will not be in secret. It will not be seen by one or two disciples, who follow a teacher with insider knowledge. All will see it. No one will be able to miss it. And it will be awesome: the church will lift up her head and see the coming of Christ and rejoice; and the persecuting, antichristian world will see the same event and be terrified.

This also destroys any idea of a rapture. There is no secret, invisible coming of Christ. There is one coming of Christ at the end of history. That coming will be *after* the tribulation, not before.

The coming of Christ will be to a world completely corrupted and rotten in sin. Mankind is, spiritually speaking, a rotten, putrefying corpse ("Wheresoever the carcass is, there will the eagles be gathered together" [v. 28]).

Many have been the explanations of verse 28. Some have said that the allusion is to AD 70 and the Roman eagle on the standards of the Roman legions. The carcass would then refer to the rotten Jewish nation upon which Roman soldiers swoop in terrible vengeance. Some have suggested that the carcass refers to Christ and that the eagles are Christians. When Christ returns the Christians will flock to him. The opinion of others is that the carcass is the rotten Jewish nation and the eagles are false prophets who swoop upon the Jews to destroy them by deception. Others have said that the carcass is the rotten world and the eagles refer to Christ and his angels coming in judgment.

The best explanation is not to seek to determine the reference to the carcass or eagles, but to view the whole thing as a simile or metaphor. Eagles or vultures swoop down to devour a rotting carcass. Likewise, Christ comes in judgment upon a world that has filled the cup of iniquity. That cup is filled as apostasy, deception, and falsehood reach their height in the false prophet; and persecution, tribulation, and suffering reach their height in the antichrist—not the golden age promised by post-millennialism.

When the last drop of martyr's blood, which has been appointed, has been shed; when sin has developed to its full potential, so that sin has shown itself to be exceedingly sinful; when the last elect soul has been brought to Christ—*then* Christ shall come. Every eye will see him. Do not seek him in the secret place or in the desert, here or there. Seek him as he said he would come. He will come on the clouds. Look for him. Pray for his coming.

Chapter 10

♦

CHRIST'S GLORIOUS COMING

Immediately after the tribulation of those days shall the sun be darkened, and the moon shall not give her light, and the stars shall fall from heaven, and the powers of the heavens shall be shaken: and then shall appear the sign of the Son of man in heaven: and then shall all the tribes of the earth mourn, and they shall see the Son of man coming in the clouds of heaven with power and great glory. And he shall send his angels with a great sound of a trumpet, and they shall gather together his elect from the four winds, from one end of heaven to the other.—Matthew 24:29–31

The blessed hope of every Christian is the return of Jesus Christ:

4. I thank my God always on your behalf, for the grace of God which is given you by Jesus Christ;

5. That in every thing ye are enriched by him, in all utterance, and in all knowledge;
6. Even as the testimony of Christ was confirmed in you:
7. So that ye come behind in no gift; waiting for the coming of our Lord Jesus Christ:
8. Who shall also confirm you unto the end, that ye may be blameless in the day of our Lord Jesus Christ. (1 Cor. 1:4–8)

"For they themselves shew of us what manner of entering in we had unto you, and how ye turned to God from idols to serve the living and true God; and to wait for his Son from heaven, whom he raised from the dead, even Jesus, which delivered us from the wrath to come" (1 Thess. 1:9–10). "Looking for that blessed hope, and the glorious appearing of the great God and our Saviour Jesus Christ; who gave himself for us, that he might redeem us from all iniquity, and purify unto himself a peculiar people, zealous of good works" (Titus 2:13–14).

Throughout this book, we have heard Christ's answer to two questions: When will Jerusalem and her temple be destroyed? What will be the sign of Christ's coming and of the end of the world? Christ answers both questions by blending the answers. The destruction of Jerusalem in AD 70 was not the end of the world. Rather, the end of the world is described in terms of the end of Jerusalem.

We have reached the apex of Matthew 24. The waiting is over. We have heard about many signs. Now we receive a beautiful view of his coming, as Christ describes his actual return—his one coming at the end of history. That must thrill our souls. That must kindle our hope. That must take our hearts off this world. Let us look up; let us crane our necks; and let us consider the return of our Savior.

The Manner of His Return

The return of Christ will be visible and audible, indeed seen and heard by all.

First, Christ will be seen: "Then shall appear...and they shall see" (Matt. 24:30). The first thing that will be seen is the sign of the Son of man in heaven. Since the events described here are future and miraculous, it is difficult to know exactly what Christ means. Some expect that just before Christ returns, a visible token or a distinguishing mark will appear in the sky, pointing to his arrival. Some have even suggested that a cross or a bright light will appear in the sky. A better explanation is that the sign is indistinguishable from Christ himself. That is, Christ, the Son of man, *is* the sign. People who are alive at that awesome moment will see Christ himself. Matthew 24:30 reads, "Then shall appear the sign...and they shall see the Son of man." When Christ says "the sign of the Son of man," he means the sign *that is* the Son of man. What a glorious sight that will be! One moment Christ will be invisible, hidden in the highest heavens. The next moment Christ will shine across the sky: every eye will see him. Will you, will I, will our children see him?

Scripture makes clear that when Christ returns, all, both saint and sinner, alive at that time will see him. Moreover, even the dead will be raised to see him. The Lord declares, "Then shall all the tribes of the earth mourn, and they shall see the Son of man coming" (v. 30); Revelation 1:7 promises, "Behold, he cometh with clouds; and every eye shall see him." Therefore, we do not expect this to be done in a corner, but to be a worldwide event.

What a contrast to his first coming: when he came into the world, he was born in obscurity, in a backward village called

Bethlehem. Hardly anyone noticed, and fewer cared. Then he came in shame to suffer; he will come in glory to judge!

Second, Christ will not only be seen, but he also will be heard, for "he shall send his angels with a great sound of a trumpet" (Matt. 24:31). A trumpet makes a loud, long, sharp blast that no one can miss. In the Old Testament, God chose a trumpet made from a ram's horn (shofar) to represent his voice. At Mount Sinai, with the giving of the law, shofar blasts were heard. When Israel had to move camp, the shofar was blown. When Israel was called to battle, the shofar was used. The fact that Christ will come with the sound of the shofar indicates that Christ's return will have everyone's attention. This is the final call of God to all men: Stand to attention, for my Son is here! Lift up your eyes, church, and see your salvation. Look up, ye wicked, and behold your doom!

The trumpet is a feature of other passages about the second coming of the Lord, and especially about the future resurrection: "The Lord himself shall descend from heaven with a shout, with the voice of the archangel, and with the trump of God" (1 Thess. 4:16). "In the twinkling of an eye, at the last trump: for the trumpet shall sound, and the dead shall be raised incorruptible, and we shall be changed" (1 Cor. 15:52). This trumpet will be the announcement of the coming of Christ and will be loud enough to wake the dead.

The resurrection of all the dead will be the first great event that Christ will perform at his coming. This text does not explicitly mention this, but other passages do. The shofar blast of Christ will bring all dead saints out of the grave, uniting those resurrected bodies with their souls. At the same time, the wicked dead shall come forth out of their graves; and the souls of the damned will be reunited with their bodies to face judgment. As we saw in a previous chapter, 1 Thessalonians 4 makes clear that the dead in Christ shall rise first, albeit on the same day, and even before those who are alive at the coming of Christ. *All* the saints of God, both dead and alive, will meet Christ bodily in the air as he descends from heaven. What an awesome event that shall be!

This visible and audible coming of Christ conflicts with both the postmillennial and premillennial dispensational interpretations of Matthew 24.

Remember that postmillennialism teaches that Matthew 24 describes *only* the events of AD 70. Everyone agrees that Christ did not return finally, personally, and visibly in AD 70, so, argues postmillennialism, the text must be teaching something else. Postmillennialism *does* teach a future coming of Christ, although many postmillennialists are content to push that day into the distant future. Here in Matthew 24, insist the postmillennialists, Christ comes in judgment *only on the city of Jerusalem.*

Briefly, the postmillennial explanation is this: first, the sign of the Son of man in heaven is the sign or proof that the Son of man is in heaven—that proof, says postmillennialism, is the destruction of Jerusalem. Second, when Christ says that people will see the Son of man, he means that they will perceive Christ's hand in their judgment. But that interpretation is surely strained. The unbelieving, ungodly Jews did not see, recognize, or acknowledge that Christ was judging them in AD 70, or even that God was judging them for rejecting Christ.

Premillennial dispensationalism has difficulty fitting this visible, audible return of Christ into their scheme also. All Christians, whether pre-, post-, or amillennial, believe that there will be a future, personal, visible coming of Christ, although *hyper*-preterists deny it. However, the premillennial dispensationalist view is complicated because according to it there will be (at least) two future comings with (at least) two future resurrections and (at least) two future judgments.

Premillennial dispensationalism teaches one secret coming of Christ at the rapture, then a visible coming after the tribulation. Each coming has its own resurrection and judgment, one of the righteous and then one thousand and seven years later of the wicked. However, the question for premillennial dispensationalism is, *which* coming is Christ describing here? Reformed amillennialism teaches but one future, personal, visible coming of Christ, so we do not face that dilemma. However, it is not as simple for the premillennial dispensationalist as you might imagine.

Matthew 24 does not provide a neat distinction between a secret rapture and a second coming seven years later after the great tribulation. That is imported artificially from Daniel 9, as I explained in the chapter on the abomination of desolation. Matthew 24 simply does not mention a secret rapture. We have seen wars, famines, earthquakes, pestilence, apostasy, persecution, the abomination of desolation, great tribulation, and terrible deception, but no secret rapture. In fact, Christ never hints in Matthew 24 that Christians will be taken from the earth.

Moreover, the problem for the premillennial dispensationalist is the trumpet. According to 1 Thessalonians 4:16, the rapture is accompanied by a trumpet, which will raise the dead. The trumpet by which the saints are raised is the "last trump" (1 Cor. 15:52). Therefore, if the "rapture trumpet" (the last trump) is blown in 1 Corinthians 15:52, which trumpet is blown in Matthew 24:31? How could God blow the "last" (rapture) trumpet, and seven years later, at the "revelation" (the visible coming of Christ at the end), blow another "last" trumpet? The answer is, of course, that there is only one future coming, only one future trumpet, only one future resurrection, and only one future judgment immediately after the tribulation. The amillennial position, which makes perfect sense of the biblical material, is less complicated. It does not require complex and ingenious charts to explain the future.

The one, future, personal coming of Christ will be visible and audible—and glorious. That is how Christ described it: "They shall see the Son of man coming in the clouds of heaven with power and great glory" (Matt. 24:30). Glory is the radiance of God, the reflection of all God's perfections. Christ will come in his own glory, which he has by virtue of being the Son of God, coequal with the Father and the Son. Christ will also come as the Son of man. This title, a favorite of Christ's, refers to him as the man, Jesus, the mediator:

13. I saw in the night visions, and, behold, one like the Son of man came with the clouds of heaven, and came to the Ancient of days, and they brought him near before him.

14. And there was given him dominion, and glory, and a kingdom, that all people, nations, and languages, should serve him: his dominion is an everlasting dominion, which shall not pass away, and his kingdom that which shall not be destroyed. (Dan. 7:13–14)

Thus Christ will come in the glory that God has invested upon him, his glory as the mediator and head of the covenant.

The context of Matthew 24 is important. Christ is not speaking immediately before his ascension, but just prior to his deepest humiliation in death. Jesus links glory to the cross in John 12:23: "The hour is come, that the Son of man should be glorified." The teaching of scripture is, first the cross; then the crown. That is true for Christ and that is also true for us. First we suffer; then we are glorified.

On the Mount of Olives, hours before his crucifixion, Christ can say with absolute confidence, "I shall be glorified. I shall come with power and great glory." That must thrill our hearts. Christ came the first time in obscurity and shame, bearing our sins, and suffering on the cross because of our sins. All that was preparation for his glorification and for ours (Phil. 2:9–11). On that day, all men will see him in his glory—no man will scoff at him again, no man will despise him again, for he is done with death, with suffering, and with shame, forever!

Our Lord describes his glory as "coming in the clouds of heaven." We must not imagine white fluffy clouds but awe-inspiring billowing thunderclouds, which are the trappings of deity: "Lo, I come unto thee in a thick cloud" (Ex. 19:9). "It came to pass on the third day in the morning, that there were thunders and lightning, and a thick cloud upon the mount, and the voice of the trumpet exceeding loud, so that all the people that was in the camp trembled" (v. 16). "He made darkness his secret place; his pavilion round about him were dark waters and thick clouds of the skies" (Ps. 18:11). "Clouds and darkness are round about him" (97:2). "The LORD...maketh the clouds his chariot: who walketh upon the wings of the wind" (104:1–3).

The book of Revelation often depicts Christ's coming in or with the clouds of heaven: "Behold, he cometh with clouds" (1:7). "I looked, and behold a white cloud, and upon the cloud one sat like unto the Son of man, having on his head a golden crown" (14:14). Thus Jesus Christ, the Son of man, will come in the glory of God.

The Events at His Return

Christ's return will be accompanied by signs and strange phenomena in the heavens: "There shall be signs in the sun, and in the moon, and in the stars; and upon the earth distress of nations, with perplexity; the sea and the waves roaring; men's hearts failing them for fear, and for looking after those things which are coming on the earth: for the powers of heaven shall be shaken" (Luke 21:25–26).

The sun, moon, and stars will fail. Christ says that "the sun [shall] be darkened, and the moon shall not give her light, and the stars shall fall from heaven" (Matt. 24:29). These events at Christ's coming are not natural, but supernatural or miraculous. Man is powerless before them, for science cannot explain them.

The book of Revelation indicates that there will be irregularities in the sun, moon, and stars for some time before Christ finally returns. For example, about the effects of the fourth trumpet we read: "The third part of the sun was smitten, and the third part of the moon, and the third part of the stars; so as the third part of them was darkened, and the day shone not for a third part of it, and the night likewise" (Rev. 8:12). About the effects of the fourth vial we read: "The fourth angel poured out his vial upon the sun; and power was given unto him to scorch men with fire. And men were scorched with great heat, and blasphemed the name of God, which hath power over these plagues: and they repented not to give him glory" (16:8–9). The total breakup of the creation occurs at the very end:

12. And I beheld when he had opened the sixth seal, and, lo, there was a great earthquake; and the sun became black as sackcloth of hair, and the moon became as blood;

13. And the stars of heaven fell unto the earth, even as a fig tree casteth her untimely figs, when she is shaken of a mighty wind.

14. And the heaven departed as a scroll when it is rolled together; and every mountain and island were moved out of their places. (Rev. 6:12–14)

The sun, moon, and stars were created on the fourth day of the creation week to "be for signs, and for seasons, and for days and years" (Gen. 1:14). With the coming of Christ, human history has come to an end. These heavenly bodies are necessary for life on this earth, but with the coming of Jesus Christ, the physical universe is broken up and dissolved to make way for the new creation, which God has promised. With the failure of the sun, moon, and stars, the powers of the heavens will be shaken. The Lord will shake the entire universe—the heavens and the earth—and only the eternal kingdom of God shall remain:

25. See that ye refuse not him that speaketh. For if they escaped not who refused him that spake on earth, much more shall not we escape, if we turn away from him that speaketh from heaven:

26. Whose voice then shook the earth: but now he hath promised, saying, Yet once more I shake not the earth only, but also heaven.

27. And this word, Yet once more, signifieth the removing of those things that are shaken, as of things that are made, that those things which cannot be shaken may remain.

28. Wherefore we receiving a kingdom which cannot be moved, let us have grace, whereby we may serve God acceptably with reverence and godly fear:

29. For our God is a consuming fire. (Heb. 12:25–29)

Clearly, such physical shaking of the heavens and earth with the darkening of the sun and other celestial bodies did not occur in AD 70 with the fall of Jerusalem. The postmillennial explanation is to interpret the text as a prophetic account of the eclipse of Jerusalem and Judaism as spiritual powers. Christ, says postmillennialism, is not speaking about the actual sun, moon, and stars of the sky, but about the political and religious rulers of the Jews. Christ, says postmillennialism, is not speaking about the shaking of the physical creation, but *the earth-shattering ruin of Israel as a nation*. Now, says postmillennialism, with the eclipse of Judaism, the end of Israel and the destruction of the temple, the church is free to preach the gospel. That is, to put it mildly, a very strained exegesis of the Bible.

Appeal is made to certain prophetic passages that link the breakup of the physical universe to the fall of individual nations:

9. Behold, the day of the LORD cometh, cruel both with wrath and fierce anger, to lay the land desolate: and he shall destroy the sinners thereof out of it.
10. For the stars of heaven and the constellations thereof shall not give their light: the sun shall be darkened in his going forth, and the moon shall not cause her light to shine. (Isa. 13:9–10)

4. And all the host of heaven shall be dissolved, and the heavens shall be rolled together as a scroll: and all their host shall fall down, as the leaf falleth off from the vine, and as a falling fig from the fig tree.
5. For my sword shall be bathed in heaven: behold, it shall come down upon Idumea, and upon the people of my curse, to judgment. (Isa. 34:4–5)

3. Thus saith the Lord GOD; I will therefore spread out my net over thee with a company of many people; and they shall bring thee up in my net.
4. Then will I leave thee upon the land, I will cast thee forth upon the open field, and will cause all the fowls of the heaven to remain upon thee, and I will fill the beasts of the whole earth with thee.

5.   And I will lay thy flesh upon the mountains, and fill the valleys with thy height.
6.   I will also water with thy blood the land wherein thou swimmest, even to the mountains; and the rivers shall be full of thee.
7.   And when I shall put thee out, I will cover the heaven, and make the stars thereof dark; I will cover the sun with a cloud, and the moon shall not give her light. (Ezek. 32:3–7)

Appeal is also made to the word "immediately" in Matthew 24:29. Postmillennialism says that Jerusalem's destruction in AD 70 is described in the previous context, and therefore these things must also have taken place at that time. However, the tribulation of Matthew 24 is *not* a reference only to the events of AD 70, but also those events are a type of a greater tribulation immediately prior to Christ's return. Furthermore, we know that the Old Testament passages were types of the final judgment; and we must interpret the Old Testament in light of the New Testament, not vice versa. The fall of Babylon, Egypt, Tyre, Edom, and other places in the Old Testament prefigured or foreshadowed not the fall of Jerusalem in AD 70, but the destruction of the entire world at the second coming of Christ.

The second great event accompanying the return of Christ is the gathering of the elect to Christ ("He shall send his angels with a great sound of a trumpet" [v. 31]). This, if we might use the word, *is* the rapture, not a pretribulational rapture, not a secret rapture, but the rapture. The word *rapture* has its source in the Latin translation of the Greek word translated as "caught up" in 1 Thessalonians 4:17 ("we…shall be caught up together with them in the clouds"). The word means to seize, to snatch, or to take away suddenly and forcefully. The idea in Matthew 24 is that as Christ is descending from heaven, he takes his saints out of the earth to meet him in the air, which happens at the last trumpet, immediately after the tribulation and in the midst of a visible and audible display of Christ's glory.

Christ mentions in Matthew 24 that the angels will gather the elect. The angels are the servants of almighty God and therefore also the servants of the Lord Jesus. God sends them out to gather his people "from the four winds," that is, from every nation where they have been living under the tyranny of antichrist. Not one elect soul will be missing—the dead elect will be gathered out of the graves, the elect hiding in caves will meet Christ in the air, the elect languishing in dungeons will be snatched from their tormenters. What a day!

Although the text says nothing specifically about the gathering of the wicked, the rest of scripture does. Matthew 13:38–43 speaks of the end of the world, of the angels gathering the wicked, and of the angels casting the wicked into hell after the judgment:

38. The field is the world; the good seed are the children of the kingdom; but the tares are the children of the wicked one;

39. The enemy that sowed them is the devil; the harvest is the end of the world; and the reapers are the angels.

40. As therefore the tares are gathered and burned in the fire; so shall it be in the end of this world.

41. The Son of man shall send forth his angels, and they shall gather out of his kingdom all things that offend, and them which do iniquity;

42. And shall cast them into a furnace of fire: there shall be wailing and gnashing of teeth.

43. Then shall the righteous shine forth as the sun in the kingdom of their Father. Who hath ears to hear, let him hear.

Thus we see *one* glorious coming, *one* day in which *all* men—elect and reprobate—are resurrected and *one* day of judgment followed by the eternal states of heaven and hell.

Postmillennialism has its own peculiar explanation for this gathering of the elect by the angels. Angels, the postmillennialists contend, are literally messengers. It is true that the word *could* be translated that way, if we completely disregarded the context. Matthew 24:31 would mean that after Jerusalem is destroyed, the messengers of God, his preachers, are sent by Christ to trumpet forth the glad tidings to all nations. The exegesis is strained, however: verse 14 has already spoken about the worldwide preaching of the gospel, and there is nothing here to indicate that by angels Christ means preachers. The event described here is the final, visible, glorious coming of Christ for his elect church. That is our blessed hope.

The Reaction to His Return

Such a visible, glorious return accompanied by such earth-shattering events in the physical world will have an effect on all human beings alive at Christ's coming.

First, we see its effect on the wicked: Christ will not return to a christianized world, but to the world under the tyranny of the Satan-inspired antichristian kingdom. Those wicked will mourn: "Then shall all the tribes of the earth mourn" (v. 30). This mourning is not a true sorrow over sin, for it is not a godly sorrow that leads to repentance (2 Cor. 7:10). It is the mourning of horror-struck despair.

Some have tried to link Matthew 24:30 with Zechariah 12:10: "I will pour upon the house of David, and upon the inhabitants of Jerusalem, the spirit of grace and of supplications: and they shall look upon me whom they have pierced, and they shall mourn for him, as one mourneth for his only son, and shall be in bitterness for him, as one that is in bitterness for his firstborn." Premillennial dispensationalism places that prophecy at the visible coming of the Lord Jesus after the tribulation. Its idea is that Zechariah 12 refers to a mass conversion of the Jews when they see their Messiah coming in power and great glory. Christ will then rule for one thousand years in Jerusalem over those converted Jews. Premillennial dispensationalism sees a second chance for Jews, and also for Gentiles, the so-called tribulation saints, who live between the rapture and the premillennial coming of Christ.

But Zechariah 12:10 is not fulfilled at the return of Christ. It is fulfilled throughout the New Testament age when elect sinners come under conviction of sin, repent of sin, and are converted and saved. This is clear from Zechariah 12:10: "I will pour...the spirit of grace and of supplications." *When* did God pour out his Holy Spirit? On Pentecost! On that day three thousand souls were saved (Acts 2:37, 41)! Furthermore, the first fulfillment of Zechariah 12:10 was at the cross:

35. One of the soldiers with a spear pierced his side, and forthwith came there out blood and water. And he that saw it bare record; and his record is true: and he knoweth that he saith true, that ye might believe.
36. For these things were done that the scripture should be fulfilled, A bone of him shall not be broken. And again another scripture saith, They shall look on him whom they have pierced. (John 19:35–36)

When Christ returns there will not be a mass conversion of Jews or of anyone else. Christ comes not to convert the world, but to judge it. "Behold, he cometh with clouds; and every eye shall see him: and they also which pierced him: and all kindreds of the earth shall wail because of him. Even so, Amen" (Rev. 1:7).

Throughout history, there is a twofold reaction to the death of Christ, for some are pricked in their hearts and repent, while others are hardened and perish. But there is no repentance of the wicked in Matthew 24:31, and there will be no repentance of the wicked at Christ's return. "Mourn" in verse 31 is to beat one's breast, a sign of grief, anguish, or despair. When Christ appears in all his glory, the day that the wicked fear will come, and there will be no escape. Revelation 6:15–17 depicts their horror-struck reaction:

15. And the kings of the earth, and the great men, and the rich men, and the chief captains, and the mighty men, and every bondman, and every free man, hid themselves in the dens and in the rocks of the mountains;

16. And said to the mountains and rocks, Fall on us, and hide us from the face of him that sitteth on the throne, and from the wrath of the Lamb:

17. For the great day of his wrath is come; and who shall be able to stand?

The wicked will no longer be able to deny it. No longer will they laugh and mock, for they will realize that their doom is sealed. How dreadful to be in the unbeliever's place on that day. Naked he will stand before Christ, in his sins, with nowhere to hide. Well might he beat his breast in anguish, but it will not avail him. It will be too late, foreve, too late!

The effect of Christ's return on the saints is altogether different.

Are you tempted to fear? There is no need. God's people will not be beating their breasts in despair. Instead, Christ says, "Look up, and lift up your heads; for your redemption draweth nigh" (Luke 21:28). It is very sad that much end-time writing and preaching makes God's people fear. This must not be your response to these chapters. Christ wants us to be adequately warned, but at the same time he leaves us abiding comfort.

The comfort is not that these things will not happen, that the church will escape these things in a secret pretribulational rapture, or that these things have happened already in AD 70. The comfort is that these things are all necessary to prepare for the coming of Christ. The comfort is that when Christ returns, our salvation will be complete. The glorious return of Jesus Christ means an end of suffering, tribulation, and persecution; it means an end of the antichristian kingdom and all the blasphemies of the wicked; and it means an end of sin itself. Finally, it means for us that we will forever be with Jesus Christ, our bodies will be raised incorruptible, and we will see him, the one whom our souls love, coming in his glory. We will not be terrified to meet the Lord Jesus Christ in his glory. We will not shrink back in horror when the trumpet sounds and the angels gather us either out of the grave or out of the clutches of our enemies.

> What comfort is it to thee that Christ shall come again to judge the quick and the dead?
>
> That in all my sorrows and persecutions, with uplifted head I look for the self-same One who has before offered himself for me to the judgment of God, and removed from me all curse, to come again as Judge

from heaven; who shall cast all his and my enemies into everlasting condemnation, but shall take me, with all his chosen ones, to himself, into heavenly joy and glory.[1]

When we stand before the Lord, it will not be in nakedness. We will be clothed in the perfect splendor of Christ's righteousness. Christ came the first time to die for our sins; and he returns the second time to bring us into the fullness of salvation. We will have nothing to fear and every reason to rejoice.

So we pray, "Come, Lord Jesus, yea, come quickly." And we lift our heads because we know our redemption draws near.

---

1   Heidelberg Catechism Q&A 52, in ibid., 3:323–24.

Part Two

WATCHING
FOR
CHRIST'S
RETURN

🔥

Chapter 11

THE PARABLE
OF THE
BUDDING FIG TREE

Now learn a parable of the fig tree; When his branch is yet tender, and putteth forth leaves, ye know that summer is nigh: so likewise ye, when ye shall see all these things, know that it is near, even at the doors. Verily I say unto you, This generation shall not pass, till all these things be fulfilled. Heaven and earth shall pass away, but my words shall not pass away.—Matthew 24:32–35

In Matthew 24:1–31 Christ has answered the disciples' questions concerning the signs of his coming: the coming of deceivers, turmoil in nature and among the nations, the church hated by all men, the cooling of the love of many, the worldwide preaching of the gospel, the abomination of desolation, the great tribulation, and false reports of Christ's coming. The passage climaxes with the final, glorious coming of Jesus Christ at the end of history. Moreover, we have seen that all of this is revealed under the type of the destruction of Jerusalem in AD 70.

With verse 32 Christ switches gears and continues in this gear until the end of Matthew 25. Thus there is a new theme for part two of this book. The focus changes from "The Signs of Christ's Coming" to "Watching for Christ's Return." Christ is really applying what he has taught earlier: "I have not given you these signs to satisfy your curiosity. I have given you this instruction so that you are prepared. Watch! Watch for two reasons: my coming is near, and my coming is at a day and at an hour that no man can know. Because you know I am coming but do not know *when* I am coming, you must always be watchful."

The parable of the fig tree is not a sign of Christ's coming as such. Rather, it is an illustration about the nearness of Christ's coming and a call to be watchful. A parable is a comparison. The literal meaning of a parable is "to throw beside." Our Lord takes two or more ideas and throws them beside one another, so that one idea sheds light on the other idea. Moreover, a parable usually has one main thought. It is a mistake to try to interpret all the details of a parable. Many of the details are incidental to the main thought.

You will not find this parable, the parable of the budding fig tree, in the standard works on parables. It is not in the same class as the parable of the sower or the parable of the good Samaritan. At the same time, Jesus does not interpret the parable of the budding fig tree. He expects it to be self-evident, a simple illustration that needs no elucidation. Literally, Jesus says, "Learn from the fig tree the parable." In other words, simply by looking at a fig tree, the spiritual truth must be self-evident. This parable, although surely simple in itself, has suffered at the hands of many men with overactive imaginations, who have wrested it from its context.

The Fig Tree

The premillennial dispensational understanding of the fig tree is that Christ promises a reblossoming of Israel. Let us examine the elements of their interpretation so we understand their argument.

First, the fig tree in scripture, it is claimed, is a symbol of the nation of Israel. However, the more common symbol of Israel is the vine, not the fig tree. The evidence is certainly not overwhelming. In addition, most commentators agree that the fig tree cursed in Matthew 21 is a picture of Israel, of Israel's spiritual barrenness and hypocrisy. What in the context of Matthew 24 suggests that the "fig tree" *here* is the nation of Israel? After all, the entire context of Matthew 24 is the *destruction* of Israel in AD 70 as a type or picture of the final judgment!

Second, the fig tree, a symbol of Israel, will bud, put forth leaves, and bear fruit after it has been temporarily set aside by God. The premillennial dispensationalist's basic thesis is that national Israel is and always will be the elect people of God. Therefore, the kingdom of God belongs to national Israel. Although national Israel rejected the kingdom of God, one day in the future God will return to Israel and she will accept the kingdom of God. Meanwhile, God is dealing with the Gentiles in the church-age "parenthesis."

In fact, says premillennial dispensationalism, Israel has reblossomed already. On May 14, 1948, Israel became a Jewish state again. After over 1,800 years without a homeland, the Jews returned to the land. In 1967 Israel defeated the combined armies of Egypt, Jordan, and Syria, then successfully annexed Jerusalem.

The problem is the timing: premillennial dispensationalism asserts that Matthew 24, the great tribulation, the abomination of desolation, the destruction of Jerusalem, and the destruction of the temple all refer to a future rebuilt Jerusalem, which will be destroyed by the future antichrist. But the rebudding of Israel, if it happened in 1948 or 1967, took place *before* her *future* destruction.

The significance for many of the reblooming of Israel—the fig tree putting forth leaves when her branch is tender—is that this indicates that we are in the final generation before the coming of Christ.

The rebirth of Israel, teaches premillennial dispensationalism, is only the beginning of a greater summer, a spiritual harvest in the future. Soon antichrist will come. He will speak peaceably to Israel, and he will even make a peace treaty with her for seven years. During that time Israel will build her temple (somehow the Muslims will have to be expelled from the Dome of the Rock!). Halfway through antichrist's rule, he will break his peace treaty with Israel, and he will defile her temple (with the abomination of desolation) and inflict the great tribulation on the Jews—recall their interpretation of the seventy weeks of Daniel 9. Conveniently, during this time, the church will be in heaven, having escaped the great tribulation in the rapture.

Matthew 24:34 says, "Verily I say unto you, This generation shall not pass, till all these things be fulfilled." The premillennial dispensationalists understand this verse to teach that the generation living at the time of the budding of the fig tree will not pass away until all these things are fulfilled. In scripture a generation usually means forty years. By this time, however, "this generation" has been stretched beyond all limits of credulity.

When Israel was reborn in 1948, excitement among premillennial dispensationalists increased because that meant, they said, that within forty years the rapture would occur. A simple calculation shows that 1948 plus forty years equals 1988.

Predictably, men claimed exactly that. A man called Edgar C. Whisenant published a book entitled *88 Reasons Why the Rapture Will Be in 1988*. He mailed 300,000 copies to pastors all across America, and when the rapture failed to happen, he followed up with other books predicting 1989, 1993, and 1994 as the year of Christ's return. He died in 2001.

The second possibility is that 1967 plus forty years equals 2007. That date has also come and gone. Finally, some suggest a generation can be as much as 120 years, with the result that the end will be sometime between 2068 and 2087.

Premillennial dispensationalism has missed two things. First, no one knows the time of Christ's return. Second, if the generation that witnessed the budding Israeli fig tree cannot pass away until all these things occur, "all these things" must include the abomination of desolation, the great tribulation, and the other signs. This means that that generation must live *through* those things. What, then, of the *pre*tribulational rapture?

Others have a different view of the meaning of "this generation" in verse 34.

Some, including the famous dispensationalist *Scofield Bible Notes*, interpret "this generation" to mean the Jewish race. The Jewish race will not pass away but will be preserved until the end. However, the word *generation never* means the Jewish race, especially not in the book of Matthew. It means a group of people living at the same time. "This generation" would refer to the people living when Christ spoke those words on the Mount of Olives.

The following are passages from Matthew where "generation" has that meaning: "All the generations from Abraham to David are fourteen generations; and from David until the carrying away into Babylon are fourteen generations; and from the carrying away into Babylon unto Christ are fourteen generations" (1:17). "Whereunto shall I liken this generation? It is like unto children sitting in the markets, and calling unto their fellows" (11:16). "The men of Nineveh shall rise in judgment with this generation, and shall condemn it: because they repented at the preaching of Jonas; and, behold, a greater than Jonas is here" (12:41). "Verily I say unto you, All these things shall come upon this generation" (23:36).

Others, not necessarily premillennial dispensationalists, teach that this generation means this kind of people—either this kind of believing people or this kind of unbelieving people. "Generation" means a kind of people in the following passages: "An evil and adulterous generation seeketh after a sign; and there shall no sign be given to it, but the sign of the prophet Jonas" (Matt. 12:39). "Jesus answered and said, O faithless and perverse generation, how long shall I be with you? how long shall I suffer you? bring him hither to me" (17:17). "Ye serpents, ye generation of vipers, how can ye escape the damnation of hell?" (23:33).

These interpretations of the parable miss the entire point. It is not about the rebirth of the state of Israel. That has nothing at all to do with it. The Bible nowhere teaches such a rebirth.

The premillennial dispensational interpretation cannot be correct for several reasons. First, the fig tree, which represents national Israel, was cursed. In Matthew 21:20 Christ cursed the fig tree because it had leaves but no fruit. Fig trees, unique among trees, bring forth fruit first, then sprout leaves to shade the fruit. That the fig tree displayed leaves meant there should have been fruit. When Christ found no fruit, he cursed the tree. Similarly, when Israel displayed a vain show of works but without fruit, God cursed the nation. In Matthew 21:40–43, Christ warns that the kingdom of God will be taken away from Israel and given to a nation that will bear fruit. That nation is the New

Testament church of believing Jews and Gentiles: "Ye are a chosen generation, a royal priesthood, an holy nation, a peculiar people; that ye should shew forth the praises of him who hath called you out of darkness into his marvellous light" (1 Pet. 2:9).

Second, the curse Christ pronounces on national Israel is permanent and irrevocable, which means that national Israel will *never* be restored as the nation of God. It does not mean that there will be no Jews saved in the New Testament age. There will be many Jews saved throughout the New Testament age. The fullness of the Jews and of the Gentiles will be gathered until the coming of Christ. Nor does this phrase mean that Israel will not be restored politically as a nation. Although political restoration has occurred, it has absolutely no significance prophetically. Christ's cursing of the barren fig tree means that Israel's favored position as the nation of God has finished, forever, and will never be restored. God will not return to Israel. Listen to what Christ says: "Let no fruit grow on thee *henceforward for ever*" (Matt. 21:19, emphasis added).

Nevertheless, premillennial dispensationalism looks for Israel's future spiritual restoration. Some try to circumvent Christ's final, permanent curse on the barren fig tree. Some have said that "for ever" in Matthew 21:19 means "until the age," and therefore the curse will be lifted at the end of the age of the Gentiles, the so-called church age. That is absurd because the phrase means forever in every other place in the Bible.

Others find a "second chance" for Israel in Luke 13:6–9:

6. He spake also this parable; A certain man had a fig tree planted in his vineyard; and he came and sought fruit thereon, and found none.

7. Then said he unto the dresser of his vineyard, Behold, these three years I come seeking fruit on this

fig tree, and find none: cut it down; why cumbereth it the ground?

8. And he answering said unto him, Lord, let it alone this year also, till I shall dig about it, and dung it:

9. And if it bear fruit, well: and if not, then after that thou shalt cut it down.

There the Lord suggests that if Israel repents and brings forth fruit after one more year of digging and fertilizing, God will spare the fig tree. Nevertheless, the parable ends without a promise that the fig tree would bear fruit after the fourth year; and the "second chance" for the fig tree was immediately after the third year. It is not that God cut down the fig tree in AD 70, and then some two thousand years later he will allow the vinedresser to dig and dung it and give it another chance. God gave space for repentance in the period of time leading up to AD 70. Israel did not repent. God cut her down, just as John the Baptist had warned.

There is also the parallel passage in Luke 21:29–30: "He spake to them a parable; Behold the fig tree, and all the trees; when they now shoot forth, ye see and know of your own selves that summer is now nigh at hand." If the fig tree refers to national Israel, what does the phrase "all the trees" refer to? Did all nations blossom and bud in 1948 or 1967? Some premillennial dispensationalists argue that many new nations formed at that time, but "many" is not "all," and dispensationalism at this point is surely clutching at straws!

The Significance

The fig tree in Matthew 24:32 is, quite simply, a fig tree. "All the trees" in Luke 21:29 are trees. The fig tree is not a symbol of Israel or of any other nation. It is a tree. Christ points to a fig tree as an object lesson, an illustration, of something. Jesus often did that, without any hidden meaning.

If I said: if you see frost, you know that winter is here or that it is cold, I would not be making a point that frost is a symbol of something spiritual. Similarly, Christ speaks of the weather in various places: "When it is evening, ye say, It will be fair weather: for the sky is red. And in the morning, It will be foul weather [stormy] to-day: for the sky is red and lowering [gloomy]" (Matt. 16:2–3). "When ye see a cloud rise out of the west, straightway ye say, There cometh a shower; and so it is. And when ye see the south wind blow, ye say, There will be heat; and it cometh to pass" (Luke 12:54–55). We do not think that red sky, gloomy sky, clouds, or south winds are symbolic of something. They are signs in the sky that indicate the weather. That is all!

When Christ points to the fig tree, he is pointing to the nearness of summer. That is true of all the trees, but of the fig tree in particular. When a fig tree puts forth leaves, it is an unmistakable indication that winter is past and summer is on the way. The presence of leaves indicates either very early fruit or last year's fruit. The point is simply this: ye know that summer is nigh. So near is the summer, and with summer comes harvest, says Christ, that this generation will not pass until all these things be fulfilled. This generation means this generation. There is no way to avoid this meaning.

"This generation," therefore, does not mean the generation that will live to see the restoration of Israel, whether that began in 1948 or 1967. This generation does not mean the Jewish race, nor does it mean this kind of people, whether believers or unbelievers. It means the generation of people living at the time Jesus spoke these words. That generation of people did not die off until all these things were fulfilled.

179

The postmillennial explanation of verse 34 is that everything mentioned in Matthew 24 to this point—the eight signs, including the events of verses 29–31—happened within one generation (forty years). Therefore, everything of which Christ speaks was fulfilled *finally and exhaustively* by AD 70. In fact, verse 34 is the text that drives and determines the postmillennial interpretation of the entire chapter.

That interpretation is impossible, however. All the events recorded in Matthew 24:4–31 were *not* fulfilled by AD 70, especially not the events of Christ's glorious return. The key is the word *fulfilled*. The Greek says simply "happen," as in, "This generation shall not pass away until all these things happen." However, they do not happen exhaustively, completely, or entirely. They happen in historical type. Do not think, warns Christ, that you can foist all of this on some future generation. You will see it, experience it, and live through it. Within one generation, you will have confirmation of my words. But that will not be the end. You cannot foist it all on the past either. In AD 70 it happened only typically as a dim reflection of the real thing, which will happen throughout the age and culminate at the end. It will continue and intensify until it is fulfilled, not only in type upon Jerusalem, but in reality upon the world.

Calvin's interpretation is compelling:

> Though Christ employs a general expression, yet he does not extend the discourses to all the miseries which would befall the Church, but merely informs them, that before a single *generation* shall have been completed, they will learn by experience the truth of what he has said. For within fifty years the city was destroyed and the temple was rased, the whole country was reduced to a hideous desert, and the obstinacy of the world rose

up against God. Nay more, their rage was inflamed to exterminate the doctrine of salvation, false teachers arose to corrupt the pure gospel by their impostures, religion sustained amazing shocks, and the whole company of the godly was miserably distressed. Now though the same evils were perpetrated in uninterrupted succession for many ages afterwards, yet what Christ said was true, that, before the close of a single *generation*, believers would feel in reality, and by undoubted experience, the truth of his prediction; for the apostles endured the same things which we see in the present day. And yet it was not the design of Christ to promise to his followers that their calamities would be terminated within a short time, (for then he would have contradicted himself, having previously warned them that *the end was not yet;*) but, in order to encourage them to perseverance, he expressly foretold that those things related to their own age. The meaning therefore is: "This prophecy does not relate to evils that are distant, and which posterity will see after the lapse of many centuries, but which are now hanging over you, and ready to fall in one mass, so that there is no part of it which the present *generation* will not experience." So then, while our Lord heaps upon a single *generation* every kind of calamities, he does not by any means exempt future ages from the same kind of sufferings, but only enjoins the disciples to be prepared for enduring them all with firmness.[1]

Having cleared away the pre- and postmillennial misunderstanding, let us examine the true meaning. The main idea of

---

1 Calvin, *Commentary on a Harmony of the Evangelists*, 3:151–52.

the parable of the fig tree is this. Just as a fig tree putting forth leaves tells you that summer, and therefore harvest, is near, so the signs that Christ has been explaining in verses 4–31 tell you that his coming, and therefore the final judgment, is near: "So likewise ye, when ye shall see all these things, know that it is near, even at the doors" (v. 33).

The objection to this has always been that Christ's coming was *not* near: "We have been waiting for two thousand years, and still he has not come." We must understand that the second coming of Christ *is* near, but not near in the sense of *our* experience of time. Peter explained that in 2 Peter 3:8: "One day is with the Lord as a thousand years, and a thousand years as one day."

God is outside of time. He inhabits eternity. He is in no hurry. Although he seems to delay from our perspective, everything is on his schedule. Many things must happen before that day can arrive. However, it will come, as surely as a budding fig tree indicates summer. Christ's coming is near: conceive of him as standing just outside the door with his hand on the doorknob about to come in (Matt. 24:33).

To illustrate the idea of biblical "nearness" consider some passages from the prophets. "Thus saith the LORD of hosts; Yet once, *it is a little while*, and I will shake the heavens, and the earth, and the sea, and the dry land; and I will shake all nations, and the desire of all nations shall come: and I will fill this house with glory, saith the LORD of hosts" (Hag. 2:6–7, emphasis added). The writer to the Hebrews quotes these verses:

> 25. See that ye refuse not him that speaketh. For if they escaped not who refused him that spake on earth, much more shall not we escape, if we turn away from him that speaketh from heaven:

26. Whose voice then shook the earth: but now he hath promised, saying, Yet once more I shake not the earth only, but also heaven.

27. And this word, Yet once more, signifieth the removing of those things that are shaken, as of things that are made, that those things which cannot be shaken may remain.

28. Wherefore we receiving a kingdom which cannot be moved, let us have grace, whereby we may serve God acceptably with reverence and godly fear:

29. For our God is a consuming fire. (Heb. 12:25–29)

Whether you interpret Haggai's words, "yet once…a little while," to refer to the first or second coming of Christ or even to both comings of Christ, the prophecy was not fulfilled in a short period of time, but after the passing of many generations.

"My salvation is near to come, and my righteousness is to be revealed," declared the prophet Isaiah many years before the Babylonian captivity and return, and centuries before the coming of Christ, in whom salvation and righteousness are accomplished, and millennia before the final, perfect revelation of salvation and righteousness at the second coming of the Lord (Isa. 56:1).

That nearness means that Christ's second coming is the next great event on God's agenda. The reason Christ's coming is now near in the New Testament is that everything else has been accomplished, for Christ has come in our flesh, Christ has been crucified for our sins, Christ has risen and ascended, and Christ has poured out the Holy Spirit. Now Christ's second coming *is* near, and with every day it becomes nearer.

Christ having accomplished that, he can promise that his coming is near. There are no more wonders of grace to be performed by God before the consummation of all things. Once the elect church has been gathered, sin has developed to the full, and the church has filled up the sufferings of Christ, the Lord will return. From our perspective that is a long time, but from God's perspective it is near.

Christ illustrates that with the parable of the fig tree. Do you want to know that the coming of Christ is near? Look at a fig tree! Does it sprout leaves? Do you then doubt that summer is coming soon? Then when you see *all these things,* do not doubt that Christ's coming is near.

The Assurance

The budding fig tree in nature is a sure sign of approaching summer, but there is something surer. The physical creation of heaven and earth is sure, for the world expects it to last forever, and it will surely last until God's purpose with it has been fulfilled. What is more stable, more firm, and more reliable than heaven and earth? Do we not expect that every day the sun will rise and set, and that the earth will remain firm under our feet? Nevertheless, even the heaven and earth will pass away. God promises in 2 Peter 3 that they will be destroyed by fire and renewed in the new creation.

But, says Christ, my words are surer: "My words shall not pass away" (Matt. 24:35). What mere man can dare say that? The words of Alexander the Great, Plato, Aristotle, Julius Caesar, Karl Marx, and Charles Darwin pass away. Christ is the eternal Son of God and his word is God's word. Therefore, none of his words pass away. They are true forever.

Matthew 24:35 is powerful proof of the authority, permanence, and preservation of the scriptures. When Christ spoke, none of his words were recorded. Christ himself wrote no books; Matthew, Mark, Luke, and John had not yet written their inspired accounts of Christ's life and ministry; and none of the apostles had written any of the New Testament books. Yet Christ's words did not—and never will—pass away. What Christ said has been recorded in the holy scriptures. Christ promised that the Spirit would accomplish the great work of the inspiration and preservation of his word: "The Comforter, which is the Holy Ghost, whom the Father will send in my name, he shall teach you all things, and bring all things to your remembrance, whatsoever I have said unto you" (John 14:26). If "holy men of God spake as they were moved by the Holy Ghost" (2 Pet. 1:21), the holy apostles and prophets of the New Testament were moved in the same way, so that, as Peter remarks concerning Paul's writings, they are on a par with "the other scriptures" (2 Pet. 3:16). That is, they too are "given by inspiration of God" (2 Tim. 3:16).

To that one might object that not everything Jesus said has been preserved in the New Testament. Jesus lived for thirty-three years, and even if we only include the words spoken during his public ministry of three and a half years, not every single word he spoke has been recorded and preserved. Indeed, John writes, "There are also many other things which Jesus did, the which, if they should be written every one, I suppose that even the world itself could not contain the books that should be written. Amen" (John 21:25).

It is not necessary for every single word that Jesus ever spoke to be recorded and preserved. What is necessary is that the words ordained by God the Father and inspired by the Holy Spirit are recorded and preserved. The Bible contains all the words that we must know for our salvation and for our life in this world. All those words have been recorded and preserved. What Christ taught about God, man, himself, salvation, the church, and the last things has been and shall be forever preserved. That means that the Bible has been preserved, so that the church will never lose the word of Jesus Christ.

It also means that what God has promised will stand. "Not as though the word of God hath taken none effect" (Rom. 9:6). Not as though the word of God hath taken none effect! When the words of all other men perish, the word of Christ will stand forever. What he has said about his coming *shall* be accomplished.

Therefore, do not doubt Christ's words. When you hear of wars and rumors of wars, do not be alarmed. When the world shakes for fear from famines, pestilences, or earthquakes, do not be frightened. All these things must come to pass exactly as Christ said. When deceivers of every kind assault the church, when many fall away from the truth of the gospel, do not be terrified, and do not follow them into apostasy. When antichrist comes and lays the church waste through persecution, stand firm. All these things are part of Christ's words, which will not pass away. All these things are simply, like the budding fig tree, signs that summer and harvest are on their way, the great harvest of the final judgment. Christ has died for our sins; he has defeated Satan; he has set up his eternal kingdom—he is on his way back to us. When all is completed, he will come.

Do not be distracted by the nation of Israel. Believe the imperishable word of Christ.

Chapter 12

♦

THE UNKNOWN
TIME OF
CHRIST'S RETURN

But of that day and hour knoweth no man, no, not the
angels of heaven, but my Father only.—Matthew 24:36

Ever since Christ ascended into heaven, the church has
longed for his return, because then she will be with her
husband. The church is a bride espoused to Christ, and she is
waiting and longing for the marriage feast of the Lamb. Christ
has left the church on the earth and has gone to heaven, but he
has left her with his Spirit, with his word, and with the sacra-
ments as tokens of his love. Do you long for his return? Does
the mention of his return thrill your soul?

Christ promised that he would come back soon; and perhaps
we wonder in our weakness whether he really meant "soon." He
certainly did, but he meant he would return as soon as everything is ready. He meant that the next thing on God's agenda
is the second coming of Christ. He did not mean "soon" as in

a few weeks, months, or years. We see that he has been absent from us for some two thousand years.

Two great temptations confront the church in Christ's absence.

One is to think that he is not coming again. That is unbelief. When the church begins to imagine that Christ is not coming again, she loses hope. When the church begins to imagine that Christ is not coming again, she is tempted to give up her calling and to compromise with the world or to live carelessly. When we are tempted by unbelieving despair, let us remember the word of God, and let us observe the signs Christ has taught us.

The other temptation is to become impatient and, through pride and unlawful curiosity, to attempt to predict the second coming. Christ cuts off that possibility in the text: no man can and no man may predict it. When the church spends time trying to calculate the date, she is not only foolish and proud but she is unfaithful, for she is not doing what the Lord told her to do while she waits for his return. The church must teach and preach, she must watch and pray, but she may not meddle in things rightly hidden from her.

What Is Unknown

The text concerns "that day and hour" (v. 36). This refers to Christ's second coming, the subject of the entire preceding discourse. On a day and in an hour future to us, the Lord will return in the body and in great glory. This will be at a certain time on our calendar, and with it time and history will come to an end. The day, month, year, and hour are fixed in God's eternal decree. One day, history as we know it will end. Christ might return in the summer or winter, in the early morning, noon, midafternoon, evening, or even in the middle of the night:

"Watch ye therefore: for ye know not when the master of the house cometh, at even, or at midnight, or at the cockcrowing, or in the morning" (Mark 13:35).

After his coming—after that day and hour—there will be no more days or hours or years of human history. The sun, moon, and stars, by which we measure time, will cease. When Christ returns, he will return to our earth, which is a globe. One part of the human population will be experiencing daytime; the other part, night. Some will be working, while others will be sleeping: "I tell you, in that night there shall be two men in one bed; the one shall be taken, and the other shall be left. Two women shall be grinding together; the one shall be taken, and the other left. Two men shall be in the field; the one shall be taken, and the other left" (Luke 17:34–36).

Many—indeed the majority—will be engaged in sin, whether it is day or night, because sinners never sleep. Perhaps some will be caught in the very act of adultery or fornication, and others will be drunk or under the influence of drugs. What will *we* be doing? Matthew 24:46 says that we will be happy, if the Lord finds us busy in his service. In all likelihood when Christ comes and antichrist is at the height of his power, many of God's saints will be in prison or in hiding. It will be a glorious day of redemption for us and a dreadful day of reckoning for the wicked.

The day and hour of Christ's return are unalterably fixed in God's eternal decree. History is not a random sequence of events, but the beginning, every event in between, and the end are all eternally planned by our good, wise, and holy God. God will not announce, "That is enough. Time is up," when he feels that he has had enough. The earth will not be destroyed in a nuclear holocaust or by an environmental disaster; nor will the universe simply perish in heat death. God has determined everything. Therefore, the world cannot end one moment earlier or later than God has planned, and neither sinners nor the devil can cause God to steer off course. The end of the world will be victory for Jesus Christ, glory for the triune God, and judgment for the ungodly world.

Although God has told us some, indeed much, about that day and hour, he has not revealed to us when that day and hour will occur. We know that the second coming will be announced by various signs—we know that that day cannot come unless the gospel be preached to all nations, there be a great falling away, and we see the rise and temporary triumph of antichrist. Therefore, we look for these signs that we are approaching the end. We know that the end of history will not be a golden age of earthly prosperity and peace, nor an escape for Christians in a secret rapture, but something like the destruction of Jerusalem of AD 70, which was a historical type of the end. Nevertheless, we do not know in what year, what month, what day, or what hour Christ will return: "of that day and hour knoweth no man" (v. 36). God has determined for his own glory and for our own good to keep that information hidden within himself.

We ought not to be surprised or grieved at that. God has secrets (Deut. 29:29). There are many things about God's counsel that we do not know. For example, God has revealed to us in his word that he has chosen some (elect) and rejected others (reprobate). He has told us that the elect and reprobate are a certain, definite, unchangeable number of persons, but he has not told us who they are.[1] God has revealed to us an outline of some important future events, but many of the details remain hidden. Closer to home, God has not told us, and he will not either, how long we will live, whether we will be alive next year,

---

1   Canons 1.11, in Schaff, *Creeds of Christendom*, 3:583.

whether we will marry, or whether we will have (more) children. God gives us only the sketchiest of outlines: the elect will be gathered, the cup of iniquity will be filled, the church will be persecuted according to the measure of Christ's sufferings, but the details are hidden.

That this is the case is blatantly obvious from the text and other passages. In the Old Testament, for example, God told his people about the Messiah, but he did not reveal the exact time of Christ's birth, although God's people longed to know (1 Pet. 1:11). Moreover, just before Christ ascended into heaven, he declared, "It is not for you to know the times or the seasons, which the Father hath put in his own power" (Acts 1:7). Given this truth, it is nothing short of inexcusable pride and breathtaking arrogance to attempt to predict the time of Christ's return. Alas, church history is littered with examples of men and women who have fallen into the snare of the devil in this regard. The most famous example in modern times was Harold Camping of Family Radio.

Harold Camping devoted many decades of his life to an intense study of the Bible in an attempt mathematically to work out the day and the hour. He came to the conclusion that 1988 was the end of the church age. After that date, God was supposedly no longer employing churches to bring salvation to the world. Later he promoted the idea that 1994 would be the end, but that was because he tried to factor into his calculations a shortening of the days for the elect's sake. When nothing happened in 1994, he started promoting 2011. Camping plastered billboards all across the world with the message, "MAY 21, 2011. JUDGMENT DAY. THE BIBLE GUARANTEES IT." In fact, he predicted that on May 21, 2011, a series of devastating earthquakes would destroy the world, millions would die, and God's people would escape in the rapture. When nothing happened, he spiritualized the earthquakes and waited for October 21, 2011, as the final day.

Initially, when Camping was challenged that no man knows the day or the hour, he retorted, "But we can know the month and the year." How did he come to calculate the day and the hour as six o'clock in the evening on May 21, 2011? Let us examine a few of Camping's arguments, especially his abuse of Matthew 24:36. We do this to learn how *not* to interpret the scriptures and to be warned not to twist God's word, as Camping did, to his own destruction (2 Pet. 3:16).

First, Camping noticed that in Matthew 24:37 the coming of the Son of man would be like the days of Noah. Unfortunately, he did not ask, *in what way* will it be like the days of Noah? Camping jumped to Genesis 7:4: "For yet seven days, and I will cause it to rain." Then Camping jumped to the conclusion that from the flood to the day of judgment would be seven days. Why not one hundred twenty years; why not forty days? Next Camping jumped to 2 Peter 3:8, "one day is with the Lord as a thousand years," and concluded that exactly seven thousand years after the flood the day of judgment would occur. Camping missed the word "as" in 2 Peter 3:8. Camping also calculated that the flood took place in 4,090 BC and that exactly seven thousand years later to the day would be May 21, 2011— the equivalent of the seventeenth day of the second month. You will notice that Camping chose various proof texts from the Bible and ignored their contexts.

In response to Christ's denial that man can know the day and hour, Camping had the following arguments. First, he argued that the Greek verb in Matthew 24:36 means no man knew, but that God is opening the understanding of true believers to know what was hidden before. This is an example of where a little knowledge (of Greek) is a dangerous thing. The

Greek verb is in the perfect tense, but in that form it is always translated as the present tense.

As further proof he appealed to Daniel 12:9, "the words are closed up and sealed till the time of the end," and Revelation 5:5, "behold, the Lion of the tribe of Juda, the Root of David, hath prevailed to open the book, and to the loose the seven seals thereof." In Daniel's day the book was closed, but in Christ's day the book is opened. Notice the illogical leap: Camping assumed that both passages speak about the *same* book.

Moreover, he compared Acts 1:7, "it is not for you to know the times or the seasons, which the Father hath put in his own power," with Ecclesiastes 8:5, "a wise man's heart discerneth both time and judgment." It was not for the apostles to know, but it *was* for Camping to know.

Finally, Camping said that we *must* know, otherwise the day would come upon us as a thief: "Yourselves know perfectly that the day of the Lord so cometh as a thief in the night. For when they shall say, Peace and safety; then sudden destruction cometh upon them, as travail upon a woman with child; and they shall not escape. But ye, brethren, are not in darkness, that that day should overtake you as a thief" (1 Thess. 5:2–4). Again, Camping did not ask in what sense the day of the Lord will be like a thief. This is an excellent illustration of how *not* to exegete!

To Whom It Is Unknown

The ravings of men like Harold Camping notwithstanding, Christ is crystal clear. The information concerning the second coming is hidden in God and is unknown to any creature.

First, Christ says, "But of that day and hour knoweth no man" (Matt. 24:36). Literally, Christ says "no one" or "nobody," neither man, woman, or child. Christ repeats this in verse 42 and in Matthew 25:13. Christ's whole point is that no man knows, so we must always be in a state of readiness. The day of Christ's coming will take men by surprise: he will arrive unexpectedly, for no man will be able to calculate it; and no theologian or Bible student will be able to predict it. All attempts to do so—whether from the seventy weeks of Daniel 9, the numbers in Revelation, or the idea that Christ comes seven literal years after the rise of antichrist—are futile.

Nor will Christ reveal this at some future date to certain favored disciples. He did not reveal it to Peter, John, or any other inspired writers of the New Testament, so why would he reveal it to someone today? In fact, anyone who says, "Lo, here is Christ, or there" (Matt. 24:23) is a liar and a false prophet, and indeed, he himself is one of the signs of Christ's coming. Remember that the risen Christ, moments before his ascension, said to the apostles literally, "*not to you to know* times and seasons" (Acts 1:7, emphasis added).

Second, the angels do not know, "no, not the angels of heaven" (Matt. 24:36). That is a startling statement. The angels are more intelligent, wiser, and mightier than we, and they dwell in heaven in God's glorious presence, but they are not privy to this information. We, down below, see in a glass darkly, for we see and know only in part, but the angels dwell with God. Whereas fallen human beings are on earth, Jesus declares, "In heaven their angels do always behold the face of my Father which is in heaven" (Matt. 18:10). Yet they do not know the time. The angels are intensely interested in God's work of redemption. First Peter 1:12 speaks of "things...which the angels desire to look into." Yet they do not know. The angels as God's servants have been involved in many of God's purposes: they sang for joy at man's creation (Job 38:7); they rejoiced at the birth of Jesus in Bethlehem (Luke 2:14); they strengthened

Jesus in his temptations and in Gethsemane (Matt. 4:11; Luke 22:43); they rejoice over repenting sinners (Luke 15:10). Yet they do not know the time of Christ's second coming.

Do not forget that the angels will be involved in the second coming. They will not be idle spectators. Christ has mentioned the angels in Matthew 24:31. He will mention them again in Matthew 25:31. They are a feature of 2 Thessalonians 1:7 and throughout the book of Revelation. The angels are ready when the command goes forth from the throne of God, "It is finished. Time is no more. Go forth with my Son and gather my elect." But they do not know the time. If the angels can be content not knowing, so must we. Not even the glorified saints in heaven know:

> 10. And they cried with a loud voice, saying, How long, O Lord, holy and true, dost thou not judge and avenge our blood on them that dwell on the earth?
> 11. And white robes were given unto every one of them; and it was said unto them, that they should rest yet for a little season, until their fellow-servants also and their brethren, that should be killed as they were, should be fulfilled. (Rev. 6:10–11)

Calvin describes the foolish madness of one who tries to find out the time of Christ's return in these words:

> The chief part of our wisdom lies in confining ourselves soberly within the limits of God's word. That men may not feel uneasy at *not knowing that day*, Christ represents *angels* as their associates in this matter; for it would be a proof of excessive pride and wicked covetousness to desire that we who creep on the earth should know more than is permitted to the *angels* in heaven...

That man must be singularly mad, who would hesitate to submit to the ignorance which even *the Son of God himself* did not hesitate to endure on our account.[2]

Only one knows, the Father, who is the triune God. When Jesus is speaking on the Mount of Olives, he is speaking as a man, and his Father is the triune God. Thus he speaks of "my Father only." Father, Son, and Holy Spirit together planned everything in eternity: part of that plan was that the Son assume a human nature, with all the necessary limitations, to suffer and die for our salvation. So, of course, the Father, Son, and Holy Spirit know exactly when Christ will return, because just as they determined when and where he would be born and when, where, and how he would die, they also determined together when he would usher in the end of history. Therefore, we conclude that only God, the omniscient, perfectly wise, sovereignly free, almighty Creator and ruler of all things, knows the moment of Christ's return. We must never forget this. It is part of the glory of God that only he knows. Never may we allow curiosity to lead us to set a date for the second coming. Never may we be tempted to believe any man or even an angel from heaven. They do not know, they will not know, and they cannot know.

The Father only!

To underline this truth, Jesus says something else, not mentioned by Matthew but recorded in Mark. No man knows, no angel knows, but "neither the Son" knows (Mark 13:32).

The Son, as all sensible commentators agree, is the Son of man, the man Christ Jesus. Harold Camping, however, was not a sensible Bible commentator. Camping contended that there is nothing in the verse to suggest that Jesus Christ is talking about

---

2   Calvin, *Commentary on a Harmony of the Evangelists*, 3:153.

himself when he says "neither the Son." Why? Because Christ says, "Son," not "Son of God" or "Son of man." Camping searched the Bible for another who is called the "Son." The conclusion he reached was that Lucifer is called "son of the morning" in Isaiah 14:12, and Judas is called "son of perdition" in John 17:12, and the antichrist is called "son of perdition" in 2 Thessalonians 2:3. Therefore, declared Camping, Mark 13:32 means that *the devil* does not know the time of the second coming!

Camping's exegesis was absurd. There can be no doubt that by "neither the Son" Jesus refers to himself. In Mark 13:26 Jesus refers to himself as the Son of man. Nothing in the contexts indicates a change in subjects. In many places in the New Testament, Jesus calls himself simply the Son, without further qualifying the description with the words "of God" or "of man" (Matt. 11:27; John 5:23; 8:36; Heb. 1:8; 1 John 4:14). Besides this, how anticlimactic would be the declaration that even the devil is ignorant of the time of Christ's return! If the angels do not know, of course the devil, who is a fallen angel, could not know!

Clearly then, even Jesus Christ did not know the date of his own return. The words "my Father only" exclude even Jesus Christ himself! Does that not leave us with a terrible problem? How could Jesus Christ not know the time of his own second coming? Is Jesus Christ not *God?*

Jesus Christ is God, the eternal Son of God, but as he speaks to his disciples on the Mount of Olives, he speaks as a man, in our flesh, with all the limitations of our human nature except sin. Remember that Jesus Christ as a man had, and still has, a human body, mind, soul, and will. He is sinless, he is perfect, but he was in a state of humiliation. Willingly, the eternal Son of God humbled himself, became a helpless baby, and had to grow up. Part of that process of growth was an increase in knowledge (Luke 2:52). The eternal Son of God knows all things, but in his human nature the man Jesus Christ does not. An omniscient human nature is no more possible than an omnipresent human nature. Sometimes the divine nature communicated knowledge to the human nature, but not always. The precise date of his own return is one of the things of which Christ as a man remained ignorant.

There are mysteries to Christ's person—he is the eternal Son of God with two distinct natures—that we can never fully understand. We humbly worship. We worship because Christ was content to be ignorant with a view to our salvation. Ignorance was part of his suffering. Christ's suffering was for us: he suffered and died to pay for our sins, and while he lived in that state of humiliation and condition of misery and shame and suffering, he was limited in power and knowledge according to his human nature. Now, with his resurrection, ascension, and session at God's right hand, he does know. He knows everything that a glorified human nature is able to know. As the Son of God, he is omniscient, but he will not tell us, the angels, or the glorified saints. We remain ignorant until we see him.

Why It Is Unknown

Do not conclude that God has done us a disservice in not telling us the day and hour of Christ's return. God sees in his infinite wisdom that it is better that we do not know. The wider context of the rest of Matthew 24 provides the main reason for this. Christ would have us watchful, always ready, always waiting, and always longing: "Watch therefore, for ye know not what hour your Lord doth come…If the good man of the house had known…Be ye also ready: for in such an hour as ye think not the Son of man cometh" (vv. 42–44). "The lord of that servant shall come in a day when he looketh not for him" (v. 50). "Watch therefore, for ye know neither the day nor the hour wherein the Son of man cometh" (Matt. 25:13).

Cannot we watch better for Christ's coming if we know the day and hour? Alas, our human nature is such that if we knew we would misuse the information. We tend to procrastinate, to put things on the back burner because we have no sense of urgency. The fact is, if the Lord had given us a date, we would become careless, complacent, and idle. We would not be diligent in observing the signs. We would say, "I will prepare for the Lord's coming later. I have plenty of time."

Christ would have us *not* know so that we are *always* ready and in a state of expectation. Christ is coming soon, and we must always be ready to meet him. It is easy to see how the unknown time of Christ's return is God's way of keeping his people ready and exposing and condemning the hypocrites in the kingdom of God. The rest of the Olivet Discourse will illustrate that.

We all have the same information—we all know that Christ is coming again and we know the signs to observe, but none of us know *when* our Savior will return. Some are careless, for they do not watch; they walk in sin and refuse to repent, but they tell themselves, "I will be able to repent later." Others remain always ready, for they keep their garments pure and use God's good gifts to serve the Lord while they wait.

If your employer informed you that the government inspector was coming on Friday, you would most likely do nothing until Thursday evening or Friday morning. But if your boss warned you that the government would be doing spot checks, you would keep your records in a constant state of readiness. In the military, spot inspections of soldiers' quarters improve discipline. If the teacher tells his students that at any time he may give a pop quiz, every sensible student will be prepared every day. So much more is it the case with those who profess to believe in Christ.

Imagine if Christ had said he would return on February 17, 2096, to choose a date at random. Much of the church would have said, "He is not coming for ages." Thus the church would have fallen asleep. Then in 2096, many would have said, "This is the year. Better get serious this year. Better pray more this year. Better be more faithful this year. Better read more this year. Better be a good witness this year." The point is that most would do *nothing* until it was almost February 2096. That kind of last-minute service is not what the Lord Jesus demands of us.

Every day we must be obedient out of love and gratitude, for God demands readiness of heart at all times. Let us therefore be ready, not with a calculator, but ready doing God's will. Let us not be ready by idly waiting for the day, but by serving God faithfully every day and always praying, "Come Lord Jesus, yea, come quickly."

Chapter 13

✸

CHRIST'S COMING AS IN THE DAYS OF NOAH

But as the days of Noe were, so shall also the coming of the Son of man be. For as in the days that were before the flood they were eating and drinking, marrying and giving in marriage, until the day that Noe entered into the ark, and knew not until the flood came, and took them all away; so shall also the coming of the Son of man be. Then shall two be in the field; the one shall be taken, and the other left. Two women shall be grinding at the mill; the one shall be taken, and the other left. Watch therefore: for ye know not what hour your Lord doth come. —Matthew 24:37–42

It is instructive to note that Christ believed and confessed the flood of Genesis. Jesus Christ, the Son of God, knew and believed the Old Testament scriptures. He did not believe that Genesis was a book of myths, fables, and legends. He confessed the historicity of Genesis, that is, he confessed that Genesis is history. He did that here, and he did that elsewhere. In a parallel passage, he confessed the historical truth of the destruction of Sodom and Gomorrah:

26. And as it was in the days of Noe, so shall it be also in the days of the Son of man.
27. They did eat, they drank, they married wives, they were given in marriage, until the day that Noe entered into the ark, and the flood came, and destroyed them all.
28. Likewise also as it was in the days of Lot; they did eat, they drank, they bought, they sold, they planted, they builded;
29. But the same day that Lot went out of Sodom it rained fire and brimstone from heaven, and destroyed them all. (Luke 17:26–29)

Because Jesus believed and confessed the Old Testament scriptures as history, so do we. In our catechism classes, we teach our children Old Testament and New Testament history. We teach and preach that the stories and the miracles happened exactly as they were recorded in scripture. Men might scoff and mock, but we accept the Bible by faith, on God's authority.

The flood and the destruction of Sodom and Gomorrah are not only history, but are also *typical* history that foreshadows a greater fulfillment in the New Testament. This is true of Old Testament history in general. All of it foreshadows Jesus Christ, and all of it prepares for Jesus Christ. It is not simply a list of random, meaningless stories. Many events in Old Testament history have a deeper spiritual significance. For example, the exodus is a type or a picture of Christ's redemption of us out of sin's bondage; and the flood is a picture of the final judgment.

We must be careful with types and our interpretation of them. In any type or picture there is usually one main point of comparison. Therefore, it is foolish to find hidden, spiritual meanings in all the details. For example, David is a type of Jesus Christ, but not in everything he did. Therefore, it is foolish and vain to pick apart David's life to find comparisons in every detail.

The question we need to ask with respect to the type in Matthew 24:37–41 is this: how, in what way exactly, will Christ's coming be as in the days of Noah?

The Character of Those Days

The days leading up to the second coming of Christ will be like the days before the flood, which were days of terrible wickedness. "The LORD said, My spirit shall not always strive with man, for that he also is flesh: yet his days shall be an hundred and twenty years" (Gen. 6:3). God set a limit of one hundred twenty years, after which he would destroy all mankind. However, it is important to note that God did not tell anyone about the one hundred twenty years. Not even Noah knew the timeline of God's purposes. God determined to destroy man because man's wickedness was great, for the earth was filled with violence and all flesh had corrupted itself on the earth:

5. And God saw that the wickedness of man was great in the earth, and that every imagination of the thoughts of his heart was only evil continually.

6. And it repented the LORD that he had made man on the earth, and it grieved him at his heart.

7. And the LORD said, I will destroy man whom I have created from the face of the earth; both man, and beast, and the creeping thing, and the fowls of the air; for it repenteth me that I have made them.

8. But Noah found grace in the eyes of the LORD. (Gen. 6:5–8)

God would have destroyed every man alive, except that he determined to keep his promise to send the seed of the woman. Accordingly, he kept his covenant with Noah, in whose generations he would send Christ. So wicked was the world that when the flood came the church had been diminished to eight people. One of the reasons was that the godly line of Seth had been almost persecuted out of existence by the ungodly line of Cain. Another reason was the mixing by intermarriage of the two lines: the sons of God (the members of the church) took wives of the daughters of men (the women of the world). The result was apostasy, a great falling away of those who once belonged to the line of Seth in their generations. But for the flood, the godly line of Seth (from which the seed of the woman, who is Christ, must come) would have been eliminated.

It is remarkable to note, however, that Jesus does not focus on *that* aspect of the days before the flood. He does not mention the gross corruption, the terrible violence, the apostasy, or the persecution. You might have expected Christ to say, "As in the days that were before the flood they were guilty of murder, pillaging, and gross immorality." He does not deny that they were doing such things, but that is not his focus in the comparison. Instead of that, Christ speaks about ordinary, seemingly harmless everyday activities: "They were eating and drinking, marrying and giving in marriage" (Matt. 24:38). Then he remarks that they were doing ordinary, everyday work: laboring in the fields and grinding grain at the mill. In Luke 17 Christ adds concerning the men of Sodom that "they bought, they sold, they planted, they builded" (v. 28).

None of these (eating, drinking, weddings, commerce, agriculture, or work) are evil in themselves. Nevertheless, they were symptoms of serious underlying wickedness.

First, the people's whole lives were absorbed in and consumed by these things. Their eating and drinking and everything else they did were in the service of sin and in the pursuit of pleasure. One word described that world: materialism.

Second, their eating and drinking were not done to the glory of God: with their eating and drinking they should have been praying, worshiping, singing God's praises, and serving him. They were not walking with God, as Enoch and Noah were.

Third, their eating and drinking were symptomatic of their false security. They were prosperous, and they believed they would always remain so. Because they could lead a normal life, they felt secure. Given the circumstances of the day, eating, drinking, and marrying were not appropriate. There is a time for eating, drinking, marrying, giving in marriage, buying, selling, planting, and building, and it is not when God has pronounced judgment. Given the circumstances, they should have been repenting, wearing sackcloth like the Ninevites of Jonah's day, crying out to God for mercy, and seeking salvation in the promised Christ.

They had one great sign, the sign of Noah: a man building a huge wooden vessel on dry land to escape a flood. Nevertheless, they ignored that sign; they laughed at it, mocked it, and carried on eating and drinking. Does that kind of world, does that society, and do those kinds of people sound familiar? We have progressed a great deal from the society of Noah's day, but spiritually speaking mankind has learned nothing. Jesus warns us that it will always be so.

Our world is just like the world of Noah's day, which is another deathblow to the dream of postmillennialism. The days of Noah were not days of spiritual vitality, of revivals, and of mass conversions. The days of Noah were not days when the people of God dominated culture, commerce, and politics. They were not a golden age of earthly prosperity and peace for the church. The seed of the serpent was mighty in the earth. The days of Noah were characterized by gross wickedness, widespread apostasy, and terrible persecution—things of which Jesus has warned us already in this chapter.

Our day is especially one of carnal security and materialism. On the Lord's day people are eating and drinking and they are shopping: very few are in public worship, and even fewer are worshiping in a true church where the gospel is faithfully preached. Most in our western, industrialized nations are living as if God did not exist. God is not in their thoughts, and they have done their utmost to suppress what knowledge of him they do have. When you tell them about Jesus Christ and his coming, about salvation and the forgiveness of sins in his blood, they wave the hand as if they do not care, for they would rather be eating and drinking. Or they scoff. Their attitude is described by Peter: "Knowing this first, that there shall come in the last days scoffers, walking after their own lusts, and saying, Where is the promise of his coming? for since the fathers fell asleep, all things continue as they were from the beginning of the creation" (2 Pet. 3:3–4).

What about us? Are we eating and drinking, marrying, buying and selling, building and planting? Of course, these things are part of our lives on earth and they must be. God has given us the good things of this creation lawfully to enjoy: "Every creature of God is good, and nothing to be refused, if it be received with thanksgiving: for it is sanctified by the word of God and prayer" (1 Tim. 4:4–5).

We must examine ourselves. Is God in our thoughts as we eat and drink, play and work, and plan for the future? Is God *first* in our thoughts in all these things? Is God in our thoughts as we worship him? What about our marrying and giving in marriage? Is God first in our dating and in our choosing a mate? Are we dating, and are we teaching our children and young people that the goal in dating is not having a good time, but marriage? When we date or plan marriage, do we seek a godly spouse, one who believes the scriptures, the gospel and the doctrines that we believe? Do we pray together and do we read scripture together? Do not date anyone, and certainly do not marry someone, with whom you cannot pray and with whom you are not spiritually united. Remember, it was intermarriage between the sons of God (professing believers) and the daughters of men (the unbelieving world) that led to the corruption and apostasy of the church and the ultimate destruction of the old world.

The Sudden Judgment

There is something tragic, solemn, and pathetic about verse Matthew 24:39: "[they] knew not..." That is Christ's assessment—they were spiritually clueless about what was coming. The idea is that the flood took the men of Noah's day, the fire and brimstone took the men of Lot's day, and the coming of Christ in judgment will take the men of our day completely by surprise.

When God determined that mankind had one hundred twenty years left before judgment would fall, they knew not. When Enoch and then Noah preached righteousness, they knew not. When Noah and his sons patiently built an ark to preserve themselves in the floodwaters, they knew not. When seven days before the flood the animals came to Noah, and Noah entered into the ark, and God shut the door, they knew not. They went on eating and drinking, marrying and giving in marriage, buying and selling, planting and building, and harvesting and grinding grain until the flood came. Up to that point, they knew not.

Tragically, the men of Noah's day "knew not" until the windows of heaven opened and the fountains of the great deep were broken up. Then they knew, but it was too late. The same will be in the future—the vast majority will not know until Christ actually comes: they will be completely surprised. The first they will know of his coming will be when they actually see him on the clouds of heaven. Then they will mourn, and they will wail tragic, bitter cries of horror and despair. It will be too late—the door of salvation will be shut. The time to repent and believe, the time to seek the Lord, and the time to cry out for mercy is now!

How could they not know, and how is it possible that men today do not know? The antediluvians, that is, the men before the flood, knew. They were the descendants of Cain, the first-born, wicked, reprobate son of Adam and Eve. If Enoch was seventh from Adam (Jude 14), Noah was tenth from Adam. In their generations the antediluvians had known God, but they hated God, for they belonged to the seed of the serpent, and they opposed the seed of the woman. They knew that God was holy and righteous, for they had heard the preaching of Enoch and Noah, and they had the witness of Noah's ark building, but they imagined that God would tolerate their high-handed rebellion forever. They promised themselves victory. The words of 1 Thessalonians 5 are true of them:

1. But of the times and the seasons, brethren, ye have no need that I write unto you.
2. For yourselves know perfectly that the day of the Lord so cometh as a thief in the night.
3. For when they shall say, Peace and safety; then sudden destruction cometh upon them, as travail upon a woman with child; and they shall not escape.

4. But ye, brethren, are not in darkness, that that day should overtake you as a thief.

5. Ye are all the children of light, and the children of the day: we are not of the night, nor of darkness.

6. Therefore let us not sleep, as do others; but let us watch and be sober. (vv. 1–6)

Their ignorance, then, was the willful, deliberate ignorance of unbelief, a kind of spiritual madness. That is the same ignorance we confront today: God has not left himself without a witness; those who perish have been left with no excuse. The men of Noah's day had the witness of God in their generations as well as the witness of godly Noah. We have the witness of God through two thousand years of church history, a completed Bible, and the gospel preached in the entire world. But what does man do with this knowledge? He scoffs and he denies the very existence of God. Therefore, he will not know until either God opens his heart or he sees Christ coming in judgment.

The destruction was swift and terrible ("the flood came, and took them all away" [Matt. 24:39]). The destruction came in the form of a flood of waters, which drowned all men outside the ark and swept the men of Noah's day into hell. Notice the universal nature of this judgment: took them *all* away. The flood was a worldwide, catastrophic, cataclysmic, devastating judgment that swept away every man, woman, and child alive except Noah and his family. Similar was the judgment on Sodom and Gomorrah: "The same day that Lot went out of Sodom it rained fire and brimstone from heaven, and destroyed them all" (Luke 17:29).

The difference between Sodom and the antediluvians was this: Sodom received no warning, no preacher of righteousness. Only Lot was present, and he was terribly compromised in his witness by living in Sodom. But even the Sodomites knew that there was a God and that their lives were displeasing to him.

The future judgment will be swift and terrible ("so shall also the coming of the Son of man be" [Matt. 24:39]). This time, as 2 Peter 3 explains, the judgment will not be by water, but by fire. The entire universe will be burned up, and the elements will melt with a fervent heat. Out of those melted elements, God will form the new creation. Despite the warnings, despite the signs, all is explained away and denied. The majority of men will be swept away by that fiery judgment into the everlasting fires of hell. There will be no escape—as the flood took away all the wicked, and as fire and brimstone destroyed all the Sodomites, so the judgment of Christ will destroy all unbelievers:

> 7. And to you who are troubled rest with us, when the Lord Jesus shall be revealed from heaven with his mighty angels,
> 8. In flaming fire taking vengeance on them that know not God, and that obey not the gospel of our Lord Jesus Christ:
> 9. Who shall be punished with everlasting destruction from the presence of the Lord, and from the glory of his power;
> 10. When he shall come to be glorified in his saints, and to be admired in all them that believe (because our testimony among you was believed) in that day. (2 Thess. 1:7–10)

The judgment of God will take people unawares. They will be eating and drinking, marrying and giving in marriage, buying and selling, planting and building, working in the fields or at the mill, when suddenly they are taken in judgment. "One shall be taken, and the other left" (Matt. 24:40–41).

It is common for premillennial dispensationalists to appeal to verses 40–41 for proof of their rapture doctrine. That doctrine is this: before antichrist appears and the great tribulation occurs, true believers will be snatched away to heaven to escape the judgments described in Matthew 24 and in the book of Revelation. This rapture will happen at a secret, invisible coming of Christ, for Christ will come in silence, believers will disappear, the world will descend into chaos, and antichrist will arise to offer solutions in the panic.

One day, so the argument, two will be in a field, working side by side: the believer will be taken to heaven, and the unbeliever will be left behind. Two women will be working at the mill, and the believer will be taken to heaven, while the unbeliever is left behind. Two will be in one bed, and the believer will be taken to heaven, while the unbeliever is left behind. The famous series of novels called the Left Behind books, written by Tim LaHaye and Jerry B. Jenkins, are based on these verses.[1]

Although such a view might seem plausible, it is false, because that interpretation ignores the context. Thus the Left Behind explanation fails.

First, the Left Behind explanation has it backward: the one taken in the context of verse 39 is the one taken in judgment, while the one left behind is preserved in Christ. Noah was left behind because he was kept safe in the ark; the antediluvians were taken in the flood. Therefore, we want to be "left behind," for to be "taken" is not to escape God's judgments by a rapture but to be swept away in God's fierce wrath!

Second, Jesus warns that this will all take place at his

---

1 Tim Lahaye and Jerry B. Jenkins, *Left Behind: A Novel of the Earth's Last Days* (Carol Stream, IL: Tyndale House, 1995) is the first of a series of sixteen novels published between 1995 and 2007.

coming, not in a secret rapture before his visible coming. Matthew 24 knows *nothing* about a secret, invisible, silent coming. The coming in Matthew 24 will take place immediately after the (great) tribulation at the end of the world, not seven years before his coming.

Third, there are three words for Christ's coming in the New Testament: the first is *parousia* (presence or arrival), the second is *apocalypse* (unveiling, uncovering, or revelation) and the third is *epiphany* (manifestation or appearance). The three words are used interchangeably in the New Testament. *Parousia* is used both here and in verses 3 and 27. This has nothing to do with a secret, invisible rapture![2]

The solemn truth is not that there will be a premillennial, dispensational rapture, but that judgment day will bring final separation between believers and unbelievers. On that fearful day, two people will be working side by side. One will be ready to meet the Lord, but the other, an unbeliever, will be taken. The wheat and the tares must grow together until the harvest, but on the judgment day, the angels will take away the tares *first* (Matt. 13:41). What an awful day that will be for the wicked! They will not escape.

---

2 The New Testament writers employ three main Greek words to describe the coming of the Lord, and they use them interchangeably. All attempts, especially by premillennial dispensationalists, to make out of these different words multiple future comings of Christ fail. *Parousia* (coming or arrival) appears in the following passages: Matthew 24:3, 27, 37, 39; 1 Corinthians 15:23; 1 Thessalonians 2:19; 3:13; 4:15; 5:23; 2 Thessalonians 2:1, 8; James 5:7–8; 2 Peter 3:4, 12; 1 John 2:28. In addition, there are also non-technical uses of *parousia* referring to the coming or arrival of others than the Lord Jesus (1 Cor. 16:17; 2 Cor. 7:6–7; 10:10; Phil. 1:26, 2:12; 2 Thess. 2:9). *Epiphaneia* (appearing or epiphany) appears in the following passages: 2 Thessalonians 2:8; 1 Timothy 6:14; 2 Timothy 4:1, 8; Titus 2:13. *Apocalypsis* (revelation or apocalypse) appears in the following passages: Luke 17:30; 1 Corinthians 1:7; 2 Thessalonians 1:7; 1 Peter 1:7, 13; 4:13.

The Calling to Watch

The calling in light of all this is to watch: "Watch therefore" (Matt. 24:42). To watch is to pay attention or to be alert. The men of Noah's day were not watching: they ignored all the warnings. They were indulging their flesh; spiritually they were asleep, indeed dead. But Christ commands us to watch, to look for signs, and to interpret the signs as tokens of Christ's promise. Each natural disaster, each war, each false teacher, each example of abounding iniquity, and each example of persecution is another footstep of Jesus Christ. As he approaches, the footsteps get heavier, louder, and more frequent.

We watch by standing against the materialism of our modern society, by praying, by studying the word, and by active, lively membership in a true church. We watch together, so that we encourage one another when we become spiritually drowsy. We watch, exactly because we do not know when Christ shall come. Noah did not know when the flood would come. Noah was told to prepare—God waited for Noah to build the ark (1 Pet. 3:20), and then seven days prior to the flood, Noah entered the ark at God's command. We do not even have seven days' notice: we certainly cannot calculate the date based on the seven days in Genesis 7:4, which Harold Camping attempted without success. We know Christ is coming. He has said so, and we know what signs to watch for, but watching is still important, because we do not know the time.

We do not fear the second coming, because it is the coming of our Lord ("ye know not what hour your Lord doth come" [Matt. 24:42]). As our Lord, Christ has purchased us with his own precious blood. Therefore, the one who loves us is coming for us. He is not coming to destroy us. Will he destroy those for whom he died? Of course not! Instead, he is coming to bring us to himself, for we cannot receive our complete salvation until we are glorified body and soul. That cannot happen until God has finished his purpose with the wicked and until all the elect have been gathered. *Then* he will come, for there is no delay.

Watch! Christ is coming. Let us not be found sleeping when he returns, but looking for his return. Let that watchfulness begin today if it has not been our habit before, so whether he comes on the clouds or calls us in death, we will be ready to meet him.

Come Lord Jesus, yea, come quickly.

♠

Chapter 14

UNPREPARED
FOR THE
THIEF

But know this, that if the goodman of the house had known in what watch the thief would come, he would have watched, and would not have suffered his house to be broken up. Therefore be ye also ready: for in such an hour as ye think not the Son of man cometh.—Matthew 24:43–44

The theme of the latter part of Matthew 24 and of Matthew 25 is preparedness. That preparedness or that state of constant readiness is necessary. It is necessary because of the unknown time of Christ's return. It is necessary because of the consequences of unpreparedness. Many, the majority, are unprepared for Christ's return. This was the case in Noah's day: "They…knew not until the flood came" (24:38–39). This will be the case with every person who dies in unbelief. This will be the case when Christ finally returns. In order to underline the seriousness of unpreparedness, Christ likens his coming to a thief.

Are we prepared for the thief, who, when he comes, will take everything the unprepared man possesses and leave him penniless, broken, and ashamed?

The Thief's Coming

It is vital that we do not overinterpret the illustration of a thief. Christ is not like a thief *in every respect*. Too many Bible interpreters miss this vital point and allow their imaginations to run wild. Do not be tempted to think abstractly about a thief or a burglar, and then to think in how many ways Christ could conceivably be like a thief. To do so would lead to absurdity. Christ is like a thief in one respect—in his coming, *only* in his coming. This is clear from all the passages in which Christ is likened to a thief: "Yourselves know perfectly that the day of the Lord so cometh as a thief in the night. Ye, brethren, are not in darkness, that that day should overtake you as a thief" (1 Thess. 5:2, 4). "The day of the Lord will come as a thief in the night; in the which the heavens shall pass away with a great noise, and the elements shall melt with fervent heat, the earth also and the works that are therein shall be burned up" (2 Pet. 3:10). "Remember therefore how thou hast received and heard, and hold fast, and repent. If therefore thou shalt not watch, I will come on thee as a thief, and thou shalt not know what hour I will come upon thee" (Rev. 3:3). "Behold, I come as a thief. Blessed is he that watcheth, and keepeth his garments, lest he walk naked, and they see his shame" (16:15).

Christ's coming is like a thief in two respects, both taken directly from Matthew 24:43–44.

First, Christ comes suddenly, unexpectedly, and without warning. No thief takes out an advertisement in the local newspaper that reads, "Dear householder, I intend to burgle your house on Thursday evening at ten o'clock. Kindly leave your valuables on display and your window open. Signed, the thief." Thieves do not want to be detected, so they sneak in, steal, and leave. The first time you know that you have been burgled is when you return home, or you wake up the next morning to discover your valuables gone.

Second, the one upon whom Christ comes unexpectedly suffers loss. Thieves are not welcome, because they do not come to do you good. They are not friendly elves who clean your houses while you sleep. They are not tooth fairies who leave money under your pillows. They steal and leave you poorer. The point of the illustration is not that Christ steals, for he is not a thief in that sense. The point of the illustration is to underline the danger of being unprepared when a thief comes. The unprepared man will suffer the loss of his valuables.

The thief, who is Christ according to his own illustration, does not come secretly in the sense of a secret rapture. It is not that Christ sneaks into the world, steals away the Christians, and leaves silently. That is not the point of the illustration either, for Christ's coming in view here is not the secret, silent, pretribulational rapture, but his glorious second coming. That is clear from the context of Matthew 24 and 25, as well as other passages, such as 2 Peter 3:10: "The day of the Lord will come as a thief in the night, in the which the heavens shall pass away with a great noise." Certainly, the dissolution of the entire universe is incompatible with a so-called secret rapture!

Christ's coming as a thief brings "sudden destruction" upon the wicked (1 Thess. 5:3), which is the same coming as when Christ descends with a shout (4:16). Thus the rapture theory falls apart again under exegetical scrutiny.

Christ makes the point that the *fact* that Christ is coming as a thief is known, but the *exact moment* of his coming is unknown. Matthew 24:43 does not say, "If the goodman of the house had known that the thief would come," but it says, "If the goodman of the house had known *in what watch* the thief would come" (emphasis added). The knowledge of the goodman in verse 43 was limited, but he knew something. The goodman is the householder, the owner, or the manager of the house, who is responsible for everything in the house, including the security. The householder knew there was a good possibility the thief would come during the night. Perhaps he had heard or seen signs of the thief's activity, or he had received a tip-off. However, there was one important detail that the householder did not know. He did not know *in what watch* the thief would come.

In former days the night was divided into four watches. Mark 13:35 identifies the four watches as "even" (6:00 p.m. to 9:00 p.m.), "midnight" (9:00 p.m. to 12 midnight), "the cock-crowing" (12 midnight to 3:00 a.m.), and "morning" (3:00 a.m. to 6:00 a.m.). Therefore, if Jesus walked on water during "the fourth watch" (Matt. 14:25), that was between three o'clock and six o'clock in the morning. These time periods are called watches because during night watches watchmen watched, and at the end of each watch, the watchmen changed shifts (Judges 7:19).

Nevertheless, the householder, although he knew that burglaries usually happened at night, did not know in which of the four watches the thief would come. If he had known, he would have watched. He did not know, so he did not watch.

We are like the goodman of the house in Christ's illustration. We know that the thief, Christ, is coming and that his coming will be sudden. Christ (and here the illustration reaches its limit) has told us that he is coming again and that when he comes many will suffer loss, because they will be overtaken by him, just as a thief catches a sleeping householder by surprise. But he has not told us *when* he will come, and we will not receive a prior warning some years, months, or days before the event. Notwithstanding, we have no excuses, because we know the signs to anticipate: signs in nature, among the nations, and in the church that indicate that Christ is on the way.

Harold Camping appealed to 1 Thessalonians 5:4 to support his thesis that Christians must know the time of Christ's coming. Camping insisted that Christ would come as a thief only on the ungodly and unbelieving world, but that that day would not come upon us as a thief. However, Camping's conclusion was flawed, because the reason Christ does not come upon us as a thief is not that we know something that the ungodly do not know (we know the day and the hour), but because we will be watching and they will be sleeping. The difference is between those who do not know the hour and therefore do not watch, but sleep and get drunk; and those who do not know the hour and do watch.

The Householder's Unpreparedness

The householder knew the thief was coming. Therefore, he knew or ought to have known that his valuables would be at risk. However, because he did not know in which watch the thief would come, he did not watch at all.

Christ describes for us a foolish, negligent, and lazy householder. There were twelve hours from the beginning of the first watch (6:00 p.m.) to the end of the fourth watch (6:00 a.m.), but the householder could not and did not stay awake. Perhaps he believed that the thief would not come that night but on another night. He imagined he had more time. Perhaps he believed that his house was well defended against thieves, for no thief, he imagined, could break into *his* house. Perhaps his neighbors' houses were at risk but not his ("When they shall say,

Peace and safety; then sudden destruction cometh upon them" [1 Thess. 5:3]). Perhaps he believed that it would do no harm to sleep because he was a light sleeper, and surely he would wake up in time to catch the thief before he could steal.

Moreover, Christ does not describe the rank unbelieving householder, who really knows almost nothing about the coming of Christ, but the hypocrite in the visible church. That is really the context of the Olivet Discourse: the foolish householder, the evil servant in Matthew 24:48, the foolish virgins and the slothful servant in chapter 25, and even the goats on the day of judgment are hypocrites in the visible church. They know something about the coming of the Lord, but they do not watch. They have heard about Christ, they have heard the call to repent and believe, and they even appear to belong to Christ for a time. But like all hypocrites in the church, this householder imagines that he can watch later, that he has time enough to care for his soul. Thus the Lord comes suddenly upon him ("in such an hour as ye think not" [Matt. 24:44]).

Unpreparedness is the attitude of many, certainly those in the world, but also many in the church. Paul describes them in 1 Thessalonians 5, where he makes extensive use of the figure of a thief. The thief comes in the night, when those who are of the night or of the darkness are not watching.

Night, in every culture, is the time when sin abounds, when men and women indulge their passions, and when drunkenness increases. Sinners, says Paul, are in their element at night: they sleep, they are drunk, but they do not watch; and the more drunk they become, the less they watch. Life, says the world, is a party. Life is too short for watching, the reasoning goes, or for being alert, so enjoy it.

The reasons for the world's unpreparedness are many, but fundamentally the reason is unbelief. Unbelievers simply do not expect the Lord to come. They imagine that what the church has been preaching for two thousand years is nonsense. Therefore, they mock, they scoff, and they go back to their pleasures. Moreover, the longer the Lord delays his coming, the less likely they are to watch. Perhaps the householder began to watch, but he became bored or disillusioned, and the temptations of sin were too great. So in the midst of his sleeping, when the householder should have been watching, the Lord returns. Thus the thief arrives and catches him unprepared, unready, vulnerable to attack, and easy pickings for the thief.

Implied in Christ's illustration, and explicit in 1 Thessalonians 5, is the truth that not all householders are foolish, negligent, and lazy. Some watch and are ready. So must we be. That is how Jesus sums up his teaching in Matthew 24: "Be ye also ready." Notice the reason Christ gives for the need to be ready: "For in such an hour as ye think not the Son of man cometh" (v. 44). No householder, no matter how wise and watchful he is, knows in which of the four watches of the night the thief will come.

Suppose the householder *did* know that the thief would come in the fourth watch, that is, between three and six o'clock in the morning. What will he be tempted to do? He will be tempted to fall asleep and plan to wake up at two thirty, so that he is ready for the fourth watch. But that is not the Lord's will for us: we must be awake not for one or two or three of the four watches, but for them all. We must be like a wise householder, sitting with his eye on the door for the entire night. There can be no taking forty winks, because at the moment we think not, the Lord might arrive.

Watchfulness is a spiritual state of constant readiness so that whether the Lord returns or calls us away in death, we are prepared to meet him. Readiness implies, first, repentance and faith. We believe, and believe daily, on the crucified and risen Jesus Christ. We trust in him, casting off confidence in all other would-be saviors. Only a believer is ready to meet Christ and only a believer is ready to die. Readiness also means living in close communion with Christ. The Christian ready to meet the Savior is one who spends time in prayer and the word, who attends the means of grace, especially the preaching, who does not walk in sin, and who daily turns from sin to the Lord. The Christian, to use the words of Revelation 16:15, keeps his garments. He does not allow his Christian profession to be spotted, spoiled, and defiled by the world. When Christ returns we do not want to be found in some shameful activity of the darkness. We are the children of light, and we walk in the light.

The Loss Suffered

The loss that the foolish, negligent, and lazy householder faced was that "his house [was] broken up" (Matt. 24:43). The householder slept soundly, securely, but when he woke up the next morning, his valuables were gone. He had been burgled! Christ makes clear that he was responsible for his own loss: "he suffered [by his own foolishness, negligence, and laziness] his house to be broken up." He allowed it to happen. He did nothing to prevent it, although he could have prevented it. If only he had watched, the thief could have been stopped. The next morning the householder looked at the ransacked and destroyed house and discovered that precious possessions were gone, and he mourned and lamented his foolishness.

Spiritually, that will happen to the wicked when Christ returns. Their house will be broken up. They will lose everything, for Christ will take it all; not because he is a thief, but perhaps we could change the figure slightly. He is a bailiff, one who comes to confiscate the belongings of a man who is in debt. The point is that when Christ returns, that foolish, negligent, lazy householder will lose his life, his soul, his possessions, his family, his friends—everything! That man will be cast body and soul into hell, where he will have occasion to lament his foolishness forever! What a frightful warning, and yet how few are watching.

Nevertheless, we have this great hope. Watchful householders will suffer no loss. They will be richly rewarded. Perhaps there were times during that long vigil from six o'clock in the evening to six o'clock in the morning when they were tempted to stop watching. The devil came to them and said, "Why are you watching? There is time. Look at what the world is doing. Why not join them instead of wasting your time watching? You are missing out on all the fun." Worldly friends and relatives came too: "What a fool you are, sitting up all night watching. Your Jesus will not come. You do not need to worry. Join us at the party." Have you felt that pressure: why must I watch, pray, read my Bible, worship the Lord, and say no to so many things my flesh desires? Is there any point?

Nevertheless, by God's grace, we watch as the psalmist: "My soul waiteth for the Lord more than they that watch for the morning: I say, more than they that watch for the morning" (Ps. 130:6). Everything I have is his, for he has purchased me body and soul on the cross. He does not come to steal from me. He comes to take me from my little house here below, which I have guarded and kept for him, to his Father's house above.

When he comes, I will be glad that I watched. It will be worth it.

Chapter 15

WATCHING AS SERVANTS WITH RESPONSIBILITIES

Who then is a faithful and wise servant, whom his lord hath made ruler over his household, to give them meat in due season? Blessed is that servant, whom his lord when he cometh shall find so doing. Verily I say unto you, That he shall make him ruler over all his goods. But and if that evil servant shall say in his heart, My lord delayeth his coming; and shall begin to smite his fellow-servants, and to eat and drink with the drunken; the lord of that servant shall come in a day when he looketh not for him, and in an hour that he is not aware of, and shall cut him asunder, and appoint him his portion with the hypocrites: there shall be weeping and gnashing of teeth.—Matthew 24:45–51

In this parable Jesus contrasts two kinds of servants in the visible manifestation of the kingdom of God, the church, and he warns us not to be evil servants, but to be faithful and wise. This parable is another application of the truth that Christ taught in verse 36: "of that day and hour knoweth no man." That was true of Noah's contemporaries. They did not know until the flood came. Watch, therefore, for no man knows the day or the hour! That was true of the foolish householder, who did not know in which of the four watches of the night the thief would come. Watch, therefore, for no man knows the day or the hour! That is true of this parable. Neither the faithful and wise servant nor the evil servant knew when the Lord would return, but one served the Lord diligently, while the other indulged his lusts.

Watch, therefore, for no man knows the day or the hour!

The Responsibilities They Had

In the parable Jesus describes two kinds of servants or slaves. These two men are not simply employees. They are slaves. A slave belongs to his master, who has bought him and therefore has complete authority over him. A slave, strictly speaking, does not belong to himself: his time, gifts, and resources belong to the master and must be used in the master's service to promote the master's name and wealth. The slave in the parable is a particular kind of slave, a high-ranking slave, one who has been placed in a position of authority above other slaves. He is in a position such as Joseph was in Genesis 39:4–6:

4. And Joseph found grace in his sight, and he served him: and he made him overseer over his house, and all that he had he put into his hand.

5. And it came to pass from the time that he had made him overseer in his house, and over all that he had, that the LORD blessed the Egyptian's house for Joseph's sake; and the blessing of the LORD was upon all that he had in the house, and in the field.

6. And he left all that he had in Joseph's hand; and he knew not aught he had, save the bread which he did eat. And Joseph was a goodly person, and well favoured.

The steward determines the daily running of the household, he works out duty rosters, and he organizes the budget. However, at the end of the day he is a steward: everything belongs to the master. Part of the duties of this high-ranking slave is to give meat to the other servants: he must feed, clothe, and generally take care of those under him. He does not have the liberty to take the master's goods and do what he wants with them. Instead, he must work for the good of his master and of the other servants or slaves. The slave must be careful, because he must give account to the master when he returns.

The slaves in the text are people who profess to belong to Jesus Christ and who have positions of authority in the visible church and the kingdom of God. First, Christ refers to office-bearers: ministers, elders, and deacons who occupy positions of leadership and authority in the church. The pastor must give meat to the other servants in due season; he must be diligent in his study of the word of God. He must feed the sheep and lambs of Christ's flock. With the pastor come the elders and deacons, who together form the council. They together, especially the elders, lead the church in the way of God's word. The first application of this is to the twelve disciples on the Mount of Olives listening to Jesus, but it really refers to all officebearers in the church of all ages.

We must not end the application there, because all of us are servants of God. All who profess to believe in Jesus Christ and are members of the church and kingdom are called to serve. Husbands and fathers are called by Christ to lead their wives and children, to give them meat in due season. They must provide, by diligent labor outside the home, for their families; and they must lead them in the ways of God's word. That is a heavy responsibility. Wives are called by Christ to serve in the home, and if they are mothers they are called to feed, nourish, and instruct their children in God's word.

This calling comes to every member, young and old. Serve Christ! Serve him in your home. Serve him at school and university. Serve him in the church. Serve him in the workplace. All your time and resources belong to him.

Nevertheless, says Christ, as the church and kingdom appear in history, there are two kinds of servants or slaves: the faithful and wise (Matt. 24:45) and the evil (v. 48). The faithful and wise servant does his master's will. When the Lord makes the faithful and wise servant ruler over his household, the servant considers this a great privilege and an awesome responsibility. Christ gave us all responsibilities and entrusted us all with tasks to do and service to perform. Therefore, we must be busy in them until he returns or until he calls us home.

Christ will not be pleased if, instead of serving him, we spend our days staring into heaven wondering when he will return. It is good to long for the return of Christ, but it is very wrong to become so speculative that we do nothing useful. Some people are like that: they spend their time speculating about signs or useless questions but are idle busybodies who neglect their calling in this world. Let us be in the kingdom doing the Lord's work.

To be faithful and wise servants we must be busy. Every Christian must be busy. The faithful pastor must work: he must spend his days studying the scriptures, not in idle speculation, so that he can feed the flock entrusted to him by preaching and teaching the wholesome doctrines of God's word. The faithful elders and deacons must be busy, serving the church, ruling, and showing mercy to the poor and miserable. Faithful husbands and fathers must be busy working at a calling and then leading their wives and children. Faithful wives and mothers must be busy at home, cleaning, cooking, and serving their husbands and children. Faithful children and young people must be busy helping their parents and siblings and doing their school or university work.

They do this, and we do this, because they, and we, are faithful and wise. A faithful person is dependable, trustworthy, and reliable. He does what he says he would do when he said he would do it. He is not constantly late, not constantly making excuses. Moreover, he is wise: he lives in accordance with reality. That is the difference between knowledge and wisdom. He knows that he is a steward who must give account and he lives in that consciousness. This man, spiritually, is prudent, sensible, a man you can trust, and a man worthy of having important responsibilities entrusted to him.

There is a second kind of servant, the opposite of the first, and he serves as a terrible warning to us all: he is "that evil servant" (v. 48). He is evil in that he lacks all the basic good qualities of the other servant. This man is unfaithful: he cannot be trusted, and, as we shall see, he proves unworthy of the great privileges and responsibilities laid upon him. This man is not busy in the Lord's service: he is lazy, idle, good for nothing, and base.

This man is also foolish, for he knows the Lord's will. He knows that the Lord will return. He knows he must give account. However, he does not live in that consciousness. For all that, he is a servant. Outwardly, he belongs to the household of servants, and he even gains a position of leadership above other servants. This servant therefore is no heathen, but a member of the visible church, even a baptized, confessing officebearer. If you ask him he will say, "I am a Christian." This servant is a minister, an elder, a deacon, or a professor in the theological school who is not wise, not faithful, but a hypocrite. This servant is a husband, a father, a wife, a mother, or a church member who claims to serve Christ but, deep down, has no interest in such service. He is a professing Christian who does not care that Christ is coming but who, for whatever reason, remains a member of the church.

The Service They Rendered

These two servants, one faithful and wise, the other evil and base, behave very differently in the absence of the master who has entrusted his household to them.

The wise servant gets to work as soon as he waves goodbye to his master. The faithful, wise servant organizes the lord's household for the master's good. He prepares good, nourishing meals for the other servants, and he makes sure they eat at the regular times ("in due season" [v.45]). He keeps his master's household in good order, careful to do nothing that will bring dishonor or shame on the good name and reputation of his master or will harm his master's profits. The wise servant does all this faithfully, diligently, gladly, and with a sense of his unworthiness, because he knows he works imperfectly.

This is a beautiful picture of the faithful, prudent Christian in his various offices and stations in life. The minister prepares a balanced diet for the people of God: he feeds them with sound doctrine; he applies the word to their hearts and lives; he teaches the children and young people; and he brings the word of God to the saints in their afflictions. The elders and deacons rule wisely, with a view to the glory of Christ, the Lord. Husbands, fathers, wives, mothers, and children fulfill their various callings in the workplace, home, and school with an eye on the return of Christ.

The faithful and wise servant does so because, quite simply, he is faithful and wise. However, this faithfulness, wisdom, and prudence are not natural to him, but fruits of grace, spiritual virtues worked in his heart. We must not think that some are faithful and wise by nature, that some merit a place in God's favor because of their faithfulness, wisdom, and prudence. By nature, we are all foolish: "For we ourselves also were sometimes foolish, disobedient, deceived, serving divers lusts and pleasures, living in malice and envy, hateful, and hating one another" (Titus 3:3).

Nor may we think that faithfulness, wisdom, and prudence are prerequisites or conditions the servant must fulfill to be or to remain a servant of Jesus Christ. Rather, Christ saved a faithless and foolish person, dying on the cross to pay for his faithlessness and folly and all his other sins. Faithfulness and wisdom are gifts of Christ worked in that servant's heart and life by the Holy Spirit sent by Christ. Because of Christ's love shown on the cross, the faithful and wise servant loves the Master and gratefully serves him out of love.

Therefore, it is no drudgery for this servant to be left in the house with these many tasks to perform. What would seem to be drudgery is a labor of love. The faithful and wise minister, elder, and deacon serve the church and serve Christ out of gratitude and love. The faithful and wise husband and father serves his family and his church out of gratitude and love. The faithful and wise wife and mother serves her husband and children out of gratitude and love. The world cannot understand that. The hypocrite in the church cannot understand that. We can understand it, because we know the love of Christ. It is an honor and a privilege to serve him.

The other servant, the evil, base servant, is really the opposite of this first servant. It would appear that the evil servant, as all hypocrites, makes a show of serving the Master at the beginning. Only gradually does he begin to show his evil character ("and shall begin to smite his fellow-servants, and to eat and drink with the drunken" [Matt. 24:49]).

There are servants like that in the visible church and kingdom of God. Some men start off as ministers, but the rigors of sermon preparation bore them. Their sermons are shallow at best, because they really make no effort. After a while they bring fluff and silly stories, because they could not be bothered. Such unfaithful men have no real interest in teaching the Bible. They neglect the preaching, catechism, Bible studies, and pastoral work. They would rather take it easy, and they stay in the church because they want to collect their salaries and pensions. Such are elders and deacons who do as little work as possible; such are husbands and fathers who are lazy and neglect their families; wives and mothers who prefer gossiping with the neighbors to cooking meals and looking after their children; students who do not study.

Neglecting their calling is one thing, but these evil servants go one step further: they abuse the privileges given to them when Christ made them rulers over his household. We have a saying about idle hands: idle hands are the devil's tools. The evil servant "smite[s] his fellowservants and eats and drinks with the drunken" (v. 49). He becomes a tyrant: instead of feeding and caring for his fellows, he beats them, he lords it over them, and he is violent toward any who get in his way. He is especially cruel and harsh toward that church member who dares say to him, "Pastor, your sermons are not faithful to the Bible," or "Brother, you are neglecting your calling as husband and father," or "Sister, you are neglecting your calling as wife and mother."

We have another saying: "When the cat's away, the mice will play." When Christ is away, the evil servant reveals his own evil heart: he really never had any interest in serving Christ.

Therefore, he will serve sin, and he will be found with the ungodly of this world, eating and drinking with the drunken!

Christ gives us the reason for this wicked behavior: "That evil servant shall say in his heart, My Lord delayeth his coming" (v. 48). That is the great temptation against which the parable warns us. The Lord has not returned; two thousand years have passed and Christ is still absent. The evil servant began to say, "My Lord is delayed. He is not coming soon, and perhaps he is never coming back. I can live it up. I can do what I want." We must never be tempted to use the perceived delay of Christ as an excuse to sin, an excuse to abuse our positions, or an excuse to live like this wicked world. We must never imagine, as this evil servant does, "My Lord delays his coming. There will always be time later to repent. I can serve the Lord later."

The deeper reason is that there is no love for the Lord in this servant's heart. He calls himself a servant, and he calls Christ his Lord, but he does not serve the Lord out of love and gratitude. He lacks those spiritual virtues of faithfulness and wisdom. He knows the Lord's will, for he knows the Lord is coming back, but he is a fool, and he does not live according to the reality of the Lord's return. He is a hypocrite. Christ is not really his master. Christ did not purchase him on the cross. He has no real interest in serving Christ, the Lord. Instead, he serves Christ only insofar as it suits him, for he loves himself.

The Reward They Received

The evil servant fools himself into thinking that the Lord's coming is in the distant future ("My lord delayeth his coming" [v. 48]). Nevertheless, the Lord returns sooner than he thinks and the evil servant is not ready to meet him. It is not as if the evil servant did not know. Christ left him with instructions, warning him of signs in the creation, the church, and the nations—things that must alert him that Christ is coming. So absorbed was the evil servant in the pleasures of the world and so drunken was he with his power that he failed to notice. "The lord of that servant shall come in a day when he looketh not for him" (v. 50). Why? He was *never* looking for him; he hoped he would never come. The lord of that servant will come in an hour that he is not aware of. Why? Because he was not watching and praying, not serving his master, but wasting his master's goods and abusing the position the master gave him. If any had said, "Sir, you know that the lord is coming back. We have heard rumors of his coming. There are indications that he is returning," the evil servant would have dismissed such words. He was enjoying himself too much to care.

Sadly, there are members of the church who are like that evil servant. They use the good things God gives, the things Christ has entrusted to them, to serve self and to serve sin. They know Christ is coming, but they do not care. They do not prepare, and they are taken by surprise when he finally appears. One moment they are enjoying life in the world while appearing religious enough to get by. The next moment Christ returns or summons them at their deaths.

Punishment from the Master falls swiftly, heavily, and justly upon that evil servant. Christ himself cuts that evil servant, that unfaithful pastor, elder, deacon, husband, father, wife, mother, or church member asunder. To cut asunder is to dichotomize, to cut into two pieces: the evil servant is cut into pieces by the sword or sawn in half in front of his Master. The word Christ uses could also mean to cut to pieces by scourging or to hack into pieces. Either way, he is put to death. Then that evil servant is thrown out of the Master's house and given the place with the hypocrites: he was a pretender; now his real character is revealed. Outside the Master's house is hell, endless misery with weeping and gnashing of teeth.

While the return of Christ brings endless misery upon the evil servant, the return of Christ brings happiness to the faithful and wise servant. The Lord returns to find the faithful and wise servant doing what he was commissioned to do ("Blessed is that servant, whom his lord when he cometh shall find so doing" [v. 46]). The Lord left him as ruler over his household to give meat to the other servants in due season. That is what he did! Consistently, faithfully, lovingly, gratefully, the faithful and wise servant has been serving the Master, always with an eye on the door, looking for Christ's return. When the faithful and wise servant has fallen into sin, he has sought forgiveness and trusted in the sacrifice the Lord made for him on the cross. That will be true of us by the grace of God: pastors will be found preaching and teaching, elders and deacons ruling and ministering to the poor, husbands and fathers working, wives and mothers caring for their families, and young people studying diligently. Why? Because by the grace of God that is what we are always doing!

The reward is promotion: "he shall make him ruler over all his goods" (v. 47). In a word, the reward is blessedness or happiness, the eternal bliss of heaven. In heaven, that faithful and wise servant will look back on the little, weak, seemingly insignificant service he performed, and with wonder he will say, "Lord, it was nothing. It was done in weakness and in sin. I am an unprofitable servant." That will be true of every faithful and wise pastor, elder, deacon, husband and father, wife and mother, and every faithful church member.

Christ will say, "Yes, my child; I know. But you are here because of me: because of my work for you, and now you have the privilege and high honor to serve me for all eternity. It pleases me to reward your service. Enter into the joy of your Lord."

Chapter 16

‹♦›

WATCHING
AS WISE VIRGINS

Then shall the kingdom of heaven be likened unto ten virgins, which took their lamps, and went forth to meet the bridegroom. And five of them were wise, and five were foolish. They that were foolish took their lamps, and took no oil with them: but the wise took oil in their vessels with their lamps. While the bridegroom tarried, they all slumbered and slept. And at midnight there was a cry made, Behold, the bridegroom cometh; go ye out to meet him. Then all those virgins arose, and trimmed their lamps. And the foolish said unto the wise, Give us of your oil; for our lamps are gone out. But the wise answered, saying, Not so; lest there be not enough for us and you: but go ye rather to them that sell, and buy for yourselves. And while they went to buy, the bridegroom came; and they that were ready went in with him to the marriage: and the door was shut. Afterward came also the other virgins, saying, Lord, Lord, open to us. But he answered and said, Verily I say unto you, I know you not. Watch therefore, for ye know neither the day nor the hour wherein the Son of man cometh.—Matthew 25:1–13

"Ye know neither the day nor the hour wherein the Son of man cometh" (Matt. 25:13). This has been the constant refrain in the latter part of the Olivet Discourse. We also read that in Matthew 24:36, 42, 44, and 50. To underline that truth, Jesus warned his people by means of parables. At the end of Matthew 24 the evil servant in the parable says in his heart, "My lord delayeth his coming," and is not ready when the master appears.

Matthew 25 contains two more parables, both of which warn us to watch and be ready, and it climaxes with a description, not so much a parable, of the final judgment. These parables have something very important to teach those who say they are members of Christ's church and citizens of Christ's kingdom. In these parables the warning is against hypocrisy or mere pretense. Hypocrisy takes many forms in the church, so Christ looks at hypocrisy from various angles. In this parable the hypocrite has no real spiritual life, just an empty claim; and in the next parable, the hypocrite brings forth no real spiritual service to the Lord.

This parable of the wise and foolish virgins is well known. Remember that its first application is not to the heathen outside the church, but to those inside the church. We know that because it begins with these words: "Then shall the kingdom of heaven be likened unto" (v. 1). In addition, let us once again be warned not to read too much into all the details, but to focus on the main idea or ideas of the parable. Let the foolish virgins be a warning to us as we seek to be like the wise virgins. This, then, is a description of the kingdom of heaven, which is the church.

Anticipating the Bridegroom

To understand the parable, we need some comprehension of the wedding customs of that day. The parable includes the various elements of Jewish wedding celebrations. The bridegroom, whose coming is anticipated, is the Lord Jesus Christ. In view of his coming, scripture often calls him the bridegroom or husband (Mark 2:19–20; John 3:29; 2 Cor. 11:2; Eph. 5:23–24) because he loves his church, he has died for his church, and he is preparing all things for the salvation of his church. Salvation is the marriage supper of the Lamb, where Jesus is the gracious host, and we are not only the blessed guests, but also the bride (Rev. 19:7–9; 21:2, 9–11). The bride, here represented by the wider bridal party consisting of ten virgins or bridesmaids, is the church. The bride, as such, is not even mentioned in the parable, but we must not read too much into that or try to distinguish between the bride proper and the bridal attendants or bridesmaids. The bride consists of those whom Christ loves, whom Christ has bought with his blood, called by his Spirit, and separated from sin and the world. Paul describes the church in 2 Corinthians 11:2: "I am jealous over you with godly jealousy: for I have espoused you to one husband, that I may present you as a chaste virgin to Christ."

The wedding festivities in the Bible focused not on the bride, but on the bridegroom. The Jewish wedding began with betrothal, which was like our engagement but much stricter and legally binding. When a man and woman were betrothed, they were legally married. Any infidelity was considered adultery. It was very difficult to break a betrothal. Mary and Joseph were betrothed, and Mary's becoming pregnant was a very serious problem for Joseph until the angel appeared to him. But a betrothed couple did not yet live together: "When as his mother Mary was espoused to Joseph, before they came together" (Matt. 1:18).

The actual coming together did not occur until the coming of the bridegroom. Until that day, the espoused bride would wait for his coming, and she must be faithful to him while she waited. On the day of the wedding, the bridegroom left his house and came to receive his bride. Both bride and groom were accompanied by attendants. The bridegroom and his attendants left his house; those accompanying him would be filled with joy and carry lights in a festive procession. The same day the bride left her parents' house and went to the house in which the married couple would live. She too was accompanied by joyful attendants.

When the bridegroom was near, a call would go out from one of the bridegroom's attendants, "Behold, the bridegroom cometh; go ye out to meet him" (Matt. 25:6). Then the bride's attendants would go out to meet him, holding their lighted lamps, and accompany him into the house to be with the bride and groom. After the coming together of bride and groom, the festivities would begin. Our modern weddings have lost some of that. Today it is, "Here comes the bride." Then it was, "Behold, the bridegroom cometh."

Jesus likens a wedding to a great spiritual reality. In so doing, he depicts the state of the professing church as she waits for the coming of the Lord. The ten virgins represent the church as the manifestation of the kingdom of God ("Then shall the kingdom of heaven be likened unto ten virgins" [v. 1]).

The description of the church and kingdom of heaven as ten virgins is significant. First, there are ten virgins, which is the number of completeness, for the Lord looks at the church as she manifests herself on earth at any given time in history. Second, they are virgins: a virgin is someone who is sexually pure, one who is devoted to one husband, and one who keeps herself separate from the world and the allures of Satan. There are not five wise virgins and five foolish harlots: there are ten virgins, which means they all profess to love Christ, all claim to be espoused to him, all claim to be devoted to him, and all claim to be virgins!

All ten virgins profess that it is their intention to go "forth to meet the bridegroom" (v. 1). We know this because all ten have lamps. Clearly, the lamp is significant, but the lamp is something common to all the virgins, both wise and foolish. Whether saved or lost in the church, all have lamps. The ungodly world do not even have lamps. The Muslim, the Hindu, or the atheist has no lamp, but every member of the visible church has a lamp. The lamp, then, is the outward profession of the church member. By having a lamp all the virgins proclaim, "We are waiting for the coming of the bridegroom. When he comes we will enjoy the heavenly wedding feast." Moreover, none of the virgins know *when* the bridegroom will return, and all of them fall asleep before he arrives.

The ten virgins look exactly alike. They all carry their lamps, they all call themselves virgins, and they are all members of the kingdom of God in an outward sense. Nevertheless, Christ shows that among the ten are two spiritually distinct kinds of virgins: five are wise and five are foolish.

Wisdom is not the same as intelligence, for wisdom is a spiritual gift. Wisdom is the right use or application of knowledge. It is to live in accordance with or in harmony with knowledge and reality. A wise person takes the fact that Christ is coming and adapts his life to that one great reality, and he lives and acts in that consciousness.

Wisdom is not natural to us because as fallen sinners we are naturally foolish. Wisdom is a grace worked in us by the Spirit of Jesus Christ. Foolishness, then, is the opposite of wisdom; it is not simply stupidity, but something sinful and wicked. Foolishness is to refuse to apply knowledge correctly; it is to live in a way that denies reality. A foolish person knows that Christ is coming, but he does not adapt his life to that truth and does not live in the consciousness of Christ's coming. A foolish person, for all his or her profession, does not have the Spirit of Christ and is an unbeliever. The five foolish virgins are unbelievers.

Prepared with Oil

The difference between the wise and foolish virgins lies in their preparedness in the form of oil. The oil here is pure olive oil used as fuel for lamps. All ten virgins have lamps, but not all ten have oil. To have a lamp without oil is to make an empty, hypocritical show of religion. A lamp can be made of pure gold, polished and admired by neighbors, friends, and family, but if there is no oil in it, it has no power and produces no light. The foolish virgins had just enough religion to please men, but there was no substance to their religion. It was vain, empty, and worthless. What Paul says in 2 Timothy 3:5 is true of the five foolish virgins: "[They had] a form of godliness, but [they denied] the power thereof."

The five wise virgins had lamps and "took oil in their vessels with their lamps" (Matt. 25:4). Oil in the Bible is often a symbol of the Holy Spirit, but here that does not quite fit, because one cannot *buy* the Holy Spirit. Oil here is an inner, spiritual, gracious preparedness that gives substance to the outward profession and empowers one to live according to that profession. This oil cannot be bought, and it cannot be earned, but we receive it freely from Christ as it flows to us by the Holy Spirit from his cross:

1. Ho, every one that thirsteth, come ye to the waters, and he that hath no money; come ye, buy, and eat; yea, come, buy wine and milk without money and without price.
2. Wherefore do ye spend money for that which is not bread? and your labour for that which satisfieth not? hearken diligently unto me, and eat ye that which is good, and let your soul delight itself in fatness. (Isa. 55:1–2)

The wise virgins have oil, but the foolish virgins have none. They bring none. Notice the difference: the foolish bring only lamps; the wise bring lamps, vessels, and oil in the vessels. It is not that the wise and foolish virgins both burn oil and then the foolish run out of oil at the last minute. No one burns the oil in the parable until they hear the cry, "Behold, the bridegroom cometh" (Matt. 25:6). There is no need to light the lamps until then. It is when they hear the cry that the wise take the oil from their prepared vessels; and the foolish, who have no vessels, are found to be without oil. The solemn fact is that the foolish never had any oil; they *never* had any spiritual life; they always were hypocrites, pretenders, or unbelievers in the visible church. Their lack of oil is only revealed when the bridegroom comes. That will be the day of exposure for hypocrites in the church.

The foolish virgins brought no oil because they assumed they would not need it, believing they could manage by using the oil of others. They deliberately neglected to bring oil, which makes them guilty of presumption. *We will get oil from the common stock*, they thought, but they were mistaken. That is why, when they heard the cry, "Behold, the bridegroom cometh," they turned to the wise virgins and said, "Give us of your oil; for our lamps are gone out" (v. 8). But there is no borrowing of spiritual graces from others. Each person must be prepared by himself or herself. You cannot borrow oil from the minister, from your spouse, from your parents, or from your children. You personally must be ready with oil, which you receive directly from Christ. You personally must repent and believe. The foolish virgins discovered that to their eternal cost.

This preparedness is necessary because of the delay of the bridegroom ("while the bridegroom tarried" [v. 5]). Two things are clear about the coming of Christ in scripture, especially in the Olivet Discourse: Christ comes quickly, and Christ tarries or delays his coming. Yet this is no contradiction. On the one hand, Christ comes quickly, as quickly as he can, in accordance with the eternal will and counsel of God. On the other hand, Christ tarries. He tarries not because he has been held up or delayed, but because much must be accomplished before he comes. Moreover, he only tarries or delays from our perspective; he merely *seems* to take a long time: "If that evil servant shall say in his heart, My lord delayeth his coming" (Matt. 24:48). "While the bridegroom tarried, they all slumbered and slept" (25:5). "After a long time the lord of those servants cometh, and reckoneth with them" (v. 19).

Christ has a purpose in tarrying or in seeming to delay his coming. It is a test. All ten virgins profess that they love the Lord and desire his coming, but how will they behave when he does not come when weddings usually begin, in the early evening, but waits until after midnight? We see that he delays so long that all the virgins fall asleep: it gets so dark and so late that they almost give up all hope that the bridegroom will come.

What will we do when the Lord delays his coming? Will we be like the evil servant in Matthew 24 and live in sin and be caught out and cut off? Will we be like the foolish, graceless virgins? Or will we remain ready with oil in our lamps like the wise virgins?

Concretely, what is this preparedness; what does it mean to have oil in the lamp? It means to live in daily anticipation of the second coming, so that one's great burning desire and the aim of one's whole life is the return of Jesus Christ. It means that we are watching—watching for any indication or any sign that Christ is coming. We are vitally interested in the signs listed in Matthew 24 and we look for them, as much as a bride is thrilled by every footstep of her coming bridegroom. It means that we believe in Christ, live a life of daily repentance, and pray fervently for the return of Jesus. We keep ourselves pure for our Husband. It means that our life is one of godliness, not a mere outward show of religion, but a life of thankful obedience from the heart. We who do that are ready to enter into the marriage.

Entering into the Marriage

At midnight a cry goes out, "Behold, the bridegroom cometh; go ye out to meet him" (Matt. 25:6), but the foolish virgins are not ready, so they are forever shut out. The final cry, "Behold, the bridegroom cometh," shakes all the virgins out of their slumber, but it is too late for the foolish virgins, who then notice their mistake. All ten virgins "trim" their lamps, but try as they might, the five foolish virgins cannot light their lamps. Again and again, they try to ignite a spark, but each time there is a dim flicker and the light goes out. Of course they cannot light their lamps: they have no oil; and without light they cannot join the festive procession that greets the bridegroom.

They turn in desperation to their five wise counterparts and ask to borrow some of their oil, but the wise virgins cannot help them: "The foolish said unto the wise, Give us of your oil; for our lamps are gone out. But the wise answered, saying, Not so; lest there be not enough for us and you: but go ye rather to them that sell, and buy for yourselves" (Matt. 25:8–9).

It is not that the wise virgins are mean and miserly: they *cannot* help them, because no one has more oil than is necessary for himself or herself. There is no extra grace, nothing that one can communicate to another. There is only one thing left to do: "Go ye rather to them that sell" (v. 9). So the foolish virgins go off into the night to look for someone who, at midnight, might sell them some oil for their lamps. We never find out whether the foolish virgins found someone to sell them oil at that late hour. We do not need to read too much into it. It is part of the story. We simply read that they came back after the bridegroom's coming.

Incredibly solemn is the conclusion. The foolish virgins return to find themselves shut outside the wedding feast. They said that they were waiting for the bridegroom and that they would join the festive procession to welcome him, but they were not ready. How could they have been ready? How could they have fooled themselves from the beginning: they brought no oil! There are people like that in the church. They go through the motions, but they do not truly believe. Therefore, they fool themselves that they will get the oil later. Without oil all they can do is to hold up dark lamps in the darkness!

Frantic, the five foolish virgins stand outside the closed door and beg to be let in, but the Lord's answer is final: "I know you not!" (v. 12). Those are terrifying words to hear from Christ on that day: "I do not know you." There will be many who were members of churches, who called themselves Christians, who will hear those words. "I know you not" means I do not have an intimate relationship of love with you; you are not part of that blessed number whom I love, for whom I died, and whom

I have saved. You do not belong with me—you belong outside! The virgins might cry, "Lord, Lord, open to us" (v. 11), but the Lord will not listen. "Lord, Lord, we were members of such-and-such a church; Lord, Lord, we sang, we prayed, we attended worship services, we were baptized, we did mighty works in thy name, we cast out devils in thy name" (Matt. 7:21–23). But the answer will be forever the same. "I know you not." Outside is weeping and gnashing of teeth (Luke 13:28; Matt. 8:12; 13:42; 22:13; 24:51; 25:30).

The five wise virgins enjoy great blessedness: "They that were ready went in with him to the marriage and the door was shut" (Matt. 25:10). They were ready. They were ready because, although their watching was not perfect because they too fell asleep, they remembered to bring oil. When the cry came they roused from sleep, trimmed their lamps, fed their lamps with oil, and held them aloft in the festive procession that welcomed the bridegroom. They had received the grace of God. They had believed in Jesus Christ. They had more than an outward profession. They had true spiritual life. Now they enter into the marriage supper of Christ not simply as guests, but as part of the bride. The blessedness is to enjoy the fellowship and joy of the Bridegroom, Jesus Christ. That is the essence of heaven—they went in with him. And the door was shut—to keep out the wicked and to show the security and eternal blessedness of heaven.

Given the dreadful consequences of being unprepared, and the wonderful blessedness of being prepared, Christ concludes the parable: "Watch therefore, for ye know neither the day nor the hour wherein the Son of man cometh" (v. 13). Watch, be alert, do not fall asleep. Pray, look for the coming of your Lord. Look for the signs of Christ's coming and keep oil in your lamps. In this way you too will be received into the eternal festivities of the wedding supper of Christ.

◆

Chapter 17

WATCHING AS FAITHFUL TALENT USERS

For the kingdom of heaven is as a man travelling into a far country, who called his own servants, and delivered unto them his goods. And unto one he gave five talents, to another two, and to another one; to every man according to his several ability; and straightway took his journey. Then he that had received the five talents went and traded with the same, and made them other five talents. And likewise he that had received two, he also gained other two. But he that had received one went and digged in the earth, and hid his lord's money. After a long time the lord of those servants cometh, and reckoneth with them. And so he that had received five talents came and brought other five talents, saying, Lord, thou deliveredst unto me five talents: behold, I have gained beside them five talents more. His lord said unto him, Well done, thou good and faithful servant: thou hast been faithful over a few things, I will make thee ruler over many things: enter thou into the joy of thy lord. He also that had received two talents came and said, Lord, thou deliveredst unto me two talents: behold, I have gained two other talents beside them. His lord said unto him, Well done, good and faithful servant; thou hast been faithful over a few things, I will make thee ruler over many things: enter thou into the joy of thy lord. Then he which had received the one talent came and said, Lord, I knew thee that thou art an hard man, reaping where thou hast not sown, and gathering where thou hast not strawed: and I was afraid, and went and hid thy talent in the earth: lo, there thou hast that is thine. His lord answered and said unto him, Thou wicked and slothful servant, thou knewest that I reap where I sowed not, and gather where I have not strawed: thou oughtest therefore to have put my money to the exchangers, and then at my coming I should have received mine own with usury. Take therefore the talent from him, and give it unto him which hath ten talents. For unto every one that hath shall be given, and he shall have abundance: but from him that hath not shall be taken away even that which he hath. And cast ye the unprofitable servant into outer darkness: there shall be weeping and gnashing of teeth.—Matthew 25:14–30

Some imagine that watching for the Lord's return is idle speculation. The apostle Paul had to counter that attitude among the Thessalonians. Some had given up working and became busybodies with nothing better to do than to wait idly for the Lord to return. Paul rebuked them sharply: he called them disorderly busybodies and warned, "If any [will] not work, neither shall he eat" (2 Thess. 3:10). In fact, idleness is characteristic of some who make foolish predictions about the Lord's return. Remember, for example, the Millerites in October 1844 and Harold Camping's followers in May 2011. We must therefore not get the wrong idea from the previous parable: the ten virgins did not sit twiddling their thumbs while they waited for the bridegroom. Watching does not mean idleness, as the parable of the talents proves.

The parable complements the parable of the wise and foolish virgins. Both parables depict the state of the professing church as she waits for Christ's return. Both the ten virgins and the three servants are a picture of professing Christians, meaning that this parable has immediate application to us in the church and not to the heathen world.

As with all parables, it is necessary to identify the main elements before we seek to give an interpretation and application to ourselves. The man traveling into a far country and returning is the Lord Jesus. The Lord, after his death and resurrection, ascended into heaven, where he is crowned with glory and honor by his Father. But he will return "after a long time" (Matt. 24:19) to judge. The three servants represent professing Christians in the visible church. They are slaves: they belong to, or at least profess to belong to, the Lord Jesus. They have been bought, or profess to have been bought, by the blood of the Lord. Thus they have the calling to serve the Lord with the Master's goods. Two servants are faithful users of the talents and one servant is a wicked, slothful neglector of the Master's talent. We must emulate the first two servants and avoid the evil example of the third.

Receiving the Master's Talents

The fundamental element in the parable is the talent. Everything centers on the talents, on the servants' receiving the talents, on the servants' doing something (or nothing) with the talents, and on the servants' giving account for how they used the talents. Fail to identify the talents and the parable becomes unintelligible. "Talent" is a transliteration of the Greek word *talanton*. However, words evolve in meaning. "Talent" in the parable is not what we have come to understand a talent to mean today.

In common language a talent is a gift or ability, whether natural or spiritual. This wrong explanation of "talent" not only makes the parable impossible to understand, but it also causes havoc in the church, for then men and women demand the right to use their "talents" in God's house. The young people are told that they have a particular gift for music or drama, and pressure is applied to allow the young people to use their gifts in the church: youth bands and sketches and skits come in, while the regulative principle of worship is abandoned. Or we hear the clamoring of women: "We have gifts of teaching and preaching; we have leadership gifts too. We must use our 'talents' in the church offices." If the church does not allow the use of such "talents" to young people and women and others, she is guilty of burying those talents in the earth, we are told.

But in this context "talent" cannot refer to natural or spiritual abilities; the parable forbids that interpretation. Verse 15 distinguishes between talents and ability. The Lord gives talents "according to his several ability." Therefore, the talent cannot be the ability. The parable also indicates that two of the servants double their number of talents, which cannot be done with natural or spiritual abilities. Therefore, we must understand talents to mean something other than abilities.

A biblical talent is not a natural or spiritual gift, but a sum of money (silver or gold) according to weight. Conservative estimates make a talent about 30 kilograms (or 66 pounds). "Talent" is used only here and in the parable of the unforgiving servant in Matthew 18, where a certain man is in terrible debt to the Lord. He owes ten thousand talents. That is not ten thousand different abilities such as novel writing, impressionist painting, shooting basketball hoops, and playing the violin. In the parable it is money, a debt of millions, and a picture of our debt of sin. Here too the three men in the parable receive a different number of talents: one receives five, another two, and a third one. These are, according to the parable, three different sums of money. Even one talent is a tidy sum.

Of course, ordinary money is not meant either. This is a parable. The talents are a picture of something else. The talents are opportunities, occasions, or positions in the kingdom, or spheres of labor and service given to every professing Christian in which he may serve God to the best of his ability.

One receives five talents: he has a prominent position, greater responsibility, greater authority, or greater opportunity of service than others. Christ gives him that position according to his ability. It is a position where he can exercise his gifts, but not a position where he is overburdened or overwhelmed. Another receives two talents: he has also an important place in the kingdom, somewhat less influential, a somewhat less prominent position, a narrower sphere of service perhaps. Christ wisely gives him fewer talents in accordance with his lesser ability, but still enough talents so that he can serve God to the fullness of his ability. The third receives one talent. He has the least ability. The Lord wisely sees that he could not cope with more than one talent, but one talent is certainly not to be despised. He has much opportunity to serve the Lord with one talent.

Pause and ask, who am I? Who are you? Are we five-talent servants, two-talent servants, one-talent servants, or somewhere in between? More importantly, what is our attitude to the talents we have received? If you are a five-talent servant, how do you behave toward the two-talent servant and the one-talent servant? Or if you are a one-talent servant, how do you behave toward the two- or five-talent servant?

Do you conduct yourself with pride and haughtiness? Do you boast of your five talents? Do you seek to flaunt your five talents in the face of the one-talent servant? Remember that we only have five talents, two talents, or one talent not because we earned them or merited them, but because Christ is pleased to give them. Listen to Paul when he writes, "Who maketh thee to differ from another? and what hast thou that thou didst not receive? now if thou didst receive it, why dost thou glory, as if thou hadst not received it?" (1 Cor. 4:7).

Do you view the two- or five-talent servants in the church with envy because you only have one talent? Are you satisfied to have only one talent, or do you grumble because the Lord did not give you the prominence that you think you deserve? Do you say to yourself, *Who is he or who is she, that he or she got five or two talents and I only got one talent?* Do you think to yourself, *This one talent cramps my style; it clips my wings. My gifts are not being recognized. If the Lord had given me more than one talent, I could do something with my life?* Then listen to the Lord: "Is it not lawful for me to do what I will with mine own? Is thine eye evil, because I am good?" (Matt. 20:15).

Do not question the Lord's wisdom. Matthew 25:15 explains that he has given you one talent, two talents, or five talents, according to your ability. These sins of pride on the one hand and envy on the other must be condemned. Every servant, whether he has five talents, two talents, or one talent, if he is a true servant of Christ, must be thankful. We are servants, that is all. We are not masters. We are not lords. All that we are and all that we have belongs to Jesus Christ.

Moreover, we are blood-bought servants. We have been delivered from the bondage and the tyranny of the devil and of our own sins. It is therefore a great honor and privilege to serve Christ. It ought to be our desire every moment to serve him who gave himself for us on the cross. We ought not look askance at others and at their many or few talents, but we ought to consider how we can use the talents or even one talent that God has given us.

Besides, it ought to weigh heavily with us that the Lord has entrusted us with some of his goods. Verse 14 says that he "called his own servants, and delivered unto them his goods." Remember that they are not your talents to do with whatever you please. They are his talents, and he only lends them to you; you must use them for his glory and to further his kingdom. They are not to give you a name or to enhance your reputation.

We cannot tell, though, whether we are a five-talent, two-talent, or one-talent kind of servant. Perhaps we will be surprised. Perhaps we think a minister laboring in a large congregation is a five-talent servant and we hardly have one talent. Perhaps a stay-at-home mother thinks that she has only one talent, but the day might reveal that she had five, while the minister or elder only had one. Do not think, either, that all the five-talent servants go to heaven, while all the one-talent servants go to hell. The issue is not how many talents you have at the beginning, but what you do with them. A man with only one quarter of a talent might surpass us all; a man with ten talents might squander the lot. There is a much wider range of possibilities not explicitly mentioned in the parable.

Trading for the Master's Advantage

In the parable two servants work diligently and faithfully. They lose no time in trading with their master's talents. They both see the trust that the master has given to them to be a great honor and a grave responsibility. Both men go to the markets and double their money. The five-talent servant is successful. Five talents become ten talents. The two-talent servant is successful too. He began with less capital, but he too doubles his money. Two talents become four talents.

These two men are representative for the sake of the story. Not all servants double their money. There are degrees of faithfulness, and all of our service is tainted with sin, for which we constantly go to the cross for forgiveness. Perhaps some five-talent servants only manage to gain an extra two, making seven talents out of their original five. Perhaps some two-talent servants only manage one extra talent, making three talents. Perhaps others even triple or quadruple their money. The point is that the servants did not steal or squander their Master's money. They entered into honest trading and gained a return.

We must aim to be like the five- or two-talent servants. We must trade with the Master's goods and receive a return for the Master while we wait for his coming. We do not literally go to the money markets. We are speaking of spiritual trading and spiritual gains for the Master. This means that God in his sovereignty and wisdom has placed each of us in various callings and stations of life. Some of us have five-talent positions, some two-talent positions, and some one-talent positions. God makes some husbands and fathers; some he makes wives and mothers; some he calls to serve him in single life, at least for a time. Others serve God in widowhood or childlessness. Others serve God as children or young people. Some are placed in long-term illnesses, and some are called to serve God in the weaknesses and limitations of old age. Some must even serve God in prison or in divinely imposed isolation. Some are officebearers, ministers, elders, deacons; some are theological professors or missionaries. Some are rich. Others are poor. Some have many opportunities.

Others have relatively few. Whatever we have, or whatever we perceive ourselves or others to have, our calling is to serve Christ in every area of life, to press everything into his service, and to gain for him a spiritual return on his investment.

The five-talent servant did not spend his time observing what the two-talent servant was doing: he was busy in his own sphere of activity and service, whether large or small. The same was true of the two-talent servant. He did not eye the five-talent servant with envy, nor did he behave toward the one-talent servant with pride, but he faithfully served his master with his master's money. That is our calling too: use Christ's talents; do not live idly, but be faithful.

This calling is underlined by the warning about the wicked and slothful servant, the one in the parable who received but one talent. He did not trade with the talent. He did nothing with it. He buried it and refused to use it. This, at first glance, might not appear to be such a terrible sin. After all, is it not better to be safe than sorry? Dare he risk investing the money and lose it?

Nevertheless, it was a terrible sin because it was disobedience. Clearly, at the beginning the servants understood that the master had given them talents for a purpose. The one-talent servant knew, as did the others, that what he had received was a sacred trust. If the master had wanted his money to lie idle in the ground, he could have buried it himself. But the reason for this servant's laziness is clear: he was dissatisfied with the one talent, especially as he saw how many talents the others received. Dissatisfied with only one talent and coveting more talents, he decided to do nothing with the one talent that the master gave him.

There are people like that in the church in every age. Dissatisfied with their one talent, they refuse to serve the Master in the position where he places them. They forget that God gave them only one talent for a reason: God sees in his wisdom that five talents or even two talents would be too great a burden for them. If such people were given the positions that they crave, they would harm the church, so it is best that they be left to serve in a position of relative obscurity, out of the limelight. However, that is not how they see it. Such disgruntled one-talent servants behave like Diotrephes: "I wrote unto the church: but Diotrephes, who loveth to have the preeminence among them, receiveth us not" (3 John 9).

The root of such an attitude is pride, the same pride that was the downfall of the devil himself, and the pride that will destroy anyone whom it masters. If the one-talent servant cannot be top dog, cannot be the five-talent servant, he will not serve at all. That is his dreadfully prideful attitude. The minister who is a one-talent servant feels himself slighted, because he never gets called to the larger and influential congregations. He refuses to work diligently among the little flock entrusted to him. The member who is never chosen to be elder or deacon feels slighted, so he refuses to do even the simplest of tasks in the church. Be a greeter? No way! Help hand out flyers? No! Help put out or put away chairs? Forget it!

In addition, idle one-talent servants who have buried their one talent invariably feel the need to criticize the other servants. If they cannot be the minister, the elder, or the deacon, they will undermine the ones who are. This is because the one talent they received from the Lord is not a prized possession, not a great honor, not a grave responsibility, but an insult. They despise the Lord's one talent. How dare God only give me one talent! One measly talent! Surely you cannot expect me to do anything with this? Be a wife and mother in the home? Be a faithful employee in the workplace? Pray from my sickbed and glorify God through suffering without bitterness? Be an encourager? Be an obedient son or daughter? No! Such church members and such professing Christians will do the bare minimum, but they will not be enthusiastic, joyful, thankful servants in the Lord's house. Let us beware lest that root of bitterness spring up in our hearts:

12. Wherefore lift up the hands which hang down, and the feeble knees;
13. And make straight paths for your feet, lest that which is lame be turned out of the way; but let it rather be healed.
14. Follow peace with all men, and holiness, without which no man shall see the Lord:
15. Looking diligently lest any man fail of the grace of God; lest any root of bitterness springing up trouble you, and thereby many be defiled. (Heb. 12:12–15)

Entering into the Master's Joy

"After a long time the lord of those servants cometh, and reckoneth with them" (Matt. 25:19). The master will hear from his servants what they have done with his talents.

We begin with "the wicked and slothful servant" (v. 26). His judgment is treated at length in verses 24–30. The one-talent servant appears with a mouthful of excuses and complaints against his master. From this we see that the motives of hearts will be revealed on that day. The one-talent servant blames the master, insulting him to his face. "I knew thee that thou art an hard man" (v. 24). That is how unbelievers in the church think of God and of Christ. They see him as harsh, strict, or cruel, and they are afraid of him. That is because they do not know his mercy. Unbelievers, when they serve, serve Christ grudgingly, because they have to, but deep down they resent God. That is because they have not tasted of his goodness. Unbelieving church members wish they did not have Christ as master, but they are too afraid to show that to others, so they continue with the pretense.

In addition, the one-talent servant gives vent to his frustration and bitterness and accuses the master of unreasonableness: "Lord, you reap where you did not sow, and you gather where you did not scatter. You expect a good harvest but you make no effort. You do not even give the proper resources to get the job done. How did you expect a return on only one talent? Sure, the five- and two- talents servants, *they* could do something, but *my* gifts were not even recognized. I was restricted from day one. Here is your one talent back, lord." Thus the one-talent servant compares Christ to Pharaoh, who demanded bricks without straw—an utterly unreasonable and cruel master indeed!

The lord sees through the man's excuses and judges him from his own mouth. This is no ill-treated servant, cruelly oppressed by an unreasonable master. Rather, this is a wicked and slothful, idle and lazy, good-for-nothing servant who sneered at his master's goods and despised his master's one talent. Did Christ not give this man his abilities, and did not Christ in perfect wisdom assign one talent to this man according to his ability? Let us even for the sake of argument agree with him about the reaping and gathering. Even then, this man ought to have taken the one talent and invested it in the bank or put it to the exchangers. Then at least it would have made interest (v. 27).

As just punishment for his wicked laziness, the servant is stripped of his one talent and cast into the outer darkness of hell, where there is weeping and gnashing of teeth (v. 30). Now the little that he had and that he despised is taken from him forever. Never again will he have opportunity to serve the Lord. Never again will he be in a position to perform even the lowliest task in the kingdom of God. He never belonged to Christ, and judgment day reveals it. How solemn: not only those who steal or misuse the Lord's talents are cast into hell. Not only the grossly immoral who never had any talents, but the lazy unprofitable servant is damned. What a warning we must heed!

But what a contrast to the other servants! Both of them, the five-talent servant and the two-talent servant, were faithful, and both are rewarded. That is the key: they are good and *faithful* servants. The Lord does not measure success, but faithfulness. The Lord makes no essential difference between the man who gained five and the main who gained only two. Both gained something! Both men hear the same commendation: "Well done" (v. 23). The five-talent servant who made five more talents receives the unused talent of the one-talent servant. He ends up with eleven talents! Both enter into the joy of their Lord.

The reward is not of merit but of grace. Christ is not teaching that good works are the ticket to heaven. That would contradict all of scripture. Christ gave the talents, whether five, two, or one. The talents were always his. Christ gave both the position in the kingdom as well as the ability to use that position; Christ constantly forgives the weakness and sin with which we serve him. How wrong the wicked and slothful servant was! Christ is not an austere taskmaster, but a merciful and gracious Lord. It is the greatest privilege to serve him. Behold the reward: eternal joy. The reward far surpasses even the greatest service. What an incentive for faithful and diligent service, whether we have five, two, or even only one of the Lord's talents!

◆

Chapter 18

THE FINAL
JUDGMENT OF
THE SHEEP AND GOATS

When the Son of man shall come in his glory, and all the holy angels with him, then shall he sit upon the throne of his glory: and before him shall be gathered all nations: and he shall separate them one from another, as a shepherd divideth his sheep from the goats: and he shall set the sheep on his right hand, but the goats on the left. Then shall the King say unto them on his right hand, Come, ye blessed of my Father, inherit the kingdom prepared for you from the foundation of the world: for I was an hungered, and ye gave me meat: I was thirsty, and ye gave me drink: I was a stranger, and ye took me in: naked, and ye clothed me: I was sick, and ye visited me: I was in prison, and ye came unto me. Then shall the righteous answer him, saying, Lord, when saw we thee an hungered, and fed thee? or thirsty, and gave thee drink? When saw we thee a stranger, and took thee in? or naked, and clothed thee? Or when saw we thee sick, or in prison, and came unto thee? And the King shall answer and say unto them, Verily I say unto you, Inasmuch as ye have done it unto one of the least of these my brethren, ye have done it unto me. Then shall he say also unto them on the left hand, Depart from me, ye cursed, into everlasting fire, prepared for the devil and his angels: for I was an hungered, and ye gave me no meat: I was thirsty, and ye gave me no drink: I was a stranger, and ye took me not in: naked, and ye clothed me not: sick, and in prison, and ye visited me not. Then shall they also answer him, saying, Lord, when saw we thee an hungered, or athirst, or a stranger, or naked, or sick, or in prison, and did not minister unto thee? Then shall he answer them, saying, Verily I say unto you, Inasmuch as ye did it not to one of the least of these, ye did it not to me. And these shall go away into everlasting punishment: but the righteous into life eternal.—Matthew 25:31–46

We have reached the end of the Olivet Discourse. This text is not, strictly speaking, a parable, yet it is parable-like—a striking description. Just consider for a moment the context of these words. Jesus of Nazareth is sitting on the Mount of Olives. The twelve disciples are gathered around him, and he is concluding a long sermon or discourse. In a few days, Jesus will be crucified. Yet he can declare that he, Jesus of Nazareth, the man who will be crucified, will be the great judge on the last day. According to his word, some will be sent away into hell by him, and others will be called into the glories of heaven by him. If that is not a claim to deity, what is it?

The whole scene emphasizes Christ's glory as the exalted Son of man. It is a scene that ought to strike terror into the wicked, and a scene that must be of tremendous comfort to us. The Judge is he whom the wicked have despised, mocked, and rejected, whose blood they have trampled underfoot, whose name they have employed as a swear word, and whose law they have broken. No clever lawyers, legal loopholes, and bribing of judges or juries will be possible on that day. Observe how Jesus is now described: no longer is he gentle Jesus meek and mild; no longer is he baby Jesus; no longer is he the despised and rejected Jesus. Instead, he shines with glory sitting on the throne of his glory, for he is the king and the Lord.

The Judge is our savior. He is the one we love, and who loved us and gave himself for us. He is our shepherd and we are his sheep. We need not fear to stand before him, because he has already stood in the place of judgment for us. So while the wicked cry in terror for the rocks and the mountains to fall on them and to cover them, we will be glad to see our Redeemer glorified as Judge on that day.

The Final Separation

The final judgment begins with a separation of all mankind into two distinct groups. From this we notice that all mankind will be judged and that they will be judged on the same day. There are not two judgments, two resurrections, or two future comings. Verse 32 speaks of "all nations" being gathered before Christ for judgment. Nations consist of individuals, so "all nations" means all individual human beings, not to mention all angels and devils. They will be assembled before Jesus Christ after he calls them all out of the graves in the miracle of the general resurrection of the righteous and the wicked:

> 24. Verily, verily, I say unto you, He that heareth my word, and believeth on him that sent me, hath everlasting life, and shall not come into condemnation; but is passed from death unto life.

25. Verily, verily, I say unto you, The hour is coming, and now is, when the dead shall hear the voice of the Son of God: and they that hear shall live.

28. Marvel not at this: for the hour is coming, in the which all that are in the graves shall hear his voice,

29. And shall come forth; they that have done good, unto the resurrection of life; and they that have done evil, unto the resurrection of damnation. (John 5:24–25, 28–29)

No one will, whether they want to or not, be able to resist this summons to stand in the judgment. Perhaps on earth they evaded the judicial system, but the call of Christ to judgment cannot be ignored. What a day that will be, when all men without exception will stand before Christ. No one will be missing. Kings, emperors, presidents, and even human judges will be there. Pontius Pilate, Caiaphas, Judas Iscariot, and the Roman soldiers who nailed Christ to the cross will be there. Notorious infidels will be there: Mohammed, Joseph Smith, Charles Taze Russell, Charles Darwin, and Richard Dawkins will all stand before Jesus Christ to hear his sentence. Rich and poor, bond and free, the powerful and the downtrodden masses, young and old, and Jew and Gentile will all stand before the Lord:

11. And I saw a great white throne, and him that sat on it, from whose face the earth and the heaven fled away; and there was found no place for them.

12. And I saw the dead, small and great, stand before God; and the books were opened: and another book was opened, which is the book of life: and the dead were judged out of those things which were written in the books, according to their works.

13. And the sea gave up the dead which were in it; and death and hell delivered up the dead which were in them: and they were judged every man according to their works. (Rev. 20:11–13)

This judgment will include believers. You and I, we who believe in Christ for salvation, will be there too. We will not be exempt from the judgment. Some deny this, or at least deny that we will be in the same judgment as the wicked. But that is because they confuse judgment with condemnation. Believers will be judged, but they will not be condemned. Their judgment will be their public acquittal, the public declaration that they are not guilty, but righteous.

The public day of judgment is necessary so that God can be seen to be just. On that day it will be clear to all, including us, that we are not worthy of salvation and yet that God is just in giving salvation to us because of the work of Christ. For our comfort the judgment day is necessary: in this life God's people are condemned, but on that day they will be commended and rewarded.

It is clear from Matthew 25 that believers are present on the judgment day. When believers first appear in this scene, they are mingled with the wicked, but before any verdict is announced, Christ separates his people from the wicked, as a shepherd separates the sheep from among the goats (v. 32). From that moment, the sheep are considered separately from the goats, but the point is this: the sheep are present with the goats to be judged in the final judgment.

Before one word of commendation or condemnation passes Christ's lips, he separates the sheep from the goats, the elect from the reprobate, believers from unbelievers, and the righteous

263

from the wicked. The sheep, on Christ's right hand, a position of honor, are the elect.

First, Christ calls them the "blessed of my Father" (v. 34). God's blessing is the effectual word of his favor pronouncing good concerning them and upon them. Christ uses the perfect participle, meaning that God has blessed them in the past with the result that his blessing continues into the present. In fact, they were always blessed, never cursed, always loved by God, and never hated by him. God's blessing flows out of the eternal decree of election according to which he chose them in love in Christ. In him, God blessed them with all spiritual blessings purchased for them on the cross:

3. Blessed be the God and Father of our Lord Jesus Christ, who hath blessed us with all spiritual blessings in heavenly places in Christ:

4. According as he hath chosen us in him before the foundation of the world, that we should be holy and without blame before him in love:

5. Having predestinated us unto the adoption of children by Jesus Christ to himself, according to the good pleasure of his will,

6. To the praise of the glory of his grace, wherein he hath made us accepted in the beloved.

7. In whom we have redemption through his blood, the forgiveness of sins, according to the riches of his grace. (Eph. 1:3–7)

Second, they enter an eternally prepared inheritance, "the kingdom prepared for you from the foundation of the world" (Matt. 25:34). Before they were born, before they were created, and before they had done any good or evil, God prepared for them a kingdom. God did not simply prepare a kingdom and leave it open concerning whom the citizens might be. Not at all: it is the prepared-for-you kingdom. These sheep did not come into possession of the kingdom by meriting it, or by working for it, or by fulfilling any condition to receive it, but by inheriting it: "Come...inherit" (v. 34). An inheritance is something received according to the gracious will of a parent, the gracious will of our Father ratified in the blood of Jesus Christ.

Third, in verse 37 they are called "the righteous." By "righteous" the Bible means someone or something in conformity to the standard of God's law. These sheep are sinners, yet God declares them righteous on that day. How? Not by ignoring the demands of the law or pretending that they had never sinned or that they had kept the law perfectly; and not by changing his standards to match their weaknesses, but by fulfilling the demands for them in Jesus Christ. The righteous are those for whom Christ died and who have therefore received Christ's perfect righteousness imputed to them through faith alone. Only because they have this status of righteousness can God bless them.

The goats, now separated from the sheep and standing at Christ's left hand, are the opposite of the sheep.

First, Christ calls them "ye cursed" (v. 41). God's curse is the effectual word of his wrath speaking evil concerning them and pronouncing evil upon them. Again the perfect participle is used. They have been cursed in the past and continue in that curse into the present. They were always cursed and never blessed, always hated and never loved by God. God's curse flows to them out of the eternal decree of reprobation, according to which God rejected them and excluded them from salvation in Christ. Accordingly, Christ did not die for them, they are not righteous, and they are not and cannot be blessed by God in time or in eternity: "For such as be blessed of him shall inherit the earth; and they that be cursed of him shall be cut off" (Ps. 37:22).

Second, the goats are separated from the sheep. For a time, they lived side by side with the sheep. Some of them even looked like and pretended to be sheep, but they were always goats, always unrighteous, and always cursed. With them stand the foolish householder, the evil servant, the five foolish virgins, and the one-talent servant of the earlier parables. The righteous are called into the presence of Christ: "Come, ye blessed" (Matt. 25:34). But the wicked are banished from him: "Depart from me, ye cursed" (v. 41). One group enters the eternal kingdom. The other group suffers the punishment of everlasting fire. Moreover, this final separation occurs even before Christ mentions any of the works the righteous have done or that the wicked have left undone.

The Final Verdict

It is clear from Christ's description of the final judgment that good works will play a role, but the question is, *what role?* We must make a careful distinction between basis and evidence.

Human courts are deliberative, that is, the judge hears evidence from both the prosecution and defense. Then he weighs that evidence and reaches a verdict. That deliberative process is not part of the judgment Christ performs. For the elect there is no prosecution, because all accusers against them have been effectively silenced by Calvary: "Who shall lay any thing to the charge of God's elect? It is God that justifieth. Who is he that condemneth? It is Christ that died, yea rather, that is risen again, who is even at the right hand of God, who also maketh intercession for us" (Rom. 8:33–34).

For the reprobate, however, there is no defense. All their sins rise up against them as witnesses, and they have no advocate to plead their case. Besides, the Judge does not need to deliberate, because he is omniscient. He knows everything that we have ever done, and he omits and overlooks nothing. All of that comes out very strikingly in the scene before us.

In light of this, we must carefully explain "for" in Matthew 25:35 and 42. Verses 34–35 read, "Inherit the kingdom…for…I was an hungered, and ye gave me meat." That does not give the reason for inheriting the kingdom. If it did, it would be a meritorious inheritance, and therefore no inheritance at all. The idea is rather evidential. By doing all these works mentioned in the text, you show yourselves to be the blessed of the Father. Therefore, these works are evidence of your blessedness, not the cause of it. We conclude that good works are the evidence but not the basis of salvation. Moreover, the works in view in the final judgment are acts of mercy performed for the relief of fellow Christians ("the least of these my brethren" [40]).

It is important to see that because this passage is misused. Some of the premillennial dispensationalists teach that the nations are judged on how they treated Israel. That is their understanding of "my brethren" in verse 40. That is patently false, because Christ never calls unbelieving Jews his brethren. In fact, he calls them the children of the devil (John 8:44). It is the believers, whether Jew or Gentile, whom Christ calls his children and his brethren: "Both he that sanctifieth and they who are sanctified are all of one: for which cause he is not ashamed to call them brethren, saying, I will declare thy name unto my brethren, in the midst of the church will I sing praise unto thee. And again, I will put my trust in him. And again, Behold I and the children which God hath given me" (Heb. 2:11–13).

Liberal churchmen and promoters of the social gospel teach that Christ has in mind humanitarian projects: helping the poor, ending racism, promoting equality, and other liberal causes. However, the poor are not Christ's brethren. Some of the poor are Christ's brethren, but not the poor as a class of people. The teaching of a universal fatherhood of God and universal brotherhood of man is false. Poverty itself does not make one a child of God. Grace makes one a child of God. Many of God's children are materially poor, but their poverty is not what makes them Christ's brethren. While we ought to do good to all men and to do evil to none irrespective of who they are, Christ focuses in the parable on doing good to fellow believers.

These acts of mercy to fellow saints are nothing spectacular and not beyond the possibility of any of us. Christ does not say, "For ye built a hospital, for ye donated a million dollars to the work of missions, for ye discovered a cure for cancer." Offering a hungry saint a meal, a thirsty saint a drink, a tired saint a bed to sleep in or a room for the night, a destitute saint some clothes to wear are the kinds of deeds that he mentions.

Notice too that he underlines doing these works of mercy to "the least of these my brethren" (Matt. 25:40). Those are the lowliest members of the church, perhaps the one always forgotten, the one who is often left out, the one with the least friends, or the one who does not have the most winsome personality. Christ remembers how we treated *them*! Very strikingly, Jesus associates himself and even identifies himself with these suffering saints. We are to see Jesus in them, because by grace and the Holy Spirit he *is* in them. This ennobles even the lowliest of acts of kindness that we perform for a fellow saint. Jesus Christ will openly reward us for these things on the day of judgment, as the angels, devils, the righteous, and the wicked look on.

It is tempting to think, if only Jesus were here, I would wash his feet, I would anoint his head, I would prepare a meal for him, or I would give up my bed for him. Do not be overly sentimental and hyperspiritual: if you do not perform lowly tasks for your brethren, if such things are beneath you, then do not think that you would do them for Jesus. "Inasmuch as ye have done it unto one of the least of these my brethren, ye have done it unto me" (v. 40).

The reaction of the sheep to this public commendation of their works is to ask when they performed such works. Believers do not enter the judgment with a list of works. That is what unbelievers, and especially the self-righteous, will do: "Many will say to me in that day, Lord, Lord, have we not prophesied in thy name? and in thy name have cast out devils? and in thy name done many wonderful works? And then will I profess unto them, I never knew you: depart from me, ye that work iniquity" (Matt. 7:22–23).

We do not even remember these works: "Lord, you say that we saw you hungry and thirsty, and we fed you and gave you drink, but we cannot remember. Lord, you say that we came to you when you were without a place to stay and destitute of clothing, and we housed and clothed you, but we do not recall ever doing that. Lord, you say that we visited you when you were sick and in prison, but we cannot think of a single example."

In fact, these works are so commonplace, so unspectacular, and so ordinary that we would think that they are hardly worthy of mention. Christ so loves his church that he remembers the lowliest acts of mercy to the least of his brethren. Christ remembers and will reward every drink of cold water that we gave to a person because he was a disciple. The world thought nothing of these brethren and even less of the works we performed to help them, but Christ overlooks nothing. All of these works are the fruit of grace in us, evidence of our faith in Christ and our love for him. He really rewards his work of grace in us with more grace.

The evidence against the wicked goats is that they did not perform acts of mercy toward the saints and therefore refused to serve Christ, whom they saw in Christ's brethren. That alone is evidence that they are devoid of grace, unbelieving, and wicked. Much more evidence could be brought against them, such as their persecution and hatred of the saints, but acts of omission are enough. The wicked have many opportunities to help the saints, and they will help their own, but they are not interested in helping the saints, because the saints represent Christ, whom they hate.

In Luke 16 we read of a rich man at whose gate sits a poor saint called Lazarus, a hungry beggar who wished to eat the crumbs from the rich man's table. The rich man never helped Lazarus. Lazarus starved to death on the rich man's doorstep. When the wicked do not help the saints, Christ takes it as a personal insult and punishes them for every time they failed to offer mercy to his people. "Inasmuch as ye did it not to one of the least of these, ye did it not to me" (Matt. 25:45). Christ keeps a record—a record of all our merciful works of kindness to the saints, and a record of all the opportunities that the wicked have neglected and despised. How much more does he not keep a record of every time the wicked have mocked, defrauded, beaten, and even killed his saints! Yet the wicked on the day of judgment have excuses: they claim ignorance. "When saw we thee an hungered…and did not minister unto thee?" (v. 44). But all their excuses are rejected.

The Final Destination

The final punishment of the wicked is just and terrible. It has been described as being cut asunder, being left outside the door, outer darkness, and weeping and gnashing of teeth. Now its full horror is revealed: everlasting conscious punishment in everlasting fire. The doctrine of hell is fearful, one that rightly causes us to tremble, and one under attack today, but it is the Bible's clear, unmistakable teaching.

First, the Bible makes a distinction between the final state of the wicked, which is the state after the judgment, and their intermediate state, which is the state between physical death and the judgment. One is called in the Old Testament *Sheol* and in the New Testament *Hades*, commonly translated as hell. The final state of the wicked is the "lake of fire" (Rev. 19:20; 20:10, 14–15). Hades (which is translated as "hell") will be cast into the lake of fire (20:14). Both hell or Hades and the lake of fire are places of burning fire, brimstone, and the undying worm (Mark 9:43–48; Luke 16:23–26). The main difference between the hell of Hades and the hell of the lake of fire is that the former is a place for the punishment of souls only, whereas the latter is a place for the punishment of soul *and body*.

Second, everlasting punishment, although dreadful, is perfectly just. The severity of the punishment of the wicked is not determined by the length of time sinners have sinned, although that will be taken into account, but by the fact that sin is a crime committed against the infinite majesty of God. At the same time, there will be degrees of punishment in hell: all will be punished everlastingly in body and soul with the fire of God's wrath and curse, but some will be beaten with fewer stripes or with less severity than others, although about the details of this we fear to speculate (Luke 12:45–48).

Third, Jesus makes it perfectly clear that hell is forever. He uses the word "everlasting," or "eternal," to describe it (Matt. 25:41, 46). It is everlasting fire and everlasting punishment. The wicked will suffer under God's wrath and curse forever. So long as God himself has being, he will pour out his fiery indignation upon them (Isa. 66:24; Dan. 12:2; Matt. 25:41, 46; Mark 9:44–48; 2 Thess. 1:9; Jude 7; Rev. 14:9–11; 19:3; 20:10). Therefore, the fire of hell will never stop burning. The wicked in hell will be burning forever.

The fire of hell is a tormenting flame, a fire that fills the body and soul of the wicked with unspeakable misery. God is present in hell as a consuming fire, inflicting upon the wicked his wrath. There is no comforting presence of God in hell, only God in his fury. The punishment of hell is especially dreadful because it is punishment away from Christ. That is how Christ begins his verdict: "Depart from me" (Matt. 25:41). Even if there were no fire, to be apart from Christ is punishment. Instead of being brought into the presence of Christ, the wicked will spend eternity with the devil and his angels, which underlines the horror of this punishment.

One of the Puritans, Ralph Venning (1621–73), describes the scene:

Depart! Depart! If they [the reprobate wicked] should then beg and say, Lord, if we must depart, let it be from thy throne of judgment but not from thee. No, says the Lord, depart from me; depart from my presence in which is joy. Depart and go to Hell. Lord, they say, seeing we must be gone, bless us before we go so that thy blessing may be upon us. Oh no, says God, go with a curse; depart, ye cursed. Oh Lord, if we must go from thee, let us not go into the place of torment, but appoint some place, if not of pleasure, then of ease. No, depart into fire, burning and tormenting flames. Oh Lord, if into fire, let it be only for a little while; let the fire soon be out or us soon out of it, for who can dwell in everlasting burnings? No, neither you nor the fire shall know an end; be gone into everlasting fire. Lord, then let it be long before we go there. No, depart immediately; the sentence shall be immediately put in execution. Ah! Lord! let us at least have good company who will pity us though they cannot help us. No, you shall have none but tormenting devils; those whom you obeyed when they were tempters you shall be with as tormentors. What misery sin has brought on man! to bring him to hear this dreadful doom![1]

In summary, hell is as eternal and everlasting as heaven is eternal and everlasting (Matt. 25:41, 46). If Christ ceases to exist or if the church ceases to enjoy heaven with him, then and only then can the everlasting punishment of the wicked cease. Let us thank our Father, who, by the blood of his Son, has delivered us from the wrath to come!

So dreadful is the doctrine of hell that many have tried to deny it. A view increasing in popularity today is annihilationism, the teaching that the wicked either cease to exist at the point of death, or that God will annihilate the wicked after a certain period of time in hell, so that eventually their punishment will come to an end. However, annihilationism is a vain hope. The word *destroy* in the New Testament does not mean to annihilate or to cause something to cease to exist. It means to ruin, to render useless, or to render inoperative. That destruction is everlasting (2 Thess. 1:9). "Punishment" in Matthew 25:46 does not mean cutting off, as the Jehovah's Witnesses cult contends. Meaning punishment, it is even translated as "torment" in 1 John 4:18. Besides, cutting off does not mean annihilation.

---

1   Ralph Venning, *The Sinfulness of Sin* (1669; repr., Edinburgh: Banner of Truth Trust, 2001), 72.

Moreover, the Bible explicitly teaches that the wicked will be tormented:

9. And the third angel followed them, saying with a loud voice, If any man worship the beast and his image, and receive his mark in his forehead, or in his hand,

10. The same shall drink of the wine of the wrath of God, which is poured out without mixture into the cup of his indignation; and he shall be *tormented* with fire and brimstone in the presence of the holy angels, and in the presence of the Lamb:

11. And t*he smoke of their torment* ascendeth up for ever and ever: and they have no rest day nor night, who worship the beast and his image, and whoso-ever receiveth the mark of his name. (Rev. 14:9–11; emphasis added)

Eternal restlessness in the tormenting flame of God's wrath is *not* annihilation. He who does not flee to Christ for mercy will *never* be released from the torments of hell. Medieval poet Dante Alighieri (c. 1265–1321) was correct when in his famous *Inferno* he wrote these solemn words on the gates of hell: "All hope abandon ye who enter here."

But for the sheep, the blessed of the Father and the heirs of an eternal kingdom, there is eternal life. They do not depart or go away, but they come into his presence. "But the righteous into life eternal" (Matt. 25:46).

Eternal life is not merely life that lasts forever and has no end. Eternal life is qualitatively different than this life. This present life, indeed, is a continual death, lived in a world under God's curse and with the presence of sin. God has prepared something much richer, greater, and more blessed for us. Jesus calls it "the kingdom prepared for you from the foundation of the world" (v. 34). Paul writes, "Eye hath not seen, nor ear heard, neither have entered into the heart of man, the things which God hath prepared for them that love him. But God hath revealed them unto us by his Spirit" (1 Cor. 2:9–10).

Jesus gives a definition of eternal life in John 17:3: "This is life eternal, that they might know thee the only true God, and Jesus Christ, whom thou hast sent." He adds in verse 24 his prayer for all his saints: "Father, I will that they also, whom thou hast given me, be with me where I am; that they may behold my glory, which thou hast given me: for thou lovedst me before the foundation of the world." To be with Christ and to behold his glory—*that* is eternal life!

Eternal life is the consummation and full enjoyment of the covenant. It is fellowship and sweet communion with God in Jesus Christ. The blessedness of heaven—or of the new creation—is described in some detail in the book of Revelation. However, we need to be careful, because Revelation presents the joy of heaven in symbolic language and uses figures to depict the beauty and richness of our promised inheritance. In addition, heaven is often described *negatively*, that is, in terms of what will be absent from the new creation. The following passages from Revelation are representative:

15. Therefore are they before the throne of God, and serve him day and night in his temple: and he that sitteth on the throne shall dwell among them.

16. They shall hunger no more, neither thirst any more; neither shall the sun light on them, nor any heat.

17. For the Lamb which is in the midst of the throne shall feed them, and shall lead them unto living fountains of waters: and God shall wipe away all tears from their eyes. (7:15–17)

3. And I heard a great voice out of heaven saying, Behold, the tabernacle of God is with men, and he will dwell with them, and they shall be his people, and God himself shall be with them, and be their God.

4. And God shall wipe away all tears from their eyes; and there shall be no more death, neither sorrow, nor crying, neither shall there be any more pain: for the former things are passed away.

5. And he that sat upon the throne said, Behold, I make all things new. And he said unto me, Write: for these words are true and faithful.

6. And he said unto me, It is done. I am Alpha and Omega, the beginning and the end. I will give unto him that is athirst of the fountain of the water of life freely.

7. He that overcometh shall inherit all things; and I will be his God, and he shall be my son. (21:3–7)

3. And there shall be no more curse: but the throne of God and of the Lamb shall be in it; and his servants shall serve him:

4. And they shall see his face; and his name shall be in their foreheads.

5. And there shall be no night there; and they need no candle, neither light of the sun; for the Lord God giveth them light: and they shall reign for ever and ever. (22:3–5)

The eternal state (the eternal home of God, Christ, the elect angels, and the elect church) will be the new heavens and the new earth. These new heavens and new earth are promised in Isaiah 65:17–25, 2 Peter 3:10–13, and Revelation 21:1–5. The present world will pass away, but it will not be annihilated as if God has to start over. God will cleanse or purge this present world with fire and bring forth a new (fresh) universe. This new universe will be a real, physical, tangible place fit for human beings to dwell with resurrected bodies, and it will bring heaven and earth together. Never again will heaven and earth be separated by an unbridgeable gulf. Heaven will descend upon the earth.

God's eternal purpose is the new heavens and new earth, a renewed and perfected universe in which God's glory in Jesus Christ is eternally displayed. The first Eden was never God's eternal purpose: Adam's sin did not spoil plan A and force God to make a plan B. Christ was always plan A, the only plan. It pleased God to make Adam and Eve, to have them fall, and then for Christ to redeem them so that God was glorified. It was never God's purpose to permit the devil to steal creation from him: God will not abandon his creation, but the entire creation will be redeemed (with elect humanity, although not every single human being, at its center [Eph. 1:10; Col. 1:20]). Therefore, Christ died not only for some human beings, but also to overturn the curse that lay on the entire creation because of our sin (Rom. 8:21). When we imagine the eternal state, we must think of a world like this one but infinitely more beautiful, in which God's glory shines from every blade of grass; a world of redeemed men, angels, and animals; of forests, mountains, and rivers.

At the center of the new creation is the glorified church or the new Jerusalem. In a vision the blessedness of the church is set forth in terms of a glorious city (Rev. 21–22). The fact that Revelation 21–22 is a vision should make us sober in our interpretation of it. The "holy city, the new Jerusalem" (21:2), is not the literal city of Jerusalem. First, she comes down from heaven (Gal. 4:26; Heb. 12:2); second, she is the Lamb's wife, the church (Rev. 21:9–10). The new Jerusalem is a symbol of the glorified church, the church as she is ideally in God's counsel, the church as she will be when she is perfectly sanctified (Rev. 21:2; Eph. 1:4; 5:27; Jude 24). The new Jerusalem is the church of all ages, consisting of Jews and Gentiles from both testaments, the patriarchs and prophets, and the apostles (Rev. 21:12–14).

The primary idea of the vision is of beauty or glory. Everything that is precious, valuable, and beautiful is found in this great city. What could be more beautiful than a city with foundations garnished with no fewer than twelve different kinds of jewels (jasper to amethyst) with the names of the twelve apostles in the twelve foundations (vv. 19–20; Eph. 2:20)? What could be more awesome than a city with twelve gates each carved in massive pearls, with the names of the twelve tribes of Israel on them, and guarded by twelve angels (Rev. 21:12, 21)? What could be more breathtakingly magnificent than a city whose streets are made of pure gold, so bright that it looks like transparent glass (v. 21)?

The size and dimensions of the city are symbolic of perfection. The city is a perfect cube and its measurements are 12,000 furlongs (1,500 miles or 2,200 kilometers). The idea is not that we will live in a city with such dimensions, but that the city is perfect, and therefore the church is perfect and complete. The number 12,000 is highly significant ($3 \times 4 \times 10 \times 10$) and indicates perfect fellowship with God. The holy of holies in the tabernacle and temple was also a perfect cube (1 Kings 6:20; 2 Chron. 3:8).

That the glorified church is described as a perfect city is significant. A city is an ordered society, a permanent dwelling place, or a community. It is a city for which the Old Testament patriarchs longed to exchange their tents (Heb. 11:10, 16). The new Jerusalem is a city with walls and gates, but these are never shut because there is neither night nor danger there. Instead, the saints enjoy perfect security, peace, safety, and permanency (Rev. 21:25).

The glory and blessedness of the new heavens and the new

earth will be fellowship with God. That is the goal of everything God has been doing for his people from the very beginning. God created Adam and Eve and gave them seed so that he could share the blessed life of the covenant, which he lives within himself, with rational, moral creatures in his image. There are various manifestations of this fellowship: walking with God; the tabernacle; Canaan; the temple; the incarnation; the indwelling of the Spirit. But in heaven God's tabernacle will be permanently, everlastingly, and perfectly with men (Rev. 21:3).

Because fellowship with God is the goal, the center of heaven will be Jesus Christ. There are many carnal conceptions of heaven. If Jesus Christ is not in heaven and if he is not the center of heaven's blessedness, heaven is not heaven and we do not want to be there. Jesus is the centerpiece of heaven because Jesus is the way to heaven. By his blood we will be in heaven; without the sacrifice of Christ, there is no heaven for any sinner. Therefore, we should not be surprised to find that Revelation 21–22 is filled with references to Jesus Christ. He is the husband (21:2), the one enthroned (v. 5; 22:3). He is the temple of the new Jerusalem (21:22); he is the light (brighter than the sun, v. 23); from him proceeds the river of life (22:1); his name shall be on our foreheads; we shall see his face (v. 4); and his coming fulfills the promise of heaven (vv. 12–13, 16, 20–21).

The activity of the saints, therefore, will be blessed rest, blessed service, and blessed fellowship *without sin* in glorified bodies and souls in the presence of God forever. There will be no sin in the new heavens and the new earth: gone forever will be even the possibility of sin. Our sinful souls and bodies will be entirely sanctified with the holiness of Christ, and we will no longer be hindered (as we are now) in our service, worship, or fellowship. That aspect of heaven is inconceivable to us now. We can scarcely imagine how we could exist in a realm where our thoughts, words, and deeds will be perfectly holy, no longer tainted with pride, selfishness, envy, or lust, and where we do everything perfectly to the glory of God.

Life in heaven will be praise and worship (thankful worship without boredom), service, and rest. When we open our eyes, there we will see the glory of God in Jesus Christ, and we will be satisfied with his likeness (Ps. 17:15). We will say, as the Queen of Sheba exclaimed when she saw Solomon's kingdom, "Behold, the half was not told me" (1 Kings 10:7). This is all ours by grace, flowing to us from the fountain of God's election and purchased for us on the cross of Christ!

Death, sin, and the curse will be absent—forever banished from the new creation. We will enjoy spiritual joy and satisfaction in abundance, for we will enter into the fullness of our inheritance.

Come, ye blessed of my Father, inherit!

That is life, eternal life, life that lasts forever and has no end. Life with Christ. Life in the presence of God, fellowshiping with him. That is blessedness and joy! That is worth waiting for!

Do not fear the judgment day. Do not be weary with watching and waiting. But pray, even for that great day.

The Belgic Confession beautifully expresses our Christian hope:

> The consideration of this judgment is justly terrible and dreadful to the wicked and ungodly, but most desirable and comfortable to the righteous and the elect: because then their full deliverance shall be perfected, and there they shall receive the fruits of their labor and trouble which they have borne. Their innocence shall be known to all, and they shall see the terrible vengeance which God shall execute on the wicked, who most

cruelly persecuted, oppressed, and tormented them in this world; and who shall be convicted by the testimony of their own consciences, and, being immortal, shall be tormented in that everlasting fire which is prepared for the devil and his angels.

But on the contrary, the faithful and elect shall be crowned with glory and honor; and the Son of God will confess their names before God his Father, and his elect angels; all tears shall be wiped from their eyes; and their cause, which is now condemned by many judges and magistrates, as heretical and impious, will then be known to be the cause of the Son of God. And, for a gracious reward, the Lord will cause them to possess such a glory, as never entered into the heart of man to conceive.

Therefore we expect that great day with a most ardent desire, to the end that we may fully enjoy the promises of God in Christ Jesus our Lord. Amen.[2]

A most ardent desire!

Is that your hope? Do you observe the signs of the times with your heart fixed on that great day? Do you watch and pray?

Come, Lord Jesus, yea, come quickly.

---

2   Belgic Confession 37, in Schaff, *Creeds of Christendom*, 3:435–36.

Index of Scripture